To Joe

A much appreciated friend

and a

Fellow past Golf Captain

Frank

CALLED TO ACCOUNT

CALLED TO ACCOUNT

Frank H. Taylor

The Pentland Press Ltd.,
Edinburgh – Cambridge – Durham

First published in 1993 by
The Pentland Press Ltd.,
1 Hutton Close,
South Church,
Bishop Auckland
Durham

ISBN 1-85821-045-3

Typeset by Carnegie Publishing, 18 Maynard St., Preston
Printed and bound by Antony Rowe Ltd., Chippenham

This book is dedicated to my wife

GLENYS MARY

With deep gratitude for all the love and joy she has brought me

May it long continue

I happily convey a sincere acknowledgement of all the encouragement and actual assistance afforded me by my old friend, David Norrie, in the preparation of this book.

TABLE OF CONTENTS

	LIST OF ILLUSTRATIONS	xi
CHAPTER ONE	EARLY DAYS IN WEYMOUTH AND DORCHESTER	1
CHAPTER TWO	ANSWERING UP	6
CHAPTER THREE	RUTLISH	11
CHAPTER FOUR	FIVE YEARS HARD	20
CHAPTER FIVE	RUTLISHIAN RUGBY	25
CHAPTER SIX	LIFE ON THE RIVER	31
CHAPTER SEVEN	CHARTERED ACCOUNTANT	41
CHAPTER EIGHT	GOLF	48
CHAPTER NINE	WAR	51
CHAPTER TEN	KEEPING THE HOME FIRES BURNING	57
CHAPTER ELEVEN	MINISTRY OF FOOD	68
CHAPTER TWELVE	THE MINISTRY OF WAR TRANSPORT	75
CHAPTER THIRTEEN	THE CASE OF THE DANCING OLIVES	90
CHAPTER FOURTEEN	THE ATHLETIC MARATHON	103
CHAPTER FIFTEEN	CITY LIVERYMAN	109
CHAPTER SIXTEEN	FARMING	115
CHAPTER SEVENTEEN	THE FIRST MILLION	124
CHAPTER EIGHTEEN	DOMESTIC LIFE	134
CHAPTER NINETEEN	PARLIAMENTARY CANDIDATE	148
CHAPTER TWENTY	THE BATTLE FOR CHORLEY AND LEYLAND	158
CHAPTER TWENTY–ONE	THE BATTLE FOR MOSS SIDE	165
CHAPTER TWENTY–TWO	PARLIAMENT	175
CHAPTER TWENTY–THREE	A HIGHLY EXCLUSIVE CLUB	190
CHAPTER TWENTY–FOUR	GLENYS	208

LIST OF ILLUSTRATIONS

The Turk's Head, Weymouth, with my father at the door   3
The Phoenix, Dorchester, again with my father standing outside   4
Surrey XV v. Berkshire XV, 1933   27
F. H. T. with punting Championship Challenge Cup   34
Start of Punting Championship Final   37
Glenys launches a 'ship'   40
Home Guard Inspection (Major Taylor extreme left)   59
Marathon Athletics – Harry Fullick with Frank Taylor   104
Training for the Athletic Marathon, 1949   106
Marathon Athletics. Start of Freestyle Swim, Fullick left, F. H. T. right 107
World Trade Centre. Laying the Foundation Stone   113
Whitnorth, Shalford, Surrey, front view   116
Monte Carlo Rally, 1959. Near to disaster in the Alps   131
Wedding of Frank and Dora, April 1936   138
Frank and Glenys at the Mansion House   145
Election publicity, 1955, Newcastle-under-Lyme   152
Telegram from Lord Woolton (but wrong result)   156
Forceful advertising by Moss Side Young Conservatives   166
The Biggest Face in Moss Side, 1961   168
The cows vote for Frank Taylor, Moss Side, 1961   169
Seeking votes. Sikh Temple, Moss Side   177
Three-line whip   179
Opening New Wilbraham High School   181
Parliamentary Delegation Greeted at RAF Bruggen, Germany, 1964   197
Winston Churchill's Funeral Invitation to St Paul's Cathedral   203
Glenys at the Palace displaying her MBE, 1978   209
Tribute by colleagues to Glenys on her retirement to marry me, 1978   210
Eightieth Birthday Gift from Sam Bryan, 10th October, 1987   215

CHAPTER ONE

EARLY DAYS IN WEYMOUTH AND DORCHESTER

I was born in a pub – no ordinary pub but the Turk's Head in Weymouth's East Street – on 10th October 1907, the elder of twins. My brother survived just three weeks. In those days it was quite normal for children to be delivered at home. Curiously, soon after I saw the light of day the Turk's Head was demolished. Whether or not any significance attaches to this I have never discovered.

My father, George Taylor, was a Cambridgeshire man, born in 1879. At the age of fifteen he ran away from home and joined the Royal Navy. At this time – the 1890s – ships were still chiefly propelled by sail and life at sea had changed very little since the days of Nelson. Living conditions were cramped and unhygienic. Leave was rare.

Father spent much of his time patrolling the coast of east Africa, intercepting the Arab dhows carrying human cargoes destined to be sold into slavery. He ultimately rose to the dizzy rank of Able Seaman. The only relic which I possess of his time in the Navy is a heavy piece of pock-marked leather, used to protect the palm of the hand from the needle employed in sail-making.

My father had one brother, Jack Taylor. Although I met him only once, Uncle Jack seems to have lacked the spirit of adventure conspicuous in his brother. He was never tempted to roam far from the city of his birth and was perfectly content managing the fruit gardens of Messrs. Chivers, the jam manufacturers, at Histon in Cambridgeshire.

*   *   *

During a period of shore leave in Portland, my Father met Emma Rebecca Hodder, a young woman born and bred there. The family lived at Fortune's Well, near the end of Chesil Beach, an eighteen-mile stretch of pebble-strewn shoreline which runs from Portland to Bridport. Emma was the eldest of thirteen children. Because

1

of the way in which family life was then structured, she had been expected to assist her mother in looking after the younger Hodders and in consequence had learned to shoulder responsibility early in life.

Emma's father, William Hodder, operated a horse-drawn carriage business, plying for trade from Portland railway station. Portland was then a thriving quarry island. The stone it produced was known and used world-wide. Consequently the station was always a-bustle with visitors seeking to be ferried hither and thither.

William Hodder found business reasonably good. He never grew rich but he and his wife, Mary, lived a steady enough life. They were hardy and they were healthy. Both survived to eighty-five years of age. As I spent many of my early school holidays at Portland I came to know them well. I also came to know their children, my uncles and aunts. The youngest, Edie, was especially kind to me. Her husband, Bob, had once worked as a quarryman. After being gassed in the Great War, ill-health forced him to retire. He afterwards became a superintendent in the St. John's Ambulance Brigade.

*   *   *

Emma Rebecca Hodder was a young woman of some foresight. When my father asked her to marry him she agreed to do so on the understanding that he first left the Navy. He bought himself out for £5, in modern terms a derisory amount. It was then a considerable sum.

Looking around for a new source of income, the newly-weds took over the Turk's Head. They reasoned that nothing could be more natural. Father had been a sailor. Sailors, when ashore, spend a great deal of time – and money – in public houses. Who better to run one than an ex-sailor? They would grow rich on the proceeds.

This was the idea in principle. In practice it worked less well. Running a pub in an area which depended for so much of its livelihood on the Navy produced its own peculiar vagaries of trade. The Fleet was often absent, sometimes for months at a time. During these periods licencees had to scratch a living as best they could. As Weymouth had more than its fair share of pubs, this was not easy. Ours was by no means the most attractive. It was a curious brick building with front-facing bay windows. It belonged to the brewers, John Groves and Sons.

Father was additionally hampered by a soft nature and an even softer heart. He found it difficult to say no to a pleading face and allowed customers rather longer credit than was wise. In some instances sailors would order drinks on 'the slate' knowing full well that they were due to sail in the morning and in all probability would never return to Weymouth.

The Turk's Head, Weymouth, with my father at the door

The Phoenix, Dorchester, again with my father standing outside

*   *   *

About 1909 these and other difficulties persuaded my parents to move to Dorchester where they took over the running of the Phoenix Hotel, a large old coaching inn with a stable yard which on market day was filled with the carriages and traps of the local farmers. The family remained there until 1911, the last year of the Edwardian era, when I was four years old.

By then it had become transparently clear that father lacked the temperament for the licensed trade. He also lacked any real facility for business. Consequently, the hotel was given up and he obtained a post as office-keeper to the Registry of Friendly Societies in London at a salary of approximately £3 a week.

On one occasion, when I was still relatively young, he invited me to come to town for lunch. At this date the Ministry had offices within the British Museum. Having some time to pass before the appointed hour, I amused myself by wandering through the Museum's cavernous halls. A short, bearded man passed me by. He delivered a piercing look. It was only in retrospect that I realised who he was – George V . . . there on a private viewing. I was utterly mortified. I had not even been allowed the time to make a bow.

*   *   *

Father took a house for us – at a rent of eight shillings and sixpence (42p) a week – near the ruins of Merton Abbey: 6 Florence Villas, 21 Phipps Bridge Road.

If this was rather on the small side, it suited our circumstances and needs. There was no money for anything more grand. From a small child's point of view, Florence Villas had the advantage of facing open fields and of standing adjacent to a small stream. Here we lived for some years.

CHAPTER TWO

ANSWERING UP

My first recollection of Florence Villas is of the lamp lighter riding past the windows at dusk, en route to illuminate the gas lamps, his long lighting-poles slung precariously over his shoulder. Where the pilot light had been extinguished through the course of the day by the wind, he would dexterously fix a match to the top of his pole. This he would then raise to the mantle, situated within a small glass door, igniting it by striking the wax match known as a 'lucifer' against the lamp-standard.

To a young boy, some of our neighbours seemed very curious. Immediately adjacent there lived a family named Carroll – husband, wife and five children. Their lives were disfigured by poverty and tragedy. The eldest son, Tom, was killed in the Great War. A second son, Jack, worked in a local sawmill where he lost an arm to one of the power saws.

The Carrolls seemed never to have any money. I recall standing in the garden and overhearing one of the boys say: 'It's just not fair, Mum. Our Jack's got half a sausage. I only got a little bit'.

This made a deep impression on me. In the way that children do, I knew that my own family was far from rich. But we had never had to make quite such draconian economies.

A second neighbour was a Mrs Murray. Like the Carrolls, she had little or no money but was a keen gardener and grew a variety of multi-coloured daisies. Each year she so arranged her flowerbeds that on Empire Day there was a wonderful profusion of red, white and blue. Binding together one flower of each colour, she would hand the finished posies to the children to carry to school.

People were more patriotic then and Empire Day was eagerly awaited. Officially recognised in 1904, it always fell on May 24, the birthday of Queen Victoria. It was observed throughout the Empire and was in some places a holiday.

*   *   *

When the Great War began in 1914 I was six years old. It was a stupendous conflict and involved all but ten of the globe's nations. In comparison, all previous wars paled into insignificance. More than thirteen million men were killed. Another twenty million were wounded or missing. A mere eighteen million came through unscathed. It is said to have cost thirty billion pounds. If one adds to this the indirect costs – the economic loss from death and injury, lost production and the damage to property – this figure is more than doubled.

It had its genesis when in August 1914 Germany demanded from Belgium the right to march through the latter's territory in order to attack France from the rear. I vividly remember a cartoon which appeared at the time on the front page of the *News of the World*. It depicted a vast and bellicose German eagle looming over a diminutive figure representing Belgium. Around the corner, hidden from the view of the eagle by a building, stood the stocky figure of John Bull, bludgeon in hand, waiting to come to the oppressed country's aid.

*   *   *

To any right-thinking man, war must always be an abomination. It is not so to small boys. Suddenly life was very exhilarating. I saw my first Zeppelin, a monstrous and frightening machine which later the same day was shot down in a dog-fight over Cuffley.

A second dog-fight involved a group of British and German aircraft. They engaged over the skies of Wandsworth. I watched as they wheeled and swooped, jockeying for position, As the aeroplane was then only eleven years old, they were, by modern standards, very curious machines. To me they appeared fantastic. Small single-seaters, capable of great speed and rapid climbing, they had machine-guns mounted in front, calibrated to fire between the whirring blades of the propeller. At the beginning of the war the supercharger had not been invented. Consequently, they had a relatively modest 'ceiling' of twenty-two thousand feet. As a result, one was able to observe their every move.

Shortly after this incident the munitions factory at Silvertown blew up. Hundreds of workers were killed and it is said that the noise of the explosion was heard for more than thirty miles around. It left a deep scar on public morale. Half a century later the incident was recreated for the television series, 'Upstairs Downstairs' – the Bellamy family's former 'tweeny' (or between-stairs maid) Ruby being employed in the factory.

War brings shortages. A limited form of rationing was introduced. Between the outbreak of war in August 1914 and October 1917 the price of most foodstuffs doubled. Meat, butter, margarine and tea became hideously expensive. There was

7

even a shortage of vegetables. At one point *The Times* carried an article pointing out that:

> 'In certain hotels, restaurants and other establishments subject to the Public Meals Order, new potatoes have been served on more than one day in the week. The Ministry of Food points out that by the terms of the Order no potatoes – or any food of which potatoes form a part – may be served or eaten on any day except Fridays.'

Meat became almost a thing of the past. When it could be had at all, the price of sirloin steak reached the unprecedented figure of 1/5d a pound. Leeds market had a weekly demand for eight hundred head of cattle. The weekly supply averaged just fourteen.

In London, restaurants and cafes were prohibited from serving meals before 10.30 in the morning. Shopkeepers suddenly found themselves the most assiduously courted group of individuals in the land. As they tended to receive their allocation in ratio to the number of their proven regular customers, many falsified their returns. For most families, the Sunday joint became a thing of the past.

Queues formed outside shops soon after dawn. The police often had to be called to keep order. Ministry of Health officials despatched enumerators to log the number of people standing in this vast national queue. There were many days when it surpassed half a million.

It was a topsy-turvey world in which tradesmen sold anything which came to hand. In my home area of Tooting, a fishless fishmonger sold home-made jam. A butcher without meat sold eggs, recommending them as a substitute. A greengrocer offered corned beef and tinned salmon. Sardines were sold at a dairy which had no milk, butter or eggs.

Unrationed provisions which found their way into the shops were usually sold within the hour. One day, shopping for my mother at a Lipton's store close to home, I heard that sugar was briefly 'off the ration'. It was limited to one ounce a customer and came in a twist of paper shaped like a cone. It cost a halfpenny (a sum so small that it is impossible to translate into modern money).

By making minor adjustments to my appearance I managed to acquire several cones – queueing firstly as myself, then as myself minus cap, then with the collar of my jacket turned up and – finally – with my jacket removed. When this little stratagem was discovered I was forcibly ejected. (I nonetheless managed to hold on to the sugar.)

*   *   *

In October 1912, on my fifth birthday, my mother took me by the hand and led me the two hundred yards to the gate of the local infant school, run by a lady named Mary Edwards. This was a busy establishment, with each class accommodating something between fifty and sixty pupils. I appear to have been a reasonably intelligent child and was usually placed in the top ten of my form. Time passed pleasantly and largely without incident.

In the course of time I moved to Singlegate Junior School at Colliers Wood, where I was subjected to an experience which left me with a feeling of resentment towards the educational establishment which I still retain. The classes at Singlegate were almost as full as those of Mary Edwards' establishment. Nevertheless, by dint of application and hard work, I managed in 1916 to finish second in a class of fifty-five. A year later I was placed first in a class of more than fifty. Naturally enough I looked forward to receiving my prize with the anticipation that only a nine-year-old can muster.

To my bitter disappointment, it was not to be. At the end of term a pompous school governor descended on us. When my name was called out he presented me with a certificate on which was printed the legend:

'In consequence of the War no prizes are being awarded. This certificate confirms that Frank Taylor was first in his class'.

* * *

Shortly after this incident, and for reasons unrelated to it, my parents decided that I should apply for a scholarship to a secondary school. Having passed the written examination I was summoned to Kingston County Hall for a personal interview conducted rather in the spirit of: 'When Did You Last See Your Father?'

A frightened and rather over-awed little ten-year-old, I was confronted by a group of eight very ancient and serious-looking men seated in a semi-circle. I was required to face them seated on a plain and very uncomfortable wooden chair.

One of my inquisitors – in appearance even more of an ogre than his companions – said:

'I want you to imagine a line of twelve men. Each man is separated from his neighbour by a distance of one foot. Kindly be good enough to calculate the length of the line – the distance between the first man and the last'.

Now I wasn't so stupid as all that and I quickly spotted that this was a trick question – the correct answer being eleven, not twelve. However, being by nature both a factual and a mischievous child, I asked:

'How fat are the men?'

9

A number of elderly mouths formed themselves into a bowl of prunes. (I now realise they were actually suppressed smiles.) Having recovered my sanity, I returned the correct answer and was dismissed. One of the witnesses to the event was friendly with my headmaster. By the next day the story was all round the school.

It seems to have done me no lasting harm because in due course I was awarded a scholarship to Merton's Rutlish Grammar School.

CHAPTER THREE

RUTLISH

I t was now the autumn of 1919. I was fast approaching my twelfth birthday and about to begin a new school life. It was a momentous year – and not just for me. At home, Lloyd George headed an uneasy government of coalition; and the American, Nancy Astor, had become the first woman to sit in parliament. Passengers had flown between London and Paris for the first time; and in the June, Captain John Alcock and Lieutenant Arthur Whitten Brown became the first aviators to fly across the Atlantic non-stop.

Bare of arm and wearing an unconventionally short dress, the astonishing Suzanne Lenglen won the first post-war women's singles championship at Wimbledon. In America a twenty-four year-old copper miner from Colorado named Jack Dempsey conducted his own Independence Day celebrations by pummelling his way to the world heavyweight title, overpowering the defending champion, the giant cowboy, Jess Willard, in three brutal rounds.

In Italy a brute of a different caste, an unknown journalist named Benito Mussolini, had founded the Fascist party, basing the appeal of this on a heady emotional mixture of socialism and nationalism. General Jan Smuts succeeded Louis Botha as prime minister of South Africa. France announced the death of Renoir.

*   *   *

In 1919 the luxury of a school bus was still fifty years away. I prefaced my first day at school by walking the mile or so from Florence Villas to the imposing gates of Rutlish in Merton's Kingston Road.

Rutlish was a curious institution, a hybrid formed through generations of evolution and compromise. In some quarters it was referred to as a grammar school, in others as a secondary school. The confusion arose because it was partly owned by the governors and in part maintained by the local authority – a state of

11

affairs which in these modern, doctrinaire times would be unthinkable. It none-theless worked very well.

The school had been founded by William Rutlish, a seventeenth-century local bigwig and embroiderer to Charles II, who in 1687 was appointed Master of the Company of Broderers. In September 1687 King Charles discharged Rutlish, his wardens and assistants from office. The following month he returned them to their posts.

The motivation behind this extraordinary sequence of events has never been fully understood. In all likelihood Rutlish and his companions lost their jobs for failing to remit money due to the King – who, as soon as they paid up, restored them to office.

At his death, William Rutlish left a sum of money for the upkeep of the poor children of the parish. Out of this bequest, Rutlish School was founded. It com-menced, I think, in 1896 under one Doctor Draper, who presided over just twenty children. The standard was high, word of this spread and by the time of my own arrival twenty-one years later the school was catering for more than four hundred pupils.

*   *   *

My entry to the School came in September 1919, shortly after the end of the First World War. The headmaster of the day was A. N. Disney, a statesman-like old gentleman with mutton-chop whiskers and a strong sense of his own dignity. He never went anywhere minus his gown. Discipline was not strong. Fortunately for us, neither was Mr Disney's arm and those of us called to his study for punishment suffered no lasting after-affects. The cane was laid on so lightly and so rapidly that it was sometimes difficult to refrain from breaking into laughter until we had reached the safety of the passage outside his study.

There were a number of very sad relics on the teaching staff at this time, many of them casualties of the war. I especially recall a gentleman named Inkpen – an appropriate name for a schoolmaster – who suffered badly from shell-shock. He found the task of maintaining discipline over some thirty boys completely beyond him. We were very cruel to him. It seems never to have occurred to us that he might have been more worthy of our sympathy.

A second incompetent was the chemistry master, Bill Fembey, a man for whom I did so little work that at the close of one term I managed the astonishing examination feat of registering nought out of a hundred. As thirteen of the thirty boys were awarded a similar mark, we all finished joint eighteenth in the form – an achievement which I still feel merits an entry in the Guinness Book of Records.

One of the most important events in the school calendar was Empire Day. This was celebrated at Rutlish by a church service presided over by Cannon Jagger, vicar of Merton, who invariably began his sermon by asking, somewhat earnestly: 'Now, boys, *what does Empire Day really mean to us?*'

Although I suspect he may have thought otherwise, he would be gratified to learn that – even to small boys – the British Empire meant a great deal. The oft-repeated slogan that it was an institution on which the sun never set was a great deal more than an empty adage. It was physically and actually true.

Great Britain was then at the zenith of her power. The British Empire controlled the lives and destinies of more than four hundred million souls. It covered a fifth of the land surface of the globe. Consequently, some part or other of it was always bathed in sunshine.

* * *

Unlike junior school, where to some extent I had been a large fish in a small pond, I found life at Rutlish a great deal more taxing. I was placed in Form 3a, with a total of thirty other boys, all of whom had also won scholarships. I lagged along somewhere around the top of the lower half of the form. As a result, at the end of the first year I was allowed to move up but placed in the lower of the two streams – Form 4b. The following year, instead of progressing to the Fifth Form I was placed in the Remove, the traditional half-way house between the two.

If I had problems, they were as nothing compared to those experienced by my brother George, who, despite being three years my senior, was struggling along a form below me. This inevitably led to a strain in our relationship. Realising that he would never make a scholar, at the age of sixteen George decided to discontinue his education and set out on a career.

* * *

If – like my brother – I sometimes felt a little disappointed at the academic progress I was making, I nonetheless enjoyed school life – especially after 1922 when the ineffectual Mr Disney retired and was replaced as headmaster by E. A. A. Varnish.

Varnish came in like a whirlwind. He scattered change before him like a dervish. Soccer was replaced as the principal sport by Rugby. Boys were organised into houses for the first time. A Cadet Corps was formed.

Basically, the new headmaster's philosophy was a simple one. He advocated pride in Rutlish, sought to instill in us a resolve not only to live up to all its traditions – both sporting and academic – but also to give of our best in our efforts to further them.

Under his guidance the school went from strength to strength. The Cadet Corps won the Nation Cup, thereby demonstrating to the world what the rest of us already knew – that it was the best and most efficient Cadet Corps in the country. In athletics Rutlish boys swept all before them, finishing ahead of all other English schools in the Public Schools Sports event two years in succession.

The esteem in which Varnish was held was perfectly illustrated when in 1970 one of his former pupils, Tom Braddock, who had gone on to become a Labour M.P., launched an unpleasant attack on his character and teaching methods in a newspaper article. He implied that pupils had led a life of terror – dominated by the cane and the prefect system – and that Varnish was a snob who had sought to create an Eton or a Harrow in miniature.

In addition to myself, a number of Old Rutlishians rushed to his defence. Among them was A. J. Doig, a member of the school staff in the 1920s and a man who knew Varnish well. He had this to say:

'When I was appointed in 1922 I found a school undergoing a revolution and filled with a community spirit that I have never seen surpassed elsewhere and seldom equalled. It was clear from the first that Mr Varnish had in some way captured the imagination of boys and staff and made them believe that all belonged to a place that was unique and bound to succeed.

'That he was unusual there is no doubt and many of the things he did were frowned on by the conventional. In fact, some of the more incredible things said of him were true. He cared little for office work or accurate records. He did not regard neat and orderly classrooms as a necessity. But the school was so alive it almost hurt.

'Academically there were some staggering results . . . Parents who had expected to send their sons to more popular and fashionable local schools began to prefer Rutlish. In sport the advance was phenomenal. For a number of years the school teams in rugby football were practically unbeatable.

'All of this would be of marginal value to the boys in the school unless they were happy and felt they belonged.

'As with other headmasters, Mr Varnish's memorial is in the lives and affections of those who taught and learned under him. Perhaps in his last years before retirement in 1942, at the age of 67, his powers may have waned a little but he remains . . . one of the most outstanding headmasters I have known.'

* * *

Varnish never promoted the physical or 'hearty' element of school life at the expense of academic success. During his time an increasing number of Rutlish boys found their way into the country's universities and some – such as David Follett and Frank Figgures – enjoyed distinguished public careers ultimately rewarded with knighthoods.

Varnish had a way of spurring boys on to higher achievement by making them his co-conspirators. One day he gathered myself and three other boys together and said:

'This long-jump record of ours . . . well, it really is quite deplorable. Do you think we might do something about it?'

It was left at that. Within three months we had extended the record by more than two feet.

My own contribution? The worst of the four. It hardly mattered. There was very little I wouldn't have done for Mr Varnish.

At my prompting, and to commemorate his twenty years' service to the school, some years later the governors commissioned a portrait of him in oils. It was a characteristic study and showed him as he was in his hey-day. One Old Rutlishian, on viewing it for the first time, said: 'That's Varnish all right – but, my word, somebody's for it!' I was then senior member of the School's Liaison Committee. This had been set up to foster a close relationship between governors, Old Boys, parents and staff. Consequently I was asked to make the presentation. I reasoned that if anyone was going to be 'for it' it would probably be me. Fortunately, Varnish thought it a good likeness. Having received it he presented it to the chairman in order that it could be hung in the main hall of the School.

*   *   *

In one quarter at least, Varnish's philosophy fell on deaf ears. I had no ambitions academically and seldom did more form-work than was absolutely necessary to get by. I did, however, endear myself to the headmaster on a personal level by being very keen on sport, notably swimming and rugby.

The highlight of the school swimming year was a two-mile swim along the River Thames. Qualification for entry for this entailed a monitored half-mile at Wimbledon Baths. As I was only fourteen years old, this was no easy task. After several abortive attempts I qualified for the main event with two days to spare. Only four others of the twenty qualifiers completed the course and as all of these were at least two years older than me I was naturally elated with my performance.

Rutlish also fostered my interest in rugby. Although I failed to make the school's First XV until my seventeenth year, I did thereafter manage to keep my place. I also became very interested in the school Cadet Corps, ultimately rising to the rank of Company Sergeant Major.

When an enclosed miniature shooting range was installed on the sports ground the Corps Commander, Major (later Colonel) Holmes, a master at the school, prevailed upon a high-ranking army general to put in an appearance and declare it open by firing the first shot.

The great day duly dawned. The school was summoned to the sports field to await the General's arrival. He entered the range, accompanied by Major Holmes and senior members of the staff. After a minute or two, we lesser mortals (gathered outside) heard the sound of a firearm being discharged. Major Holmes emerged waving a card. He said:

'The first shot has been fired. It is a bull'.

Everybody cheered.

They might have cheered less loudly had they known the truth. The day previously, I and two other members of the Corps had gone down to the range and fired single shots at virgin scorecards until we achieved a perfect bull – misrepresented the following day as the work of the General. The card at which the General had *really* fired was later retrieved by one of the more curious-minded co-conspirators. It bore no mark whatsoever.

The great man had missed.

* * *

A second farcical incident associated with the Cadet Corps occurred in 1925 during the period of our annual camp. This was held at Uphatherleigh in Devon, a sleepy unsuspecting area in which fifteen hundred cadets from a wide number of schools foregathered to spend two weeks under canvas.

The highlight of this week was a night exercise. A third of the camp was despatched to the top of a nearby hill to defend it. The remaining boys were detailed to attack it. As in everything appertaining to the Corps, preparations for the attack were taken very seriously. In order that it might be mounted by the entire force en masse, it was necessary to arrange exact times for meeting up once each unit came within reach of the hill-top.

Each section laid elaborate plans of its own on how best to advance quickly and in silence, thus preserving the element of surprise. (Quite how this was to be achieved, given that the defending source knew for certain that we were coming, is something I have never been able to fathom.)

The whole thing was rendered totally ludicrous by events which – we later swore – were quite beyond our control. In the course of its passage towards the

16

hill, the entire attacking force was routed close to a farmhouse. A light blazing from the curtainless window revealed the farmer's daughter undressing for bed.

All boys are curious. Adolescent boys are especially curious about girls. With but one thought, a thousand pairs of boots clattered to a halt to enable their owners to view this interesting event. And there we stood, rooted to the ground, as the boys defending the hill presumably grew more and more puzzled at our non-arrival. I say 'presumably' because the entire episode might, of course, have been a cunning ploy devised by the hill-toppers to distract our attention from the business in hand.

If so, we hardly minded. It was generally conceded to have been a great deal more fun than the main event.

Despite this debacle, the camp proved a great success. For my part I managed to make some amends for the farmhouse interlude by carrying off second prize in the shooting competition. For this I received a silver medal . . . which I yet have.

* * *

By the beginning of 1924 I was sixteen years of age. I may just have been aware that Ramsey MacDonald had formed the first Labour government; that Tutankhamun's sarcophagus had been raised at Luxor; that Liddell and Abrahams were leading the British rush for gold at the Paris Olympics; and that George V had opened the Imperial Exhibition by sending a telegram to himself routed around the course of the Empire in less than a minute.

Somehow I doubt it. I spent the entire year consumed by the spectre of Matriculation – success in which (I half-divined) would be of vital importance if I were to prosper in the world beyond school.

I passed – thereby surprising both myself and my tutors, who began to wonder whether they might not have misjudged me after all. I quickly disabused them. On moving into the Sixth Form I was confronted with trigonometry, calculus, and algebra. I abruptly jettisoned my new-found interest in matters academic and concentrated instead on justifying my election to the captaincy of my School House, the Kelts.

My chief rival for this was a boy named Sidney Crowson. When the matter was put to the other members of the House it was found that we had both polled 28 votes. In the normal way, this impasse would have been resolved by asking the members to vote again. On this occasion – and for reasons best known to himself – the Kelts House Master decided to refer the matter to the vote of the Common Room. This I narrowly won. Crowson later entered the Church (although not, I think, as a result of our little confrontation) where he did a great deal of sterling work, much of it in the Far East.

*   *   *

Winning the captaincy of Kelts represented one of the proudest moments of my young life. Thereafter I devoted all my energies to living up to the honour – pulling the House ahead of its rivals, especially in what I saw as the all-important aspect of sport.

For the uninitiated, Houses at Rutlish – as I believe elsewhere – were divided into Seniors, Middle and Juniors, according to the age of the members. In athletics, points were awarded on a graduated basis. The Senior members' bench-mark for the 100 yards was twelve seconds. Middle members were set a standard of thirteen seconds; and Junior members a second beyond that. Rugby, cricket and swimming competitions were decided on a confrontational basis, each House competing against every other for points.

I had an all-consuming desire to see the Kelts do well. To this end there were very few subterfuges to which I was not prepared to stoop short of actually breaking the rules.

Although I lacked any particular skill as a cricketer, I was nevertheless very keen that the House should win the school competition. In forwarding this objective, I invariably fielded an eleven composed of five left-handed batsmen and six who took guard from the right. I also made it a rule that the batting order should be regulated to ensure that there was always a right-handed and a left-handed batsman at the crease together. The batsmen themselves were under strict instructions only to score an odd number of runs – 1 or 3, never a 2 or (God preserve us) a boundary. This had the effect of demoralising, confusing and – best of all – tiring the opposition by forcing them continuously to change position.

It wasn't nice and in a curious way perhaps it 'wasn't cricket'. But we duly won the cup.

That my tactics had placed me in very bad odour with some of the other House captains bothered me not a jot.

Due to my almost Florentine deviousness, the Kelts won most of the sporting competitions that year – as the school yearbook attests:

'A feature of this year's work has been the astonishing success of the Kelts under the Captaincy of F. H. Taylor.'

Not so astonishing, really.

* * *

Shortly before leaving Rutlish in October 1925, I sought out Mr Varnish and said I should like to express my gratitude to the school by furnishing a cup for boxing, one of the few sports which did not then possess one.

Thinking I suspect of my pocket, Varnish said that he really didn't want anything too elaborate – no scrolled or engraved silver handles. A squat little ugly type of cup would do. I bought him a replica of a Georgian goblet.

Boxing was discontinued as a sport at Rutlish many years since; but the cup which I bought sixty-five years ago, as I stood on the threshold of life, still graces the table on prize-giving day.

Rutlish is like that.

CHAPTER FOUR.

FIVE YEARS HARD

B y the spring of 1925 I was fast approaching my eighteenth year. I was shortly to leave Rutlish but had no very clear idea of what I wanted to do in life. The matter was resolved for me by Mr Varnish, who took a proprietorial interest in all his charges. He suggested I might try accountancy. Having fared so badly at trigonometry and calculus, it was hardly surprising that I didn't really know what an accountant was. I knew even less of this exotic creature's functions or how one went about becoming one.

Through Varnish's connections in the City a number of introductions were arranged for me. I was not sanguine that they would come to anything. Any young man wishing to take out articles with a chartered accountant was required at that time to pay a premium, a practice which was abandoned some years ago. This was usually in the region of £300, a sum far beyond the means of my parents.

To his eternal credit, Varnish persevered and eventually found a firm, Falk, Keeping & Co., situated near Cheapside, prepared to waive its right to this honorarium. For the more manageable sum of £50 I would be accepted on a three months' trial. This I survived. I was then taken on to the permanent staff as an Articled Clerk.

Although in this manner I avoided payment of a crippling premium and slid into the profession almost unnoticed and by default, it was made very clear to me that there could be no question of the firm paying me a salary during the five years of my articles. I did in fact receive a small donation twice-yearly – at Christmas and at some point during the summer: and that was all.

The first of these amounted to two-and-a-half guineas. By the time I had entered my fifth year it had just about doubled. In theory I thus had about ten pounds a year on which to live. This was approximately what a labourer or a ditch-digger brought home every month. Nonetheless, over the course of the years I received some £70, which recouped my initial outlay to the firm with a little more besides. In return, they received five years' unpaid labour from me.

Although the practice was discontinued some years ago, the premium system existed because it was felt that articled clerks should make sacrifices in order to learn – to equip themselves for the future – and that during their apprenticeship they more often represented a liability to their employer than an asset. With the exception perhaps of some areas of the legal profession, this specious argument has long since been abandoned. Articling no doubt served a real enough purpose; but it also furnished the company with cheap labour whilst impoverishing the young employee.

The redoubtable Varnish had made the commencement of my career possible. I discovered that he was regularly putting his hand into his pocket to sustain other boys. I have never forgotten the help he rendered me at that time; and I now know I was very far from being the only boy he assisted to get started in life in this manner.

For his work at Rutlish, he was invested with the OBE. In my (biased) opinion he ought to have been rewarded at the very least with a knighthood.

*   *   *

Resplendent in my new uniform of dark suit, bowler hat and furled umbrella, I set out one bleak Monday morning in October 1925 to catch the number 5A bus to London Bridge. I crossed the bridge on foot and entered the City of London to commence work for the very first time. I was frankly apprehensive, having no idea of what might lie in store for me.

Falk, Keeping and Co had a tiny three-roomed office in Ironmonger Lane. Having absolutely no idea of what accountancy involved, I suspect I was something of an irritation to my employers (as in later years newly-articled clerks would be to me). Perhaps in consequence, I was given the most menial tasks. For many months I did nothing more than tick figures in a ledger as they were called out to me by the office manager. I had no idea what we were doing or why we were doing it.

Gradually, almost by osmosis, I absorbed a little of accountancy law. At some point I was elevated to preparing profit and loss accounts. I then moved into the heady realm of balance sheets.

One never-to-be-forgotten day I was given the task of auditing the accounts of a small farmer. Raw and inexperienced, I sought to discover the 'net balance' of his stock – which was cattle – by applying the same methods I might have used in dealing with a grocery shop. By taking the 'stock' as it stood at the beginning of the year, adding purchases and subtracting those animals sold in the course of it . . . I came to a figure which made no sense at all. At the end of the year the 'stock' was significantly greater than my calculations showed it should have been.

I wrestled with the problem endlessly . . . until it suddenly dawned on me that unlike items in a shop, farm 'stock' could be self-generating – and this farm owned a bull.

* * *

In the early days of my articled clerkship, I was sent as a junior to assist in auditing clients accounts *in situ*. Once again this entailed long days spent ticking off entries in enormous vellum-covered cashbooks weighing between thirty and forty pounds. The entries were nearly always made in beautiful copper-plate, a form of handwriting which, sadly, has now all but disappeared from the world.

The work was often boring and monotonous. Not so the people I met. Among these were Messrs Messel and Gielgud, partners in the stockbroking house of L. Messel & Co. They were both German nationals who had escaped to England at the time of the First World War. Although neither spoke more than a few words of English, they controlled their firm with great efficiency. (It survives and thrives to this day.) Both also made indirect but priceless contributions to the Arts – by way of their sons: John Gielgud and Oliver Messel.

* * *

Hours were then reasonably long – ten in the morning until six at night, five days a week, with the occasional Saturday morning thrown in for good measure.

In addition to the regular office grind, I had also to make time to study – my employers volunteering very little in the way of free tuition. I enrolled in a home correspondence course conducted by the Metropolitan College of St. Albans. In fact, in a heady moment, I enrolled in *two* correspondence courses, one to help me qualify as a chartered accountant, the other to become a chartered secretary. (I felt the latter qualification might lend me a little much-needed *gravitas* in the world of business.)

Additionally, the college ran a three-week scholarship course for newly-articled clerks. This I also took, passing out second. As a consequence, the college undertook to rebate half my examination fees for the other two courses in which I had enrolled.

This came as a great relief to my parents who, after having to find the initial £50 premium, had been left with very little money. In order further to limit their burden I resolved to pass all my exams at the first attempt. Not to do so would

22

have been to court disaster. Unlike today, when it is possible to re-sit failed sections of an examination, one had then to re-sit the thing in its entirety.

*   *   *

I embarked on a life of hard work and self-denial. It was to occupy me for the next five years. I followed the strictest of fixed regimes, rising each day at six and studying for about two hours until it was necessary to leave for work at nine. After the evening meal I again sat down with my books and worked through to midnight.

In my intermediate chartered accountancy examination – the only one which listed results in order of merit – I passed out 28th of four hundred.

I averaged six hours sleep a night – with the result that for five years I was only ever half awake. My sense of dedication – born of necessity – was such that I never allowed this to interfere with my work.

*   *   *

My only real period of recreation was the weekends. In summer I played water-polo for Wimbledon Swimming Club and took part in athletic matches organised by the Old Rutlishians. During the winter I played rugby. Even then I seldom stayed on to socialise. I was essentially a serious young man – perhaps a little too serious on reflection. I went home to my books. There was no time for girls. In many respects it was a dreary and doleful existence . . . but one which has since paid enormous dividends.

In 1929 – the year of the Wall Street Crash – I qualified as a chartered secretary. The following year, amidst great jubilation, I qualified as a chartered accountant.

The morning I received the latter result I rang Roy Burnham – an Old Rutlishian friend who worked for a firm of Mayfair solicitors – and invited him to a celebratory liquid lunch. In our rakish progress, we manoeuvred down Oxford Street, never passing a pub on principle. At mid-day closing time I weaved Roy back to the entrance to his office in Albemarle Street, where I left him clutching the railings. (Curiously, he never did qualify as a solicitor.)

I weaved off in the opposite direction. Realising that in my current condition I could hardly return home, I went to a cinema in the hope of sobering up. I then went to a second and, eventually, a third. I finally got home in mid-evening.

*   *   *

I awoke the following morning to the thought: 'It's over. I'm a chartered accountant'. Even though I was painfully aware that it would be an up-hill struggle to set up in practice for myself without money or influential friends, it came as a tremendous relief.

CHAPTER FIVE

RUTLISHIAN RUGBY

I t has been well said that none of us is ever fully weaned. In my case – and although they are now some seventy years in the past – I have never forgotten my school days and the wonderful memories and companionship they brought me. Consequently I became a life member of the Old Rutlishian Association as soon as I left school. The Association had been formed in 1906 and acquired its own sports ground in 1922. In 1925 my life membership cost me the princely sum of five guineas. I paid it willingly but – being poor – by instalments.

Two years later I formed a second association which has also been of importance to me down the years. It came about as the result of a rugby match held at Twickenham between an England XV and New Zealand's legendary All Blacks.

The visiting team contained two forwards, the brothers Brownley. Shortly after the start of the game, one of these – I forget which – was sent off for a particularly unpleasant foul. There had never previously been a sending-off in an international, nor in any match at Twickenham. As such, the incident generated considerable comment. The Press – being the Press – made a great deal of the matter.

To counter this and perhaps to defuse the situation, the England captain, the very sporting W. W. Wakefield, decided to redress the balance by organising a farewell lunch for his opponents at London's Savoy Hotel. This demonstrated that the incident was forgiven if not forgotten. Out of this the British Sportsman's Club was born. It continues to this day to provide welcoming lunches for teams from abroad, not only for those playing rugby but cricket and golf as well. The membership of the Club is by invitation only and I am proud to have been invited to join in 1950.

* * *

Through the Old Rutlishian Association I continued to develop the interest in sport, and especially rugby, which had first manifested itself at school.

In 1927–1928 I was appointed captain of the rugby section of the Association. It proved to be a marvellously successful year. We lost just one game – against the Bank of England – and amassed 728 points whilst conceding only 78. For six years I served either as captain or vice-captain, three years in each post.

Although I was fortunate enough to be selected to play rugby for the Old Boys for upwards of twenty years, I think that as scrum-halfs go, I left something to be desired. My passing-out tended to be erratic and for this I was apt to blame the backs, claiming they were incapable of catching the ball. This was something of a slander. Joe Archer, Laurie Pearce, Teddy Ericson and Peter Breed were all excellent backs and the two last-named played for Surrey. I also played for the county – as a wing forward, never a scrum-half – but, unlike Ericson and Breed, was never able to command a regular place in the side.

In order to relieve the pressure caused by my eccentric passing-back, I developed the habit of cutting the backs out completely – running with the ball straight from the scrum. In one season alone these tactics brought me twenty-eight tries, which was good for me but – as other players were being starved of the ball – bad for the club.

Peter Breed was an excellent all-round sportsman. As an athlete he won the 100 yards at the Public Schools Sports. He was a strong swimmer and, like myself, played water-polo for Wimbledon. He was captain of the Surrey water-polo team for some years. I could never match him for strength or speed in the water and I remember how in a 200 yard gala race at school he beat me by a complete length.

Like Breed I also had an interest in athletics, but in my case field sports – discus, shot and javelin. I won the occasional inter-club competition for the Association but here again I tended to be overshadowed by a more talented Old Rutlishian, Ernie Brewer, a natural discus-thrower who for some years held the British native record.

*   *   *

Rugby, however, always remained the sport I played – and loved – the best. It seemed then and seems to me still not only a wonderfully skilful and companionable pastime but a very useful outlet for controlled aggression.

Rugby tours were always great fun. I have always been fast off the mark and in the course of one tour, playing scrum-half against Bridgewater, I was frequently able to race round the scrum and flatten my opposite number before he could unload the ball. This was a perfectly legitimate tactic which relied for effect on speed. It broke no rule and did not carry me off-side. However, the Bridgewater

Surrey XV *v.* Berkshire XV

supporters failed to appreciate the finer points of this ploy and pelted me with turf.

I remember that we stayed during this tour at a local pub. Like all rugby teams, we tended to be noisy and boisterous, singing and drinking till late. The landlord appeared a jovial soul and on our departure insisted on shaking each of us by the hand. He kept repeating how much he had enjoyed having us. In fact, he repeated it so often that one of our number eventually suggested a return visit the following year.

The landlord's face dropped. 'Oh, no', he said, 'I don't think so'.

*   *   *

Although the Old Rutlishians then undertook no foreign tours themselves, I was fortunate enough to play abroad on two occasions. The first trip entailed an Easter visit to Paris as a one-day member of the famous Blackheath club, which at the last moment had found itself short of a scrum-half. The second trip, also as an adopted member, was for United Eastern Banks and also to Paris, where one of our games was against the 'Association Sportif Francais'. This encounter will remain in my memory as long as I live.

The French side was not outstanding. By half time we were leading seventeen points to nil. During the break, we waited for the customary lemons to be brought on to the pitch. They failed to materialise. Instead, we were beckoned towards two caravans situated near the touchline. The French team were taken into one, we into the other – where we were plied with a series of delicious 'fruit' drinks.

Within a few minutes of the resumption, our game began to fall apart. Thanks to the spiked drinks, players fumbled the ball, dropped it or passed it to team-mates who proved to be somewhere else entirely. They stood still. For no discernible reason they fell over.

We didn't score another point and the Frenchmen ran out the winners twenty-three points to seventeen. Given the manner of their victory, one has to wonder whether the 'Sportif' element may have been a little inappropriate.

It was certainly a long time before any of us accepted an unsolicited fruit cup again.

*   *   *

Down the years there were many memorable games, some remarkable for the outstanding quality of the rugby, others for the mishaps they produced. One of the latter resulted from a confusion over fixtures. When we arrived at our ground we found the club we were scheduled to play already changed and ready to begin. Before we could change, a second team put in an appearance – also claiming the right to take us on.

We were endeavouring to sort the muddle out when seven members of the old Mountaineers' Club – which was in the process of being disbanded – descended on us, also claiming to be booked to play us.

Confronted by the ludicrous situation of having two and a half teams – all of whom wanted to play us – we decided the most diplomatic course would be to withdraw. Consequently, we stood on the touchlines and cheered whilst our visitors – having formed two scratch teams of eighteen a side – had a thoroughly enjoyable afternoon at our expense.

There were no casualties that day. Rugby being very much a contact sport, this was not always the case. On a subsequent occasion, playing the Central Y.M.C.A., four of the visitors' players were forced to retire within the first twenty minutes.

To even up the odds I lent them two of our own players, reducing the match to a game of thirteen a side. As ill-luck would have it, both the loaned players were also soon injured. Mortifyingly, one of them was my vice-captain, Frank Green, who suffered a badly broken nose and decided as a result to give up rugby altogether. We thus had a situation where six players had been crocked in a game which hadn't produced a single incident of rough play.

If this goes to prove anything at all it must surely be that rugby is a young man's sport. Young bones tend to bend rather than break. When they do break they quickly mend. In 1927 I was just such a young man, twenty years old. I vividly recall that we then had a player of twenty-eight in the first team. I thought him ancient – more fitted for a bath chair on the touchline than a place in the thick of the fray. I was vaguely surprised that he didn't sport a long white beard. I certainly felt he should not still be playing rugby.

In the course of time – and I continued to play rugby for the Association until I was forty-two – the wheel turned full circle and the younger players, many of them fresh from school, came to view me in a similar light. At the end of the Second World War and with the termination of my journeyings abroad, I took up the sport again. But where I had formerly been in the van, calling over my shoulder to my team mates to 'Come on', I now found I was the one lagging behind, shouting 'Go on'.

In addition to this personal loss of mobility, the post-war period posed a more serious problem: that of diminishing active membership. Owing to the introduction of the grants system, many of the school-leavers who would normally have swelled the Association's ranks were proceeding to university, thereby posing the very real danger that the close association they had formed with the school would be broken and members lost.

A further problem was that those who did display any real talent for the sport tended to be poached, very early, by such giants of the game as Harlequins or Rosslyn Park, who sent out scouts to scour the countryside for new recruits. They argued – perhaps rightly – that playing club rugby at the highest level greatly increased a player's chances of being selected for his county . . . possibly even his country.

The effect of this on lesser clubs has been disastrous. Some decided to go 'open' – to admit players who had no immediate connection with the school or institution they represented. At the time of writing, the Old Rutlishians continues to close ranks. But the problem remains.

*   *   *

As a chartered accountant, it was almost inevitable that, off the field and away from sporting activities, I should be hijacked on to various committees. I served a seven-year term as treasurer and in 1939 was elected president of the Old Rut-lishians' Association. This was an annual appointment but as it was not practical to hold elections during the period of the war, I retained the post for an unprecedented six years – until the cessation of hostilities in 1945.

It is hard to believe that this election took place almost half a century ago. As a direct result I am now the club's senior past president – and hope to continue so for many years to come.

CHAPTER SIX

LIFE ON THE RIVER

At the age of twenty-one, and through some members of the Old Rutlishians' Association with whom I played rugby, I became involved with Ditton Skiff and Punting Club. The club had been formed six years earlier and by the time I joined in 1928 had attracted some forty members, all of whom were keen on the river.

It had its headquarters in Thames Ditton's Ferry Road, in a small room over the paintshop of Hammerton's boathouse. A corner of this was fenced off as a bar, the remainder as a recreation area. The atmosphere was cheerful. There was very little money.

The club's captain was a man known ironically as 'Tiny' Knight, an enormous individual who towered 6' 8" in his socks and weighed the best part of twenty stone. Despite his mature age and size he remained extremely fit and had won numerous races on the river, mostly in skiffs. He was replaced as club captain by Theo Hewitt. Theo had a brother, Sam, and a sister, Florrie, both of whom were involved with the club. Florrie trained and coached the sculling members. The boathouse was managed by Frank Buttry, a cheerful elderly man with a bald, nut-brown head.

My motives for joining were primarily social. I was then coming towards the end of the five-year period of hard studying I had undertaken in order to acquire the professional qualifications necessary for a career. Once in a while I now felt justified in tearing myself away from my books and cycling the twenty-four-mile round trip to the club-house for an evening's relaxation.

*   *   *

It was only after completing my studies that I became interested in the more active side of the club's life. Skiff racing was then very popular. Unlike the type of craft used at Henley – smooth-sided shells fitted with sliding seats – our own craft were clinker-built and had fixed seats. The doubles boats had sufficient room to accom-

31

modate a cox; although even with the help he afforded in steering, propulsion through the water was quite hard work.

By 1931 I was thought sufficiently competent to be entered for the skiff marathon championship, a coxed doubles sculling event. This was to be sculled over a course of eight and a half miles, the first half of which covered the same stretch of water as the University Boat Race, continuing thereafter up to the tideway lock at Isleworth. My partner was Colin Campbell.

We covered the course in a little under an hour. To our great surprise we won.

Given such a promising start, I had high hopes of continuing to do well at marathon skiffing. It was not to be. Entering the same event the following year, I ran third. The year after that I could only finish fourth.

The chief reason for this was the problem posed by the Offer brothers, two superb watermen from Kingston, both more than six feet tall and both enormously strong. They were to dominate the event for many years. When the elder brother retired, the rest of us felt free to hope that the race would revert to being more open. Unfortunately – at least for us – the retiring member was replaced in the boat by a third brother. The new teaming proved to be every bit as potent as the old and our hopes were dashed.

The Offers were, quite simply, unbeatable. This, coupled with the deterioration in my own form, persuaded me to abandon marathon skiff racing altogether.

It was, I think, the right decision. In the years leading up to the war it left me free to concentrate on doubles skiff racing over shorter distances. Here I enjoyed a greater degree of success, collecting along the way about a hundred tankards and forty cups, each of which represented a race won. There were then no prizes for finishing second or third. You won or you didn't.

There were Regattas most Saturdays during the summer, each on a different stretch of the Thames. Before the war, most of these concluded with a 'dongaler' race – the dongalers in question being camping punts manned by six paddle-wielding hearties, three on each side. As darkness fell, this rousing event was followed by a firework display and supper at a local hostelry or in a specially erected marquee.

These were great and glorious days, filled with sunshine and camaraderie. Unlike golf or salmon fishing, the sport was not so expensive that it fell beyond the pocket of the ordinary man. When I joined the club in 1928 the annual subscription was thirty shillings (£1.50). At the time of writing, fifty-nine years later, it is £50. It still represents excellent value for money.

*   *   *

The competition at regattas tended to be stiff. Entrants for any one race might number anything between four and sixteen and heats were rowed on a knockout basis. Consequently, by the end of the competition the winner would have taken part in four races, each of which became more gruelling and tiring as the afternoon progressed. Despite this, the standard of fitness was extremely high and many competitors enlisted for more than one event.

It was, of course, an amateur sport. As such, the prizes tended to be pint-sized pewter tankards or silver cups. Curiously, I always yearned to win a *quart*-sized tankard, an ambition which eluded me until 1932 when I was finally able to bear one home in triumph from the regatta at Teddington Reach.

At this date I was living at Shalford, near Guildford, and running a pig and poultry farm. The pigs numbered two hundred. In addition, the farm accommodated a small greenhouse in which my wife, Mabs, grew melons and cucumbers. These derived enormous benefit from being watered with the enriched liquid which drained from the pig manure.

One day – to my utter mortification – I discovered Mabs watering the contents of the greenhouse with my beloved quart tankard. It had become hopelessly corroded and the sight of it all but broke my heart. It ultimately vanished – I know not where.

*   *   *

After five or six years of skiff-racing, I began to wonder whether there might not be an easier way of passing a summer's afternoon and took up punting, another pursuit sponsored by Ditton Skiff and Punting Club.

Now punting, even in its most simple form, is a difficult art to master, as anyone who has gently propelled themselves along the Cherwell or the Cam will attest. Punt *racing* is fifty times more formidable.

Doubles punts were some thirty-three feet in length, two feet wide and propelled at speed through the water by means of fourteen-foot poles. The more skilled competitors usually graduated to the challenge of single-punt racing.

A single-punt was also thirty three feet long but a far more flimsy craft, being only thirteen or fourteen inches wide. The front and rear were canvas-covered, leaving a ten-foot well amidships in which the competitor stood. He did not walk up and down the boat but endeavoured to propel it from a fixed position.

I say 'endeavoured' because to a novice the basic premise seemed so contrary and impractical as to be almost inconceivable. Initially, I found that it was often all I could do simply to keep my feet. I didn't always succeed even in this and was frequently pitched headlong into the water.

F. H. T., with punting Championship Challenge Cup

However, with practice and application, sometimes even the inconceivable may be achieved; and within the space of a year or two I had not only mastered the art but graduated from racing the two-foot punts, to the singles craft. These were known as 'Best and Best' punts.

*   *   *

I now developed an active interest in punting and began to train in earnest. This required considerable dedication. I was living at that time at Wimbledon. Each morning I drove from there to Thames Ditton, arriving at 7.30. Having hauled out the boat, I would train for an hour under the watchful (and very critical) eye of Theo Hewitt. I would then leave for the office. On my return home in the evening I drove over to the boathouse and trained again.

It was physically gruelling, hideously time-consuming and occasionally bothersome. For anyone who sought to reach championship standards, it was also essential.

Races on the river are run on a knockout basis, in pairs. The Punting Championship on the Thames is run over a distance of three quarters of a mile and at speeds of up to eight miles an hour. Competitors race outwards to a marker pole, known as a 'peck', turning around this before commencing the run for home. 'Turning the peck' is something of a specialised art and where competitors are otherwise equally matched, races often hinge on doing so effectively.

*   *   *

In the course of my career I was fortunate enough to win a number of punting championships, among them the amateur championship held at Bray Reach near Maidenhead in 1949. A *Daily Mail* sports reporter covered the event. He wrote:

'Swans were a natural hazard on the course. Beer-drinking passengers in river steamers cheered and jeered as the punting championships were decided.

'To shouts of "Come on, Tubby" and "Well shoved, sir", stocky Frank H. Taylor won the amateur championship by pushing his narrow punt over three-quarters of a mile in seven minutes dead – and beating his friendly rival Nevill Milroy in the final.

'When he started practising this year he fell in nine times. To get pace on, the expert, working a 13ft aluminium pole, inclines the craft so that one side becomes a keel. In a sprint he can get up to 12 m.p.h.

'It seems that the English and the Japanese are the only nations who go in for this sport, and as the championship is open to all comers, Taylor is virtually world champion.'

I recall that in 1949 one of the advisers to competitors was 'Beau' Rixon, one of the great characters of the sport. Then aged eighty-three, he had thrice won the championship himself – thus fulfilling his ambition to emulate Lord Desborough's feat. He had done so for the last time in 1886, some sixty-five years previously. He remained very sprightly and was reputed to be the oldest active stockbroker in the City of London. He had fierce blue eyes and on that day in 1949 wore a panama hat. He told the Mail's reporter:

'Punting is dwindling. It's right down. Trouble is, there are too many pot-hunters now. Never a pot-hunter myself, y'know. One fellow stabbed his pole nastily through the canvas of my punt as I was beating him. Objected? Certainly not! Go in and win whatever happens. There were no ninnies about when I was punting. Trouble is, nobody tries to learn the back-shove now.'

The *Mail* described Frank Taylor as 'a man of 14st 5lbs, with big shoulders, a barrel chest and good legs'. It added:

'At the risk of giving away secrets I must record that Taylor was given three dessert-spoons of dark liquid before he won the singles – and went on to win the mixed doubles with Miss Wilkinson. Some Sunday newspapers credited Milroy with winning the championship. 'Well', said Taylor, 'I've got the cup and I can tell you it holds a surprising amount of beer.'

The dark liquid? Nothing more sinister than liver extract.

I won this competition at Maidenhead at the age of forty-two when I might more reasonably have been eligible to enter the veterans' event. In the course of a long career I also won the mens' doubles (on four occasions) and the mixed doubles (twice). My last championship win came in 1951 at the age of forty-four – more than twenty years after my success in winning the Marathon Sculling Championship on the Thames.

The immodesty of the above paragraph needs to be qualified by saying that almost no one in the amateur ranks of sport – myself included – makes the winning of championships their principal objective. It is also necessary to win friends. I should like to think that in my time with the club I made a good many; and that we share a number of happy memories, some sporting, some social, some a combination of both.

One weekend myself, Roy Burnham, Charlie Harvey and Claude Luke took two camping punts up the Thames to Hampton Court. Having tied up near the lock, we walked ashore and spent a long evening at the Caernarvon Castle pub.

Start of Punting Championship Final. F. H. T. nearest camera, with Neville Miroy

We started back to the punts around midnight. It was very dark. Perhaps as a result of this – perhaps as a result of the alcohol he had consumed – Claude Luke became detached. We separated to look for him.

At some point, Roy Burnham – who may also have been suffering from the after-affects of the evening – found himself standing in the middle of Hampton Court Bridge. Here he was spotted by a passing policeman. Said Burnham:

'Seen Luke?'

The startled bobby pondered this statement for a moment before saying: 'Who?'

'Luke', said Burnham, with a hint of irritation. 'You know. Luke. Biggish chap. Matthew, Mark, Luke and John'.

To ensure there should be no misunderstanding, he added: 'Luke'.

The policeman turned this over in his mind.

'A friend of yours, is he, this Luke?'

'Yes', said Burnham.

The guardian of the law gently turned Burnham around and with an equally gentle push in the small of the back said:

'Then maybe you'd better go and find him'.

37

*   *   *

Perhaps the most important river custom with which Ditton Skiff and Punting Club was associated was the ancient ceremony of Swan Upping.

Legend has it that the first swans on the Thames came to England as a gift to Richard I from Queen Beatrice of Cyprus. The species known as *Cygnus olor* still haunts the river. When Paul Hentzner visited England in the reign of Elizabeth I, he noted in his journal that many companies of swans frequented the Thames and that they lived:

'in great security, nobody daring to molest, much less kill, any of them, under penalty of a large fine'.

The protection which they enjoyed – and continue to enjoy – was in large part due to their being regarded as a royal bird; and the ownership of them has always been a privilege.

In 1496 a law was passed prohibiting anyone who did not possess a freehold property with a yearly rental value of at least five marks from owning a swan; and threatened anyone stealing a swan's egg with a year's imprisonment. The snaring or stealing of swans was, for the future, to be even more severely punished.

Most importantly of all, it was decreed that on every river in the kingdom all the swans were to be counted, examined and recorded. This census was afterwards re-taken every year and in the form of Swan Upping (or Swan Hopping) survives to this day.

Henry VIII commanded that all cygnets be marked with a nick on their beaks – and that any full-grown bird not so marked automatically became the property of the Crown. Henry's daughter, Elizabeth, extended this injunction by decreeing that anyone attempting to erase this mark should suffer twelve months' imprisonment.

According to one authority on the subject:

'For centuries Thames swans were regarded not only as decorative in a majestic way, but as a delicacy at royal feasts, while swan feathers were used for palace upholstery. Their economic value has declined, and it is their decorative effect which is most valued.

'Today on the Thames all the swans belong either to the sovereign or to the Dyers' and the Vintners', two of the ancient Liveried Companies of the City of London. The Queen still employs her 'Keeper of the Swans' who presides over the Swan Upping ceremony when, assisted by the swan masters of the Dyers' and the Vintners', he rounds up the new cygnets each year in late July or early August to mark their beaks – one mark for the Dyers', two for the Vintners' – and none for the Queen's.

'A small fleet of boats with banners flying and bearing the Royal Swan–Master, his assistants and the Swan–Masters of the two Liveried Companies, travels along the river to 'up' the birds, sometimes in lively scrimmages, the men all in colourful garments of red, green, blue, white and gold'.

'The annual Swan Upping takes two or three days to complete and each day the voyage concludes with a traditional banquet at a riverside inn.

'In 1980 the length of the journey, which once began at Southwark Bridge, was curtailed. It now starts at Sunbury and ends at Pangbourne'.

In the early 1950s there were almost 1,000 swans on the Thames. Owing to lead poisoning – probably occasioned by anglers' weights – this number declined drastically in the course of the next twenty years. To their credit, once the anglers were made aware of the problem, they switched to using weights fashioned from less toxic material. As a consequence, the number of swans is once more on the increase.

*   *   *

I retired from serious water-sport in 1951. However, through my association with the Thames Heritage Trust, I continue to contribute to the welfare of the river. The Trust is a charitable institution. With governmental assistance it pays unemployed youngsters a small weekly sum. In return they carry out vital conservation work – maintaining and restoring those river banks in danger of collapse from the wake of fast-moving craft. When the Ditton Club decided to build two new racing singles punts and sent out the customary appeal for sponsorship, I was pleased to be able to put something back into the sport which had given me so much pleasure by underwriting the entire cost of one of them. This Glenys was invited to launch. Due to the craft's fragility she had to settle for pouring a little champagne over the bows. To have broken the bottle across them might well have resulted in the breaking of the boat as well.

I have enjoyed my time on the river enormously. There is nothing, quite nothing, to compare with 'messing about in boats'. This said, it is not without its hidden dangers.

During my racing career, one of the river customs involved the Swan–Masters fattening up six cygnets for delivery to Buckingham Palace and – one assumes – the royal table. For at least two years they selected seven. This may have been done inadvertently. Then again it may not. In any event, the one extra somehow found its way on to the table of Ditton Skiff and Punting Club, where it formed

Glenys launches a 'ship'

the centrepiece of a cygnet supper accompanied by lashings of onion soup washed down by an appropriate quantity of beer.

I have a queasy feeling that this little dinner may have constituted an act of treason.

If so, I humbly beg Her Majesty's pardon and hope that as a result of this book I shall not be sent to the Tower.

CHAPTER SEVEN

CHARTERED ACCOUNTANT

N ow that I was qualified, Falk Keeping & Co. put me on the salary list. In 1930, the going rate for a brand new chartered accountant was three pounds a week, no great sum by modern standards, hardly enough for two pints of beer. To me it represented the riches of Lydia.

Life went on, initially, much as before. During the period of my articleship I had become fairly skilled in undertaking minor audits and these continued to constitute the bulk of my work. However, I was determined to strike out on my own as soon as circumstances permitted. My principals were aware of this and at a reduction in my weekly wage of twelve shillings (60p) it was mutually agreed that I should take one day off each week in order to found, and then to cultivate, my own practice. It was also agreed that I should devote at least a part of the time which I spent at Ironmonger Lane to coaching the junior clerk selected to take over my work when I ultimately left.

I found a small band of Old Rutlishians prepared to give me work. For this I charged a rate of ten-and-six (52p) an hour. They must have considered I was discharging this competently because they gave me more, recommended me to colleagues and business acquaintances, and within three or four months I found I had sufficient clients to form the nucleus of a practice.

It therefore became necessary to re-negotiate my arrangement with Falk, Keeping & Co. – to ask for two days off a week. In this way my practice grew, imperceptibly, until I found myself working less and less for the company and more and more for myself. Within about twelve months I was able to fill all my time independently and parted with my old employers on friendly terms.

It would be wrong to assume from all this that I achieved success overnight. I had been fortunate enough in finding my clients, but building up the practice involved working very long hours. Indeed, I found myself working harder than I had as an articled clerk when, in addition to my days at the office, I had devoted so many hours each week to study.

*   *   *

The more affluent among newly-qualified chartered accountants could rely on their families to purchase them a going practice. In my case this was, of course, out of the question. I invested two pounds in a typewriter which I installed in a make-shift office in one of the rooms of the family home in Mitcham. The possibility of employing staff was also out of the question and for a year I struggled along as best I could.

By the end of this period I had accumulated sufficient capital to acquire one room within the office of a solicitor friend, W. Timothy Donovan, in Bloomsbury's Gordon Square, situated between Woburn Place and Gower Street. For this I paid a pound a week.

In this manner the firm of Frank H. Taylor & Co. was born. Within a few months I was able to afford to employ a typist. She was paid £2 a week. This proved not to be a very good investment on my part. She was a very bad typist. As such she was soon replaced.

*   *   *

Just as I owe an enormous debt to Mr Varnish, my headmaster at Rutlish, so I shall always be grateful to Timothy Donovan. He was a great friend to me. The office which I rented from him at the back of his own provided me with a desperately-needed foothold on the first rung of the business ladder. As he would later introduce me to the fascinating world of politics, I am even further in his debt.

Donovan was a staunch Conservative. He was also the kind of man who firmly believed that it was not sufficient merely to hold political opinions. One needed to enter the fray and do one's best to see those opinions implemented. In consequence he took a keen interest in local politics and was a member of the Conservative opposition on Holborn and St. Pancras Council.

Power was then in the hands of the socialists, many of whom used the Labour Party as a stalking horse behind which to conceal an even closer affiliation to the now discredited credo of Communism. There were a number of almighty rows in the council chamber, but in the end Donovan, by now the leader of the Conservatives, succeeded in removing Labour from power – hauling, as he said, 'the red flag from down atop the Town Hall'.

He developed into an efficient and enlightened leader whose like is seldom found in politics these days, perhaps because it now attracts so many self-seekers of all denomination and party.

Donovan was the complete antithesis of a self-seeker. He cared about serving the community. Finding that he had sufficient money to be able to afford the time to do so, he saw it as his bounden duty. His work was ultimately rewarded with the C.B.E. His death in 1978 was a great loss to me.

*   *   *

Once I had reached the point of being able to afford to hire staff, I had also reached the point at which I required more office space in which to accommodate them. I took larger premises, on the other side of central London, in Kensington's Brompton Road. Here I remained for the next eight years. Curiously, I was again the sub-tenant of a firm of solicitors.

My time in Kensington is chiefly memorable now for the founding of the Brompton Finance Company. This was run by myself and a Wimbledon garage proprietor named Horace Pritchett. Its chief business was the advancing of money against the purchase of motor cars sold by Pritchett's garage. The buyers repaid their loans to the company by means of hire purchase agreements on the basis of regular instalments. Initially, we processed one transaction a week.

Over the next three or four years business might be said to have improved – were it not for the fact that I began to notice that a significantly high proportion of new clients were failing to keep up the repayments. I made one or two enquiries and learned that, confronted by a copper-bottomed borrower, Pritchett was loaning the hire purchase money out of his own pocket – thus by-passing the company entirely – and referring to it only the doubtful and the desperate.

I decided to purchase Pritchett's interest – which as a result of his own actions was practically worthless – and we duly parted company.

*   *   *

Despite this temporary set-back business in general continued to expand. Needing yet more space, I moved from Brompton Road to four first-floor rooms in an office block at Tooting Junction named Byton Chambers, built and owned by my brother, George, who retained the ground floor for the use of his business as an estate agent. George was kind enough to transfer his accountancy work to me and equally kind to pay me very well for my services. This enabled me to take on more staff, including a number of articled clerks.

43

Some of these ultimately found the period of articleship too great an obstacle to surmount and passed out of the profession. One who did not was Bill Atkins – who ironically enough long looked destined to become the greatest failure of them all.

Bill Atkins joined me as a boy typist at the age of sixteen. He was a likeable lad but a hopeless typist. He tended to take the line of least resistance, putting off until tomorrow what might easily have been encompassed today – an attitude unbecoming in a would-be accountant and one which at times I personally found intensely irritating.

At the same time, he appeared keen to learn. Consequently, after three or four months, I moved him into accountancy and gave him him his articles. Unfortunately, Bill Atkins's dilatoriness was incurable and – rather as I had done at Rutlish – he continued to do just enough work to get by. As a result, and after two or three failures, he did manage to pass his intermediate exam, but continuously failed his finals.

He religiously re-took these for the best part of two decades, initially sitting the examination twice a year and then, as he grew more and more demoralised, only once. It was not until he had been past his articled time by more than twenty years that – to my surprise and to his own utter astonishment – he passed. It was some weeks before he could bring himself to believe it.

*　　*　　*

The coming of war in 1939 brought in its wake a huge demand for the services of accountants and in consequence I was registered exempt from enlistment. However, I believed then – as I believe now – that in times of trouble one should rally to the flag; and shortly before the end of that period of unnatural calm which preceded the 'Blitz' – the months which became known as the 'Phoney War' – I contacted the War Office to see how I might best be of use.

I was summoned to an interview in Whitehall where an army officer listened in silence to my dilemma. Having done so, he pushed back his chair and said:

'No problem, old chap. We'll put you in the Pay Corps.'

This was very far from what I had in mind – and I told him so.

In a curious way, surrounded as he probably was by yes-men, he seems to have appreciated this show of forthrightness and confided that most of the ministries were desperately short of accountants to man the numerous new departments which as a result of the conflict were springing up almost weekly. As I was leaving, he said:

'Don't worry. Leave it with me. I'll ask about'.

*   *   *

He was as good as his word and very shortly afterwards I was called to several ministries for interview. One of these was the Ministry of Food, where I was offered, and accepted, the post of Finance Director. I quickly found an accountant I considered competent to run the practice during my absence and duly reported for work.

I remained at the Ministry of Food for two and a half years. I then accepted a similar posting to the Ministry of War Transport, where I saw out the war. Of both these appointments – and the trials and triumphs entailed upon them – more hereafter.

At the end of the war I returned to my accountancy practice. I found that the man whom I had detailed to run it had possessed no initiative and even less professional judgement. I wasn't ruined, but I was in a serious mess – a mess which could only be remedied by rebuilding the business almost from scratch. I found this a deeply depressing prospect.

Fortunately, soon after my return I heard that William Flower, the elderly principal of a firm of Wimbledon accountants, was considering at the very least cutting back on his activities and very possibly retiring.

William Flower was a tired man. He had been worn down by life and had never, anyway, been altogether in sympathy with it. Spiritually, he belonged to an earlier, Dickensian, era. A strict Presbyterian, he proceeded through life like a stately Spanish galleon. Modern innovations confused him. He failed to understand either their workings or their significance for the future. He enjoyed playing bowls and had a wife called Blossom – perhaps predictably, given his surname.

William Flower happily agreed to let me purchase a quarter interest in his firm. A year later I increased this stake to fifty percent. Two years after that, whilst attending a Rotarian conference at Brighton, I heard with great sadness that he had died. I bought the balance of the practice and thus became its principal.

There were now two businesses to run: one in Wimbledon, one in London. I travelled into London from Wimbledon two days a week. I prospered.

Soon, both offices were employing between fifteen and twenty people. This was very exciting, It was also a considerable responsibility because I have always believed that every employer has a duty which goes beyond keeping those who help him in work and wages. He must also be interested in their general welfare. People are a great deal more than the sum of their titles – secretaries, typists, clerks and assistants.

It is an oblique indictment of many employers that one should need to spell this out: but people desperately need to be treated as intelligent individuals who can expect as a matter of right to be rewarded for their skill and initiative. They should never be humiliated when, through minor error or lack of experience, they fail in the short-term to live up to expectations or to take an easy profit.

*   *   *

The Brompton Finance Company, the hire purchase enterprise which I had founded in Kensington in partnership with the garage proprietor Horace Pritchett, continued down the years to make only modest returns. Its existence nevertheless alerted me to the possibility of diversifying out of the hum-drum line of accountancy, which for some years had constituted the majority of my business.

To this end, and in February 1959, I founded the Wimbledon and South West Finance Co. Ltd., the share capital of which was just a thousand pounds. Almost from the date of its inception – and largely due to the amount of time and effort which I invested in it – the Wimbledon and South West Finance Company made remarkable progress. A number of my accountancy clients were persuaded to endorse it more tangibly, loaning money at what were then very acceptable rates of interest.

I found the world of finance suited my skills and temperament every bit as much as accountancy. Consequently, when I was approached with offers to hive off some aspects of the accountancy practice, usually at a handsome profit, I tended to acquiesce. I had become a little disenchanted with the profession.

Part of the reason for this was that by this time I had taken in a number of junior partners, few of whom had any ability to bring in new business. This was vital if we were to expand. They were mostly good workers – would hardly have been partners otherwise – but they were incapable of advancing the practice. I became resentful that I was the only one who gleaned new clients; that in difficult times and situations I was the only one possessed of the necessary diplomatic skills required to keep them.

It was these problems then – initially only half-understood but growing month by month – which made me think of diversifying into politics or finance. The Finance Company continued to make profits. But these were not destined to improve dramatically until Brian Howe joined the company in 1974.

It was then increasing in size very rapidly. I realised that if the momentum was to be maintained it would be necessary to inject additional capital. This I did by increasing both the number of shareholders and the number of directors.

Four new directors joined the Board and took up shares. Two of these were old accountancy clients. The remaining two were known to me from other areas of my business and social life. Each had made his way in his chosen profession. If none was exactly rich, they were all comfortably off.

More importantly, they had incisive business brains and were capable of talking what is commonly termed 'horse sense'. As such they were able to furnish me with solid objective advice regarding the direction in which the company should move and grow. I had of course to pay a price – by relinquishing sole proprietorship. Thereafter my holding was reduced to a mere twenty per cent. It was a sacrifice which in the long term was to prove eminently worthwhile.

Brian Howe proved something of a human dynamo. Having joined the firm, he was soon appointed Company Secretary and progressed to become a director. He is now chief executive. He brought to the business what others conspicuously lacked: a clear brain, a clear understanding of problems and, above all, an ability to sell the service.

He and I have jointly progressed in the venture until, at the time of writing, the Wimbledon & South West Finance Company Limited has net taxable profits in excess of a million pounds a year. There is the very real prospect of a public share issue.

To someone who began his career in accountancy some sixty years ago, commanding a wage of £3 a week, a million pounds a year is a sum almost (but not quite) beyond comprehension. However, the 1990–92 depression hit almost everybody – especially those engaged in the financial world. Alas, we did not escape, but are now striving to climb again.

*   *   *

In 1981 my career in accountancy was recognized in a letter from the Institute of Chartered Accountants, congratulating me on my fifty years' service to the profession. About the same time, I received a similar letter from the Institute of Chartered Secretaries.

Ten years have passed since then and I have now been sixty years in my joint careers. During this time I have sweated blood and I have cried tears – although never a great deal of either. I do not regret one minute. Unquestionably, I suffered seriously financially during the period I spent in public service during the war. The finance company suffered similarly during my term as a member of parliament.

Yet without these interludes my life would have been less full. I would have been significantly the poorer as a man.

CHAPTER EIGHT

GOLF

B y 1936 life seemed very good indeed. Business was developing well and I was happily married. Rugby occupied my winters and athletics and the River Thames took up much of each summer.

I had also begun to learn something of golf, one of the world's most irritating games. We were living at this time at 21 Coombe Gardens in West Wimbledon. Beyond our rear garden lay a sports ground belonging to the War Office. I found this an ideal place to practice.

Encouraged by my friends, I became a member of Malden Golf Club, where I began to spend a considerable amount of time hacking around the course. I improved my game only slowly and then with difficulty. In 1938 I joined the Royal Automobile Club, which allowed me to play their two courses at Woodcote Park, near Epsom.

In 1938 Life Membership of the R.A.C. cost £100. As the yearly subscription was £15.00, this represented an attractive long-term saving. Unfortunately, I didn't have a hundred pounds, nor did I have any hope of borrowing it. This has always been a matter of regret to me.

Nevertheless, through the club I came to be acquainted with a number of interesting people including the charismatic boxer, Bombardier Billy Wells, who a quarter of a century earlier had fought that epic match with Georges Carpentier for the European heavyweight title. Even when well past his prime, Wells remained superbly strong and was capable of hitting a golf ball enormous distances. He had an easy, charming manner and in middle-age still possessed the elegant, upright carriage which had been such a notable feature of his style in the ring.

*   *   *

My most memorable game of golf – not necessarily for the standard of play – occurred in September 1939. Jack Angle and I were half-way up the seventh fairway at Woodcote Park at eleven o'clock on a sunny Sunday morning when the calm was broken by the wailing of air-raid sirens. Britain was finally at war with Germany. The green-keeper's wife came bustling out of her little bungalow, her face ashen. 'Come in at once!', she said, 'Take shelter. The Germans are coming!'

Remembering Drake, we decided to finish our game and deal with the enemy later.

* * *

During the war there was hardly any golf, largely because so many members disappeared into the services. The absence of green staff meant the courses deteriorated. The grass grew long on the fairways. The rough became an impenetrable jungle upon which even the grazing sheep could make no great impression. A large hay-rick stood where the tenth tee had formerly been.

With Hitler's U–boat blockade seeking to starve the country into surrender, the need for home-produced food became of paramount importance. The R.A.C.'s new course was dug up and used for the growing of wheat and grass. The club-house was eerily under-populated, the car park almost devoid of vehicles. Petrol rationing was in force and only authorised journeys were permitted.

Only the shortened Old Course remained at all playable. This was nonetheless a great boon for members, especially officer members home on short leave. However, as elsewhere, the lack of staff made it a travesty of its former self and lost balls were legion.

After the war things gradually returned to normal and from 1947 to 1953 I enjoyed seven excellent years of golf at the R.A.C. In 1957 I was invited to become a member of the Committee; and in October 1961 was privileged to be appointed captain.

I was invested at the traditional Drive In ceremony, where the outgoing captain introduces the new one to the members. The new incumbent is then invited to cut a tape and to drive a ball down the fairway into a gathering of caddies. The distance the caddies stand from the tee reflects their opinion of the new man's driving prowess. This is often uncannily accurate. The ball arcs away in the direction of the assembled caddies who scramble to retrieve it. In my day, the one succeeding received a pound.

My Drive In created something of a record. It was October and the course was enveloped in thick fog. Visibility was down to a hundred yards. I drove what I considered to be a very good ball in the general direction of the invisible caddies. It was quickly enveloped by the mist. There was a great deal of distant shouting and scuffling before one man, burlier than the rest, emerged from the fog with a ball in his hand. This he represented as mine. We could not of course establish this for certain, but neither could we disprove it. My own feeling is that it *was* the right ball but taken from (the no doubt smaller) caddy who actually caught it. Whatever the truth of the matter, I had established at my Drive In one record which can never be surpassed: that of having hit the ball literally 'out of sight'.

*   *   *

My term as captain of the R.A.C. was hectic, exciting and very happy. Unfortunately, it coincided with my election to parliament as Conservative member for Manchester Moss Side. With constituency surgeries and captaincy duties conflicting, this meant that I was required to be in two places at once every weekend. I resolved the problem by alternating them. As most of the working week was spent during the parliamentary term in London, this meant that for the best part of a year my family hardly saw me at all.

Such a busy schedule also meant that I played less frequently. This in turn produced a dramatic deterioration in the standard of my game. In 1961, the year I was elected to parliament, I had a handicap of ten. Thirteen years later, when I retired from the House, it had plummeted to twenty-one.

During my term as captain of the R.A.C. I was gratified to be able to found the annual match with the Royal Scottish Automobile Club. The first of these encounters was a two-day event of twelve pairings held in 1962 in Glasgow.

Now, although they have very cunningly learned to hide the fact, the Scots have never really forgiven us for Culloden. Quite unknown to us, our opponents had scoured the entire country for outstanding players. The first day we won just one of the twelve singles matches. The following day we managed to win another and to halve one more. The slaughter of the Sassenachs was complete.

I'm pleased to say that the Scots have now ceased to take the matter quite so seriously and the event has developed into one of the most eagerly anticipated in either club's calendar.

*   *   *

These days I play golf only infrequently. But as the senior of the past golf captains of the Royal Automobile Club – and that by some years – I always endeavour to attend the annual Drive In. After this, and in company with other past captains, I play a four-ball game around a shortened course before retiring to enjoy the celebrations in the clubhouse. These usually continue for the rest of the day. This is only as it should be. Golf is a companionable game.

It must also, down the years, have made liars of more men than fishing.

50

CHAPTER NINE

WAR

The sound of the sirens which heralded the outbreak of war with Germany on that sunny Sunday morning in September 1939 came as no surprise. They had been expected for some little time. It is now fashionable to denigrate Chamberlain and to dismiss all his efforts as appeasement in its most cringing form. This may be so. It may be not.

Chamberlain's greatest 'crime' may have been that he completely misjudged Hitler's character. When in September 1938 he returned from Munich, waving the famous piece of paper which, he claimed, would bring 'peace for our time', there were many who believed him. If he was ultimately proved disastrously wrong, the year of peace which that piece of paper brought was to prove invaluable to the war effort. In 1938 we were hopelessly ill-equipped to take on the might of a fully re-armed Germany.

I knew something of the problem through one of my clients, an Old Rutlishian named Steve Mann, who, through the firm of Ralph & Mann, imported baths from Germany. He visited that country on a fairly regular basis and became very aware of the developments taking place there. He was a member of the German Chamber of Commerce in England and in 1938 invited me to attend a dinner given by this organisation at the Savoy Hotel in London. During the course of the evening I had a brief conversation with the German Ambassador, Joachim von Ribbentrop – who eight years later would be the first of the Nuremberg Nazis to be hanged.

As with all good ambassadors, von Ribbentrop made a point of discussing my career and interests rather than his own. The conversation mainly revolved around accountancy and the ways in which it differed between our two countries. He spoke excellent English. He told me that in Germany accountants were as mythical a beast as James Thurber's unicorn and simply did not exist, all accounts being audited and submitted to the revenue authorities by officials of the state.

Having begun life as a wine merchant, von Ribbentrop fancied himself as something of an epicure. Like so many Nazis, he enjoyed the high life and was a frequent guest at the dinner parties given by London Society hostesses between the wars.

At the outbreak of war he had the farcical ill-luck to be sitting in the War Office in Whitehall. His diplomatic immunity rendered him safe and he was allowed to return to the Fatherland. Hitler appointed him Foreign Minister. Captured after the war by the British, he went to his death calmly, saying: 'I wish peace to all the world' . . . a novel sentiment coming from such a source.

*   *   *

Although war is generally considered to have come in 1939, it did not in fact break out in any literal sense until August 1940, when German planes made their first bombing raids on London, heralding the onset of the Blitz.

In the late afternoon of 7 September – so sure of overcoming our puny anti-aircraft defences that they could not even be bothered to wait for darkness – three hundred bombers mounted an attack on London's East End. In minutes the docks were ablaze and more than four hundred people went to their death in a savage overture to a massive campaign of incendiary intimidation that was to last for many months. Suddenly, Londoners were in the front line. This was for me a new experience – as for many others. I didn't care for it one bit.

I came to care for it even less after finding myself at the sharp end of one of these encounters. On the day in question I was sitting in the office of a client in Merton High Street. As black comedy had arranged this little scenario, it followed that the client was an undertaker.

A wave of German aircraft flew over, bombing and strafing the High Street with machine-gun fire. I had of course heard the sound of gun-fire before – but in the Cadet Corps at Rutlish. It had not prepared me for this. The noise was indescribable, as was the sound of the exploding bombs. I found myself rooted to the spot, paralysed. In a gesture of pathetic self-protection I pressed my back hard against the wall, seeking almost to become a part of it. I was in a state of shock.

As good luck would have it, we were spared. A shed at the rear of the property, about forty yards distant, was not. It received a direct hit from a small bomb and disappeared in a cloud of dust and a shower of fragments.

*   *   *

Frightening though they were, experiences such as this fostered a spirit of great camaraderie. We were – we kept telling one another – all in this together, no longer simply individuals but a team pulling together for the common good. As such, we dug for victory; we saved for victory; we even guarded our tongues for victory because, as the posters said, 'Careless Talk Costs Lives', and spies and fifth columnists were thought to be everywhere.

The spivs and other black-market racketeers who sought to capitalise on the situation were disliked. Yet perhaps not disliked by everyone because, with the exception of the industry generated by the war effort, the Black Market became, as a result of the shortages imposed by rationing, a principal source of income.

In the country the worst effects of rationing could be alleviated. People grew their own vegetables, cultivated their own livestock, even if it was only rabbits and birds.

City-dwellers fared less well. In most cases, and with the exception of a few favours for close friends or those who had something to barter, tradesmen were compelled to adhere to the rationing regulations very strictly. There was never enough to go round and I remember that at one point the value of the weekly ration of meat fell to just eightpence (3p.). This could be supplemented by the occasional tin of corned beef and by offal, both of which were 'off the ration', but they were enormously difficult to obtain. Hitler's blockade of food imports was proving effective. Consequently, there were many children who had never seen an orange or a banana, let alone the cornucopia of exotic fruits which we expect to see on the supermarket shelves today.

People resorted to various stratagems to keep their private arrangements secret from those queuing behind. I recall one lady in particular, who operated by the use of a code. When she arrived at the counter of her butcher in Tooting she would ask him if he had repaired her 'mudguard'. He would disappear into the back of the shop and return with an ox tail, pre-wrapped to conceal it from the jealous eyes of other customers.

In November 1940 the then Minister of Food, Lord Woolton (who gave his name to the austerity 'Woolton Pie') announced that this year carrots would take the place of dried fruit in millions of Christmas puddings. He hinted at extra tea and sugar for the period of the holiday but asked people to use less milk. He said he was not prepared to place controls on such luxury food items as turkeys or confectionery. Sweet rationing was to come later.

*   *   *

Most people tended to remain on the surface at night, bravely risking the worst. A minority chose the shelters, although sleep was often made impossible by the noise of the falling bombs. As in all times of crisis, there were countless opportunities for the dry, understated humour so characteristic of the British. After one raid, a newspaper reporter was despatched to the East End to interview its victims. He found an old lady standing amidst the rubble of her former home and asked her what she made of it all.

'Well, dear', she replied, 'I really couldn't say, I'm sure. Perhaps there's right and wrong on both sides. But if 'itler goes on like this 'e's going to get 'isself disliked.'

I know of no one who was intimidated by the Blitz and to that degree it failed in its objective. The general feeling was not one of fear or apprehension, but anger and defiance. This seemed to lend us superhuman energy and overstretched rescue services performed prodigious feats almost as a matter of course.

Bombs fell impartially on rich and poor alike – six on the royal family at Buckingham Palace, prompting the Queen to make her famous remark that she and her family could 'now look the East End in the face'. In Balham a bomb dropped near the underground station. Moments later, a bus travelling along the High Street toppled into the enormous crater left by this and demolished a major water main. The water flooded into the underground. Hundreds of people were trapped and drowned.

*   *   *

At the end of November 1940, Goering changed his tactics and began attacking provincial cities. Many of his planes were now equipped with special navigational devices which allowed them to locate and destroy specific industrial targets. Six hundred tons of high explosive and thousands of incendiary bombs were dropped on Coventry, reducing the Cathedral to a charred and smoking shell. Birmingham, Sheffield, Manchester and Glasgow also suffered.

On 29 December, the Germans turned their attention towards London once more in one of the most devastating attacks of the entire campaign. With characteristic Teutonic efficiency, the raid was timed to coincide with tidal low water in the Thames. The exposed water mains were quickly shattered by high explosive parachute mines. These were followed by at least ten thousand fire bombs. For a time the fires raged out of control because the twenty thousand firemen who converged on this scene of devastation were unable to pump water from the fractured mains.

Luckily for the City, the raid was broken off just as the Luftwaffe appeared to be in sight of victory. The official explanation put out by the Air Ministry was that the aircraft were recalled due to the weather unexpectedly deteriorating over low-lying German airfields. There are those who might prefer to consider it a miracle.

*   *   *

In January 1941 sweeping new price controls were introduced to curb food profiteering. The average working-class family in Britain then had a budget of less than £5 a week, of which approximately one fifth was spent on food. Many women who before the war had been nothing more or less than housewives now found themselves the subject of a massive mobilisation programme aimed at filling vital jobs in industry and the auxiliary services.

On the night of May 10 1941 Londoners suffered an air raid which, hardened though they were by nine months of the Blitz, all but broke their hearts. In brilliant moonlight, five hundred and fifty German planes dropped bombs indiscriminately. Fourteen hundred people died that night. Parliament was hit, Big Ben scarred. St. Paul's was damaged – not for the first time – as was the British Museum. Amid the carnage, there were uplifting stories of heroism and of happy escapes. A firewatcher on duty at one of the hospitals told of being hurled from the building and landing safely, many feet below, on top of a telephone kiosk.

This raid proved to be the Germans' last desperate throw. There were other raids, but they lacked the impetus of their predecessors; and when, in the June, Nazi tanks smashed into Minsk, breaking the pact of non-aggression with Russia, Hitler found it necessary to deploy his resources elsewhere.

*   *   *

The war was beginning, imperceptibly, to turn. In a long-range sweep through the Western Desert, south-west of the main battlefield of Tobruk, the Desert Rats had penetrated eighty miles into Cyrenaica. By the spring of 1942, the R.A.F. was meting out to German cities a devastation similar to that which the Luftwaffe had visited on Britain. The Japanese were being pushed back in Burma. In the October, Montgomery scored a major victory at the battle of El Alamein. (I would later view the ghostly burned-out tanks destroyed in this battle for myself.)

By 1943 the tide had also begun to turn in the Atlantic U–boat war. In the July the Allies landed at Palermo. By the beginning of September the Italian forces were on the brink of surrender.

The Third Reich, which was to have lasted a thousand years, was now under intense pressure on every front. On June 6 1944 a terse low-key announcement from General Eisenhower's headquarters told the world that the long-awaited

55

invasion of Europe had begun. French tanks led the Allies into Paris. Berlin, battered night and day from the air, was close to collapse.

In April 1945 Hitler took his own life – complaining to the end that the whole thing had not been his fault, laying the blame on the English and the Americans, lackeys of the Jewish–Bolshevik conspiracy.

On VE Day, people took to the streets in their thousands to celebrate. The drabness and privation of five years of war were forgotten. A huge roar greeted Winston Churchill as he drove down the Mall to lunch at the Palace. Fifty thousand people went wild with joy, at first shaking hands then kissing, hugging, dancing with complete strangers. A massive hokey-cokey snaked round the statue of Queen Victoria in front of Buckingham Palace. Wearing his famous hat and siren suit, Winston Churchill appeared on the balcony of the Ministry of Health in Whitehall. The Guards' Band struck up: 'For He's a Jolly Good Fellow'.

Licensing laws were suspended for the night. Crowds gathered in front of the Palace shouting: 'We want the King!' He at last came out, holding hands with his wife and daughters. It was the first of eight such appearances he would make before the end of the evening. After dinner, Princesses Elizabeth and Margaret, escorted by two young army officers, mingled unobtrusively with the crowds and joined in the shouts for the King.

*   *   *

In August 1945 the atom bomb vaporised two Japanese cities and the war came to a complete end. The price of victory and defeat? Fifty-five million dead, many of them civilians.

Celebrations were muted at first. Then came the sound of ships' sirens and the whistling of railway trains. On VJ Day, bonfires blazed from Orpington to Ramsgate and long before dawn crowds began to descend on London in much the manner they had done to celebrate VE Day. There was more dancing, flag-waving, beating of drums and blowing of whistles. American servicemen in carnival hats waved their own national flag. It was their victory too (as they never ceased to repeat). The more thoughtful among the population began to congregate in London's churches for hurriedly-arranged services of thanksgiving.

It was over.

CHAPTER TEN

KEEPING THE HOME FIRES BURNING

By 1939 I had been living at Wimbledon for three years. I had come to like the area and formed a number of close associations with it. Consequently, with the outbreak of war, I felt that I wanted to do something to defend it. Being fractionally too old to enlist, I did the next best thing and joined the Local Defence Volunteers, the forerunner of the Home Guard. The man appointed to command this was Lieutenant–Colonel 'Taffy' Tenison.

Colonel Tenison – unless one knew him very well he was not the sort of man you called 'Taffy' to his face – was a veteran of the second battle of Ypres. Here in April 1915 the Germans had deployed mustard-gas against the British for the first time. Partly as a result of this, casualties were horrendous. Despite the heroic behaviour of Tenison in particular – for which he was rewarded with the D.S.O. – and of the British and Canadian forces in general, the Germans gained two miles along a five-mile front.

It has been said of the second battle of Ypres (as it has sometimes been said of the battle of Neuve–Chapelle, which immediately preceded it) that during it the protagonists discharged more ammunition than was used during the entire course of the Boer War, fifteen years earlier.

This was rather more firepower than the Local Defence Volunteers could muster. Initially, its members didn't even possess uniforms, the only indication of their determination to win the war from home being an arm-band bearing the force's initials.

The country in general had been ill-prepared for war. The Home Guard was even more so. We were – at least in those early days – something of a Dad's Army joke. We had no weapons, and no headquarters other than Lieutenant–Colonel Tenison's capacious haversack. Into this he stuffed the correspondence he received from his masters, the mandarins of the War Office. He never opened any of these letters until they had been given at least two weeks to mature. He realised that most of their contents were either irrelevant or seeking answers to problems which during the interim would have resolved themselves. If this was the kind of behaviour one might have expected from a military type in a novel by Evelyn Waugh, I can only say that it worked in practice very well.

* * *

As we adjusted to war-time conditions, the powers-that-be found themselves with a little more time to resolve some of our more long-term problems. Wimbledon Home Guard was allocated the former headquarters of the Territorial Army in St. George's Road. This had several good rooms – the best of which, predictably, was immediately turned into a Mess for the officers – and some passable office accommodation. It also possessed an excellent drill hall and rifle range.

Tenison appointed me section leader for the Merton Park area. This incorporated a considerable part of Wimbledon. My main duties consisted of overseeing the filling of sandbags and the positioning of redouts which – had a German invasion ever materialised – might have been a less than adequate defence against a Panzer 'blitzkrieg'.

I must have shown some aptitude for sandbag-filling, because when the Local Defence Volunteers was transformed into the Home Guard I was appointed commander of 'D' Company, one of five companies within the battalion. This brought promotion to major.

* * *

'D' company acquired headquarters in Mansel Road. This came complete with a resident warden and housekeeper, a Sergeant Tubbs and his wife, who over the months were to prove a great help to me – and to everyone else in 'D' Company.

I could not say as much for the War Office, which in fairness must, from the demands made upon it, have found its administrative arm hopelessly stretched. Sometimes weapons arrived – most of them antique carbines, relics from the Great War – sometimes ammunition. They seldom arrived together. When they did they were not always compatible. They did at least enable us to drill with some degree of credibility; and through contact with regular army units stationed in the area we gradually acquired a more acceptable military bearing and sense of discipline.

As a major, I commanded a three-hundred-strong force disposed between four platoons. These were composed of men of every age, description and physical type. For all this – and contrary to many people's image of the Home Guard – we were not permitted to enrol people indiscriminately. Recruitment was strictly regulated by the War Office. Its officials were surprisingly fussy. This posed a serious and constant problem.

Home Guard Inspection (Major Taylor extreme left)

One afternoon a gentleman of European extraction was shown into my office. He claimed to be a prince and may well have been so. As he owned Wimbledon Park House, a local mansion with extensive grounds, he was certainly affluent. He explained in what struck me as tones of sincerity that he hated the Nazis and all their causes. He desperately wanted to play his part in defeating them. Might he be allowed to join the Home Guard? Ever on the watch for spies and fifth columnists, the War Office vetoed the proposal on the grounds that he was not in possession of a British passport.

Spy or not, we could have used his money . . . if necessary to turn the tables on him, whatever his real political allegiance.

Nonetheless, we did have one or two home-grown stars of our own who could sometimes be of use. One of these was Colonel Carlisle (D.S.O. and Bar), who, like Lieutenant–Colonel Tenison, was a veteran of the First World War. Although past seventy years of age, Colonel Carlisle volunteered to become a member of the Home Guard at the lowest level. He sought no special privileges. He was no

59

longer robust and his usefulness in combat must have been questionable. He was nevertheless a great cosmetic addition to No.1 Platoon and was regularly placed in the front rank for the benefit of inspecting big-wigs. Many of these found it difficult to reconcile the row of highly impressive medals gleaming on his chest with the lowly rank of private. On reaching him, those who considered soldiers something more than a cypher, actually stopped to talk to him and learn the truth. In his modest way, Colonel Carlisle found this gratifying and so did we.

* * *

When the war entered its first active phase in September 1940, with the onset of the Blitz, life for my particular Home Guard outpost became a great deal more interesting and active.

Wimbledon is best known for its association with the All England Tennis Club. It also has an important railway junction. It was this which attracted the notice of the German bombers. They sought to immobilise it, thereby hampering the Allied war effort by hobbling the movement of vital raw materials. Night after night the enemy mounted low-flying missions to attack all three of London's principal railway stations south of the Thames. They began with Waterloo, proceeded to Clapham Junction and finally came on to us. We were alerted to their approach by the sound of wailing sirens.

Initially, these attacks were light – sticks of six bombs delivered at fifteen-second intervals. We listened for the first of these to explode – and then for the other five in rotation. From the sound they made it was possible to judge not only whether they had found their target but whether the aircraft were approaching – in which case they meant business – or merely jettisoning their bombs – in which case they were beating a hasty retreat.

It was gruelling work. Many of the men under my command were past their prime. It became necessary to walk a fine line. On the one hand I had a duty to keep them as fit as humanly possible. On the other, I had no wish to induce an outbreak of heart attacks.

We weeded out the chronically unfit by a series of route-marches. These carried us up Wimbledon Hill and around the Common, a distance of five miles. As for a part of the course the participants were required to wear gas masks, this swiftly sorted out the men from the Methuselahs.

I was abetted in these manoeuvres by Dick Holloway, one of my platoon commanders. Dick was a gentleman. He was also the senior director of the family building company, Holloway Brothers. As such he was able to keep the Home Guard supplied with essential materials.

We awaited the Germans with high expectations. We burnished our kit and oiled our guns against their arrival. They didn't come. This was very disappointing. We were spoiling for a fight. We couldn't understand it. Why didn't they cross the Channel? Could it be that they were occupied elsewhere? It was probably one of the greatest miracles of the war that they were.

*   *   *

The companies which went to make up the 54th Surrey Home Guard consisted of 'A' and 'B' Companies, commanded respectively by Majors Hastings and Wilson; 'C' Company, based at the top of Wimbledon Hill, contained a sprinkling of important businessmen, and because of this considered itself rather above the rest of us in both senses of the word. 'D' Company was my own command; and 'E' Company was composed of the employees at Wimbledon Electricity headquarters.

The battalion was extremely close-knit. Everyone appeared to know everyone else. There was, nevertheless, considerable rivalry to see which company could triumph over the rest in the all-important matter of recruitment.

Here I had something of an unfair advantage. Each week I wrote an article on the activities of the Home Guard for the *Wimbledon Borough News*. Naturally enough, this tended to concentrate on the work carried on by my own company. I didn't exactly understate our achievements and these articles brought us a steady flow of new recruits. This became an irritant to the other company commanders – and ultimately to Colonel Tenison, who mildly complained that no one ever seemed to talk about the battalion or him. Wasn't 'D' Company rather hogging the limelight? As a palliative, I arranged that the following week my article should comment on the battalion in general and Colonel Tenison in particular.

*   *   *

In 1942 I joined the Ministry of Food and was posted to Colwyn Bay. Consequently, I had to relinquish my Wimbledon command. This was a cause of great regret to me. I had been very happy there.

However, soon after my arrival in Wales I joined a Home Guard battalion operated by the Ministry of Food. As I was considered to have given up command of the Wimbledon Battalion Company of my own volition, it was not possible to retain my old rank of major and I had to begin all over again as a humble private. I had no objection to this. Within a month or so I was appointed to be lieutenant training officer, a job which I discharged with a good deal of enthusiasm, not least because I viewed it as a fast route to promotion. This it proved to be.

The four battalions which constituted the Home Guard sector in North Wales were commanded by a very pleasant gentleman named Colonel Shennon. A director of the Pen Maen Mawr slate quarry, he had a restricted grasp of military matters. When he let it be known that he wished to make an appointment to his staff of someone capable of drawing up a contingency plan to deal with the prospect of a German invasion, I was happy to accept – both the commission and the consequent promotion to brigade major.

Although the idea of a German invasion must now seem laughable, it was very far from being so then, especially in North Wales. Historically, the Irish have always had a cordial dislike for the British, possibly with some justification. At the time of the First World War they had gleefully collaborated with the Germans. Now, once more, there were deeply disturbing reports of German submarines prowling the Irish Sea. If Hitler decided to land in that faction-ridden country, it would be a simple matter for him to cross the straits to Anglesey. From there a fast and straight coastal road ran directly to the mainland.

In formulating the contingency plan against a German invasion requested by Colonel Shennon, I came to realise that the six-inch gun implacements at Llandudno might have some part to play in limiting any enemy advance. In the region of Pen Maen Mawr there were two places where the coastal road vanished into a tunnel of rock. If the weapons could be brought to bear on these and fired to pound the cliff face, they could bring large quantities of rock crashing into the road, blocking the tunnel. I therefore incorporated this into the sector contingency operation plan.

*   *   *

Time passed. My duties as finance director with the Ministry and my responsibilities as Brigade Major, G.S.O.2 kept me happy and fully occupied. At Christmas 1943 I returned home to Wimbledon. On Christmas Day I received a telephone call from Colonel Shennon offering me the command of the Home Guard's 1st Caernarvonshire Battalion.

This was a prize indeed. It meant I would be responsible for a vast amount of territory covering almost the entire western side of the River Conway, along the northern coast from Conway to Aber and down to a cluster of villages south-east of Snowdon.

I was completely at a loss for words. After a long silence I managed to blurt out: 'Thank you very much'. In the course of just a few months my fortunes had swung wildly. From a major at Wimbledon I had been demoted to a private at Colwyn Bay. I had then been elevated to the rank of lieutenant, thence to major once more and finally – as a battalion commander – to the rank of Lieutenant–Colonel.

* * *

As much of my new battalion command-area was mountainous and desolate, I commissioned a map to a scale of six inches to the mile. This was fashioned in one piece and when completed measured thirty feet by twenty. It covered the whole of one very large wall and part of the ceiling. It was initially thought of as something of a battalion joke. It later became invaluable.

By 1943 the RAF was carrying out regular night-time bombing raids on Germany. Its aircraft were inflicting terrible damage. They did not always manage to escape unscathed. Some had their landing-gear shot away, others had their direction-finding equipment incapacitated. Unable either to find their way home or a satisfactory site on which to make a crash-landing, many came to grief in the mist-enshrouded mountains of North Wales. My battalion invariably despatched a detachment to look for survivors. The map proved invaluable not only in identifying the possible location of the crash but the best route by which to approach it. At the end of the war I presented this 'joke' map to Conway Council.

* * *

Of the fifteen hundred Welshmen under my immediate command many were quarrymen. Because of the importance of their work to the national war effort they were exempt from call-up. They were all extremely fit.

Our only serious problem was one of communication. Battalion orders were issued in English. My senior officers tended to speak both English and Welsh. This was well enough. However, my section and company commanders informed me that there were villages such as Ysbyty and Ysbyty Ifan, in the rural depths of mid-Wales, where little or no English was spoken. In consequence they were unable to decipher my orders. I knew this to be nonsense. Disproving it was another matter. The problem was resolved by sending down a motor-cycle despatch rider once a week with a copy of Battalion orders which he read to the isolated local section in Welsh.

* * *

My days were now full to capacity. Recreation became a thing of the past, a word in a dictionary. But if life was hectic it was also proving very interesting, not least

63

because – in the absence of any Germans to vent our aggression on – inter-battalion rivalry was intense. Whether I laid on an exercise between Conway and Llanfairfechan or Llanfairfechan and Pen y Gwryd, there were always casualties, some of them serious enough to require hospital treatment. Swept away by the illusion that they were engaged in real warfare, men thought nothing of trying to crush the opposition by rolling boulders down the mountainside. It was all a far cry from the cosy little world of Captain Mainwairing and his little platoon of old codgers at Warmington-on-Sea.

Amusing and interesting incidents abounded. One of my companies – based at Bettws y Coed – came to the conclusion that in the event of an invasion vital communication links could be maintained by means of carrier pigeons flying low along the valley to Battalion HQ at Conway. Lofts were built and training began. It continued apace for about three weeks. At the end of that time it became apparent that many of the birds were failing to arrive at their destination. The operation *was* however proving of great benefit to an increasingly corpulent hawk, based near Llanwrst, who waited for these innocent little messengers to come flying down the valley . . . and promptly gobbled them up.

The pigeon-post was by no means the only well-intentioned if impractical scheme generated by the intense national desire to defeat the Germans. There is still on record in London's Patent Office a plan to train 'kamakazi cormorants' to fly to Berlin and peck the mortar from the brickwork of Hitler's chancellery, causing it to collapse – and at one time the Government seriously considered dropping 'effluence bombs' filled with methane gas, generated from cow-pats, on German cities.

*   *   *

In order to help the Home Guard retain some degree of financial independence, I organised Sunday evening concerts in a little cinema at Conway. I also ran a series of raffles and sweepstakes. For one of these we had thousands of tickets printed. They were sold in the battalion area at sixpence each. I anticipated we should make a bumper profit.

One day I was summoned to the office of the police inspector at Conway who told me that the tickets were in some way illegal. He had received complaints. The complaints were valid. Our tickets were not. He had to take notice.

He was very helpful and suggested I recall all those unsold. To avoid any further legal implications, I should also place an advertisement in the local newspaper offering a full refund to those who had already invested money. This, he told me, would put me as near as possible on the right side of the law.

With a grin, he added:

'I appreciate you meant well. I doubt you'll end up in the clink or even out of pocket. There won't be many people who'll go to the trouble of calling at battalion headquarters for the sake of a sixpence. And you still have the prizes. Auction them. You'll almost certainly make a greater profit than you ever would from the sweepstake'.

To my great relief he proved to be right. An even greater relief was the pleasant and helpful manner in which he handled what might otherwise have been a tricky affair. It was characteristic of the co-operation I received from the police during my time in North Wales. I appreciate it still.

*   *   *

As part of our battalion and inter-battalion training we ran a number of shooting competitions. I was pleasantly surprised to discover that the standard within my own unit was high. This further stimulated my own interest in what I had once regarded as a sport. I now came to see that in times of war it had a far more sinister application.

We practised regularly on the range at the Morfa, an open space near Conway. No one was excused. My own aptitude had the benefit of increasing my standing both with the Welsh officers under my command and with other ranks. Suddenly, I was looked upon as rather less of a foreigner. There were, however, drawbacks. On one occasion I won an officer's revolver competition with a maximum score of ten bulls. This placed me in the embarrassing position of having to present the enormous prizewinner's cup to myself.

Although I enjoyed the experience which I gained shooting in this way, it came close to costing me very dear. One day a letter arrived on my desk from the War Office informing me that a consignment of .303 ammunition was dangerous and should be returned or destroyed immediately. I passed this instruction to my quartermaster, a Captain Box.

Either through negligence, or motivated perhaps by the magpie instincts common to all quartermasters, Box failed to implement it. Some time later, practising on the range alone, I unwittingly loaded some of this faulty ammunition into the breech of my rifle. When I pulled the trigger, the cordite flashed back through the bolt, pitting itself deep into my right eye. I was rushed at short notice to a specialist at Bangor who froze the eye and literally dug the cordite from it with a probe. It was an extraordinary operation and one which left me with no permanent disability.

65

Box received a reprimand but beyond that I would not carry the matter. I understood the nature of the problem which had brought the accident about. Briefly, it was this:

The Morfa was a military transit base. Units tended to stay no longer than six months. Traditionally, each captain–quartermaster kept a surplus of equipment tucked away in some quiet corner which he held against potential deficits. Unfortunately – or perhaps otherwise – things were arranged in such a manner that he could not remove this cache when the battalion was re-posted. Consequently, and usually for a consideration, he passed it on to his in-coming colleague, who in turn added to it and in turn passed it on.

By the end of the war this had come to represent a considerable problem. Army regulations were such that it was simply not possible to admit its existence to the authorities. It was a serious offence to admit to a shortage of equipment. It implied that it must have been stolen as a result of your negligence. It was equally disastrous to admit to a surplus. This implied that *you* must have stolen it from someone equally negligent.

By the time the Home Guard was stood down in 1945 this surplus mountain had become a monstrous albatross which consumed every waking thought of the hapless captain–quartermaster left to dispose of it. He was at his wits end wondering what to do with it. He could hardly detonate the explosives. The noise could only arouse interest, suspicion and enquiry.

In the event, he commandeered a lorry which made journeys twice a week, at dead of night, to Conway Bridge. Stopping on the middle span of this, a number of shadowy figures emerged from the back and began silently to dispose of packages and boxes over the side.

The captain–quartermaster was always careful to ensure that these little sorties coincided with an out-going tide. The current was strong and the troublesome items were swiftly carried out to sea. Nearly all the surplus was disposed of in this manner.

Unofficially, I was of course aware of what was transpiring. It was a criminal waste and as such quite wrong. However there are times when regulations – no matter how well-intentioned in their formulation – positively impede the good running of a unit . . . and anyway I felt intensely sorry for the captain–quartermaster concerned. He had inherited a nightmare that was not of his making. As such I felt able to turn something of a blind eye.

*   *   *

In March 1945 the Allies crossed the Rhine. By the beginning of May, Berlin was being crushed in a vice of blood and fire. Hitler took his own life; Mussolini was strung up by his heels in Milan's Piazza Loretto. At long last peace had returned to Europe.

The Home Guard was stood down. The 1st Caernarvon Battalion, fifteen hundred strong, marched in columns of three through the town of Conway and then to a field beyond where I delivered a speech of thanks and farewell.

A few days later I was summoned to the office of the sector commander, Colonel Shennon, who confided that he found himself in a dilemma. The powers-that-be had decided that they wished to mark the sector's contribution to the war effort by recommending one of its officers for the O.B.E. This was a symbolic gesture intended less to recognise the achievements of the individual concerned than those of the unit as a whole.

Colonel Shennon admitted that the choice had been a difficult one. After a great deal of thought he had decided to put forward the name of the longest-serving of his senior battalion officers . . . the Lieutenant–Colonel commanding the Llandudno battalion.

With a wry grin, he added: 'Sorry, old chap. But I thought you'd at least like to know that you made the semi-final'.

*　　*　　*

A few days after hanging up my uniform for the last time, I left England to undertake a foreign tour in my capacity as Finance Director for the Ministry of Transport. I was about to enter an entirely different world.

CHAPTER ELEVEN

MINISTRY OF FOOD

I n 1942 I moved to Colwyn Bay to take up my appointment as a Finance Director with the Ministry of Food. As the Ministry was a large one, boasting a staff of more than fifty thousand, it had requisitioned most of the town's facilities, including several schools and practically every hotel.

I was initially billeted on a couple named Allan, proprietors of the community's largest store. I have never forgotten their kindness to me because although the arrangement lasted only a matter of weeks, I have no doubt that it must have proved a considerable inconvenience and burden to them. Realising this, in a short time I found alternative accommodation, a flat which I rented for the princely sum of £5 a week. My wife, Dora, was now able to join me.

*   *   *

At this time, the Ministry of Food acted as a form of holding company, maintaining a watching brief over a number of subsidiaries. Each of these had responsibility for a specific commodity or commodities – such as meat or coffee – and retained two principal officials: a Trade Director and a Finance Director. The former regulated the operational side of the 'business'. The latter co-ordinated expenditure within the financial guidelines laid down by the Treasury. Within these parameters both directors were allowed a very considerable degree of autonomy.

I was posted to perhaps the least romantic of these concerns – the Animal Feeding Stuffs division, where I spent the first month or so familiarising myself with the situation. This involved an almost endless reading of files.

I had also to adjust to the civil service mentality, which I found to be very different from that prevailing in the market-place. Its principal manifestation was a deeply-ingrained love of thinking and acting in a crab-like manner – never approaching matters in a straightforward way if it was at all possible to do so sideways.

I had my first experience of this almost before I had seated myself at my desk. At the various interviews I had attended aimed at negotiating my appointment it had been clearly stated that I was to go to Colwyn Bay as a Finance Director. I was aware that the former Finance Director of the Animal Feeding Stuffs division had resigned – thus creating the vacancy – leaving his deputy, an elderly man called Shears, to oversee things until my arrival.

I was not aware that in the interim, Shears had developed rather a taste for the job and, with the help of colleagues within the Ministry, had managed to have himself up-graded to the post of Joint Finance Director. We thus became the only division within the Ministry of Food to be run in tandem.

I disliked the idea but found that I was powerless to have the decision over-turned. Many ministries were run by a cabal of insiders (of which Shears was one), all dedicated to one another's support. This world of nepotism was particu-larly well entrenched within the Ministry of Food. During the First World War its Financial Secretary had been Sir George Peat. At the outbreak of the Second World War his son, Sir Harry Peat, was given his father's old job. Sir Harry was then the senior partner in the distinguished London accountancy house of Peat, Marwick, Mitchell & Co. His deputy was Ronald (afterwards Sir Ronald) Leach, also a partner in Peat's firm. With the exception of myself and one other, all twelve of the Ministry of Food's Finance Directors were members of Peat, Marwick, Mitchell.

In the event that there should ever be a third world war, I have no doubt that the executives of what was once Peat Marwick, Mitchell will once again be placed in control of finances at the Ministry of Food.

*   *   *

The reasons for my appointment swiftly became apparent. Whilst the trade section of the Animal Feeding Stuffs division was highly efficient and excellently run, the financial side had been allowed to deteriorate. By the time I arrived it was in a state of hopeless muddle which took many months of very hard work to put right.

In order to come to terms with this I had first to learn an entirely new line of business – to deal with provender merchants and millers, growers of sunflower seeds and rape, cultivators of ground nuts and those who could furnish us with the oil they produced.

I had also to co-ordinate the collection of thousands of tons of hay which was brought to central depots from farms nationwide to await distribution to areas more in need – especially the mining communities, where pit-ponies played an essential role in coal production. I have a strong suspicion that much of this strategic hay reserve was never utilised or required; and that it was afterwards sold off at a fraction of its real worth. As an accountant, this went very much against the grain. I nonetheless understood that in times of war such measures were precautionary and represented a very necessary hostage to fortune.

I was less accommodating when, one morning, an order form materialised on my desk requisitioning the import of a ton of American birdseed. The cost of this was a thousand pounds, then a very large sum of money indeed. I turned to a colleague and said:

'We are involved in a war. That war is currently costing us thousands of tons of shipping lost each week to U–boats. Some lunatic wants me to put further lives at risk importing birdseed from America.'

It was explained to me that the birdseed was required to feed the canaries used in coalmines as living gas-detectors. As such, it was considered a commodity vital to the war effort. The order went through. Once again I had learned something new.

*   *   *

Learning now formed an integral part of my everyday life. Problems came in all shapes and sizes. One concerned forty thousand tons of very old carrots. No one wanted them and no one quite knew what to do with them.

As often happened in such situations, it was decided to pass them over to my division to be disposed of as animal feed. The documentation authorising this transfer was all but complete when Jack Drummond, the Ministry's adviser on matters of nutrition, suddenly discovered – correctly – that carrots enhanced night-time vision, an invaluable asset to fighter pilots. Every last carrot was sold within the week.

Shortly afterwards, Jack Drummond was knighted – although I hesitate to associate this with any service he may have performed for carrots. In August 1952 I was greatly saddened to read that he and his wife, together with their children, had been the victims of a senseless murder whilst on a camping holiday in France.

*   *   *

Within six months I managed to return the financial affairs of the Animal Feeding Stuffs Division to a solid footing. I then approached Sir Harry Peat and said: 'My job's done. Give me something bigger – more important.'

70

As luck would have it, a group of divisions was then seeking a finance director. To my gratification (and no little surprise) I was appointed to cover divisions regulating tea, coffee, cocoa and yeast – quite a mammoth task.

My new ministry was housed in a terrace which before the war had constituted three hotels, now interlinked by means of connecting doors. I had a staff of a hundred-and-fifty.

Once again, I was forced to come to terms with a new set of rules, circumstances and values. I was greatly assisted in doing so by the Minister of Food, Lord Woolton, known affectionately as 'Uncle Fred'.

A Liverpool store-owner, 'Uncle Fred' was that strangest of anomalies – a delightful man who was also capable of achieving results. It was just these qualities which persuaded Winston Churchill to recruit him to the Ministry of Food. He summoned him to No.10 Downing Street and in his usual peremptory manner exclaimed: 'I want you to take on the Ministry of Food. I think you can do it'.

Uncle Fred said: 'What is involved?'

Churchill replied, rather testily: 'That's up to you. You think out how to do it – get the best results.'

Uncle Fred, never a man to be intimidated, replied: 'Very well. But if I'm going to be the custodian of the nation's food, you'll have to leave me to it. I don't want you or anyone else looking over my shoulder.'

After a moment's silence, he added: 'I'll have to be very severe with anyone who breaks the rules – in any way betrays my trust.' Churchill continued to stalk the room, puffing on his cigar. Finally he said: 'That's right. No dirty fingers in the people's food.'

Uncle Fred was as good as his word. He led by example and his example was magnificent. He ensured that every member of the community received each week the 2 ozs of tea to which, under rationing, they were entitled – including the legion of factory and munitions workers – and he marshalled his troops at the ministry with unparalleled success. His going was for all of us an occasion of universal lament. He shook hands with everyone.

Coming as he did in the wake of such a man, his successor, a Labour minister named Strachey, was always doomed to disappoint.

*   *   *

Coffee provided the first of my headaches. That which we imported from East Africa was shipped to Great Britain in sacks. These were often adulterated with wooden sticks, inserted as make-weight. As coffee was then purchased for about

71

£45 a ton, this represented a considerable loss of revenue. It was infuriating, but there was little I could do to eradicate the practice.

Matters were further complicated by demands from the fifty major coffee-growing estates in East Africa for increased payments to cover what they claimed were spiralling labour costs. My response was characteristically cautious. I asked the growers to submit their latest balance sheets. After much grumbling they agreed to do so. I discovered that there *had* been an increase in costs . . . but nothing like to the degree of the sum claimed.

My brief was made clear to me from the start: purchase as much of the entire stock of world coffee and tea as you reasonably can. Then bring it to England for equitable division between the twenty-eight friendly nations.

This was a noble concept in principle. Given the fallibility of human nature, it proved an impossible mandate to discharge in practice. The consignments of tea we did manage to acquire were endlessly squabbled over, some of the friendly countries seeking to increase their quota by wheedling, a few by blackmail, others by outright cheating. At the conclusion of the quarterly allocation meetings of the Tea Division of the Combined Food Board the representatives of some nations went away smiling, others scowling.

If I found it impossible to reconcile the needs of all our potential purchasers, I did at least try to ensure that almost every pound of imported tea was brought for blending to the traditional London merchants. Almost exclusively, these were situated in Mincing Lane, within the City of London. I considered it of paramount importance to ensure that such long-established firms survived in order that they might revitalise the industry once peace returned.

To this end the Ministry paid large premiums to ensure that not only the tea-blenders and their cargoes, but their insurers as well, survived the conflict in reasonable shape.

For all this, tea remained in short supply. Its acquisition was a continuous problem. We gleaned what we could from Ceylon, from India and East Africa – but at a hundred million chests a year it was never enough. It compared not at all to the pre-war figure.

There were innumerable logistical problems. Many of the Asian shipments never reached their destination – fell victim to the German U–boat blockade. Then as now, tea was a volatile commodity, subject to changes both of temperature and circumstance. Frequently, we found that the 100lb chests had been infiltrated at source by hoards of white ants, similar to termites.

Problems such as this were almost impossible to eradicate at long distance. Letters were an inadequate means of communication because we could seldom anticipate their date of arrival. It was, however, possible to correspond with the supplying countries by cable; and this at least taught us how to condense the maximum amount of information in the fewest possible words – occasionally with hilarious results aggravated by the language problem.

*　　*　　*

The Treasury fixed the price of tea to the housewife at 2/8d per pound. This not only enabled the Ministry to survive but guaranteed that the division paid its way. By and large the relationship between the Treasury and the Ministry was an equitable one. I personally experienced only one brief skirmish. This came in early 1944 when the Tamil tea-pickers of Ceylon went on strike, seeking an increase in their weekly wage from $3 to $5. Even at the higher figure, this was by any standards a pittance. It nevertheless represented a significant increase in labour costs.

After considerable deliberation, the ordnance was passed. It was assumed that the Tamils of Ceylon would now return to work. Surely they would labour even harder to reap the harvest of the increase? In fact, having finally achieved the Nirvana of being paid more for less, they stayed at home to enjoy their new-found wealth. Tea quickly became even more scarce and the cost rocketed.

In order to compensate for this, I proposed increasing the sum paid by the British housewife by fourpence a pound – a figure which would have had the effect of protecting the Ministry's modest profit whilst generating an increased annual revenue to the government of £4m.

This seemed to me perfectly justified. To my mortification the Treasury dug in its heels. It argued – with hindsight perhaps rightly – that such an increase would produce the serious risk of a knock-on effect: that any increase in the price of tea (a national institution) would automatically lead to an increase in the general cost of living. This in turn would produce higher pay demands in industry. In time of war these could simply not be countenanced.

I was forced to give way. During my last year of service this abortive battle with the Treasury cost the Ministry of Food more than £4m a year. I considered it then – as I consider it now – a major if inevitable defeat.

*　　*　　*

In some respects my time at the Ministry of Food represents a watershed in my life. It left a lasting impression on me. I became aware that I was now involved with high finance at its most rarefied level. I had sole authority to sign cheques for sums of upwards of a million pounds. The prospect of returning to my accountancy

73

practice and sending out bills for five guineas suddenly began to pall. It was this realisation which ultimately led me into the realm of politics, said – sometimes erroneously – to be the seat of all true power.

*   *   *

Late in 1944 my wife died of cancer. Her loss left me bereft. Nothing any longer seemed to have any point. I approached Sir Harry Peat and asked for a change of job and (preferably) location.

He said:

'The war's coming to an end. I hear the Ministry of War Transport wants someone to stem the appalling loss of revenue abroad. You would, of course, have to travel extensively.'

'Yes', I said. 'I don't think I should mind that.'

This was something of an understatement. It seemed to provide exactly the change of function and venue that I was seeking.

CHAPTER TWELVE

THE MINISTRY OF WAR TRANSPORT

I f my appointment to the Ministry of Food had been somewhat vague, I found that my masters at the Ministry of War Transport were equally uncertain how best to define my role. We finally determined that as the Minister's representative overseas I should seek to stem wastage – some of which was being caused by fraudulent practice, some by carelessness and some by over-caution.

The bureaucrats reasoned that if these trips cost money – so be it. We were at war. My personal expenses were of no consequence – provided, of course, they were justified by results.

This was not an attitude with which I agreed. I endeavoured to explain that money was *always* important; and that – as I had discovered in the case of the strategic hay reserve – there was never any point in stock-piling commodities beyond a reasonable assessment of requirements.

The Ministry had departments all over the world, the greatest concentration of these being in Europe, Asia and the Americas. I was asked where I thought I might best be effective. I selected the Mediterranean, the Middle East, India and Burma. Each of these zones was overseen by a controller, usually a senior retired British army or naval officer. The staff he commanded varied considerably, according to requirements.

*   *   *

I was sent for a two-week period of briefing, training and acclimatisation to the Ministry's headquarters at St. Anne's, near Blackpool. Here I learned about and talked over the problems I might expect to encounter. One of these was the strong likelihood of uncovering serious fraud. Senior officials at St. Anne's were fairly certain that this was taking place on a large scale. They could not however be sure because they were forced to rely for information on signals and messages sent from far-flung outposts. Many of these were economical with the truth, others arrived garbled. As there was no way of checking on the validity of their contents, they had mainly to be accepted as correct. It would be part of my brief to discover what was really going on.

It became clear that my schedule would involve a great deal of flying. This, I knew, would prove very gruelling. I decided to undergo a health check. The doctor pronounced me fit if somewhat overweight. I was instructed to cut down on fatty foods and to reduce my intake of alcohol. By doing so I managed to lose the best part of a stone in ten days.

*   *   *

Once again I put the wheels of change into motion. Having already found someone to look after my accountancy practice, I cleared myself from the Ministry of Food and spent many hours shopping for the kind of sub-tropical clothing which I should need in my journeyings.

During my period in Colwyn Bay one of my Home Guard company command-ers had been a Major Lockwood. Realising that I was a novice in my new career, and having no connections or friends in the areas I would be visiting, I sought his advice. Lockwood ran a guest house at which the then Secretary for India, Leo Amory, sometimes stayed. Lockwood said he felt he knew him sufficiently well to be able to effect an introduction.

He was as good as his word. I was asked to call at the India Office in Whitehall.

Leo Amory proved to be short of stature, hardly five feet tall. In an attempt to disguise this lack of inches his desk had been placed on a dais which elevated him about a foot above the rest of the room.

I found Amory to be genial and helpful. We had a long discussion concerning the places I intended to visit. He was especially knowledgeable regarding India and Burma and furnished me with some useful insights into the Asian mind.

He was also kind enough to promise me a number of letters of introduction. These arrived the very next day. Although they were mostly addressed to provin-cial governors, ministers–resident and other very highly-placed officials, they ultimately proved of limited use. They would certainly provide me with the entrée into society; but my main interest was in contacting less elevated individuals: those who might be perpetrating – or knew those who might be perpetrating – fraud. Consequently they were not all presented. I still have one or two, faded now and yellowing, still in their original envelopes.

Of far greater import was a contact I made during the early part of my time with the Ministry. Sitting in the bar of the Rock Hotel at Gibraltar, I fell into conversation with Desmond Tighe, who was then working for Reuters news agency as its Middle East war correspondent.

I divined that Tighe was trustworthy. As such I felt free to broach the subject of Amory's letters of introduction. He confirmed my worst fears. He said:

'I don't think those gentlemen will have much idea of what's going on outside their official residences. What you want', he added, fishing into his pockets and producing several scraps of flimsy paper akin to the old Bronco toilet roll, 'is *real* contacts: the head waller at Tommy's Bar in Cairo, the porters of the Turf Club, the cloakroom attendant at the Cecil Hotel in Alexandria, old Pastrudi, the Alexandrian restaurateur. Those are the people who know what's happening at ground-level – what the swindles are, who's in charge of them, who always seems to have more money to spend than they should.'

With that he scribbled notes to all these individuals and several more besides. In essence they read:

'This is to introduce my friend Frank Taylor. Please let him have information on any subject he cares to raise.'

I never saw Desmond Tighe again but his scruffy notes ultimately proved invaluable.

*　　*　　*

I composed a schedule which would allow me to travel for periods of six weeks at a time. At the end of this term I proposed to return to England for two weeks. This allowed me just sufficient lee-way to write up my notes and discuss my actions and findings with the various officials concerned.

I was destined to undertake seven such trips in all. By and large this manner of arranging things worked very well.

If there was one drawback it was the sense of disorientation which came from moving constantly and at haste from one country to another. For instance, the sixth of these tours – encompassed in just six weeks in the spring of 1946 – involved travel to thirteen countries, some of them more than once. I spent a hundred and eighteen hours in the air and covered a distance in excess of twenty-one thousand miles, much of it under uncomfortable conditions by aeroplane, flying-boat, car, train and bullock-cart.

The Sunderland flying-boat in which I often travelled had two decks and was a very homely affair – very much in contrast to the Dakota, the DC3, I also frequently used. These held about twelve passengers comfortably, but 'service rigged' – stripped to the bare essentials – it accommodated more than twice that number. Under service conditions passengers squatted or sat around the shell of the aircraft tormented by the numerous projections which protruded from its skin.

Matters were not improved by the need, in hot countries, to undertake journeys pre-dawn, to avoid the blistering effects of the sun on unpressurised cabins. Arriving day after day at a darkened airfield at four or five o'clock in the morning to begin yet another journey swiftly produced a very distorted sense of time and place. In order to make the rendezvous, it was nearly always necessary to begin the journey in the dark. On one occasion, travelling by taxi through the outskirts of Karachi en route to the airfield (airport would be altogether too grand a word), I spied two large shapes huddled on the pavement. One was an ox, the other a water buffalo. They were sleeping side by side. The taxi driver told me that they had formerly slept in the road but had learned from bitter experience that the pavement was considerably safer.

* * *

One of the most disorientating effects of almost perpetual travel was the difficulty in coming to terms with constant changes in language, temperature, attitudes and currency. Currency was especially troublesome. On two occasions I spent six consecutive nights in six different countries. In order to do so effectively, I had to carry six different currencies distributed between six different pockets.

Equally bemusing at first – at least to my masters – was the question of my salary. Being an accountant, I became aware that in my capacity as a civil servant temporarily employed abroad I was exempt from paying income tax provided only that my salary was less than £1000 a year and that I refrained from bringing any of it into the United Kingdom for at least a year after my employment had ceased. Much to the surprise of the mandarins in Whitehall, I therefore *demanded* that my salary be fixed a little under this limit; and when, in due course, it attracted the automatic increase which all other civil servants enjoyed, I was forced to go through the nonsense of writing to them and declining it.

This was not the hardship it may appear. In the first place, the increase (and no doubt some of the salary itself) would, as I have said, been gobbled up in tax. Secondly, I had, anyway, very little on which to spend it. My everyday needs were covered by subsistence payments and other benefits. When abroad, I was on occasions paid 'danger' money. This was calculated according to the degree of threat each country was deemed to pose and varied between a pound and thirty-five shillings a day. Some of my food and accommodation came free; and I was able to recoup my travelling expenses.

* * *

My first tour of duty was to Italy. I arrived at Naples having made several stops en route. The officials sent to greet me at the airport were polite and accommodating.

Anyone seeking to capture the spirit of Naples must see it first as he sails between the islands of Ischia and Capri and enters the Bay of Naples, some twenty-two miles wide. There, at the bay's northern apex, lies the largest, noisiest, most picturesque and fascinating of all Italy's historic cities.

It stands on the edge of the bluest of waters and under the bluest of skies. It is flanked seven miles to the east by the ominous bulk of Mount Vesuvius and on the west by the Heights of Posilipo. In the background an amphitheatre of volcanic hills curls away around the city. It is one of the most beautiful settings in Europe.

From a crest north of Naples, on which stands the massive bulk of St. Elmo Castle, built in the 16th century, a spiny ridge runs down to the sea, splitting the city in two. In the older and larger part to the east of this ridge, the spires of scores of ancient churches rise, intermingled with the architecture of public buildings, with here and there a factory chimney. On the western side of the ridge stand the fashionable dwellings of the rich, built on terraced hills and commanding sweeping views of the bay and the twin mountains of Capri in the far distance.

Founded by the Greeks about 450 B.C. as 'Neapolis' (the New City), for centuries the history of Naples was one of violence, intrigue and war. From 1266 to 1494 it was fought over by Angevin and Aragon princes. It next became a point of issue between the kings of France and Spain. It passed briefly under the dominance of the Austrian Hapsburgs, who in turn surrendered it to a branch of the French house of Bourbon. When Napoleon was re-making Europe, his brother, Joseph, sat briefly on the throne. After Bonaparte's fall the city returned to Bourbon rule. It continued so until 1860 when it was liberated by Garibaldi and became a part of united Italy.

*   *   *

I found the city to be very Americanised – tens of thousands of gum-chewing GIs thronged the streets, the shops and the bars. They formed a profound contrast to the indigenous population – workers from the factories, shrill-voiced pedlars, mule-drivers, fishermen and dockworkers.

Naples then represented an important supply port. Now that Italy had surrendered, the Allies were using it to off-load vital war equipment to fuel the push on Berlin. Numerous ships docked here every day, all of them under American control, as was the unloading of cargo in the harbour.

The sense of urgency was great. So was the corresponding chaos. Cargoes were off-loaded on to quays too small to accommodate them and consequently some toppled into the sea. Others got mixed up. Much was pilfered. Some cargoes disappeared entirely.

To ease this state of affairs we decided to load cargoes on to lorries straight from the holds of the ships. The idea was that these lorries would then ferry materials to a distribution depot situated about ten kilometres from the centre of the city.

This in theory. In practice, Italian civilians tended to board the lorries unobserved, usually whilst they were travelling at a snail's pace through the congested city centre. Once the vehicles reached open countryside, the stowaways frantically hurled goods overboard at specific 'collection' points from which they were spirited away by waiting accomplices. Consequently, a significant proportion of the lorries arrived at their destination almost empty.

We were never able to eradicate this pilfering entirely, but by stationing a Gurkha in the back of each truck, when swarthy hands appeared over the tailboard, he was able very deftly to relieve them of their fingers with the aid of a fearsome-looking Kukri.

*   *   *

Human cargoes also had a disconcerting habit of disappearing, notably British merchant seamen. Many of these were employed on fixed contracts. This meant that when their period of employment expired they were laid off to await another contract with another vessel. During the interim they were accommodated at Ministry expense – rent-free and all-found – at a seamen's hostel situated some ten miles from Sorento. The countryside was beautiful and the wine cheap. Girls – fairly willing girls – were everywhere. All but the most dedicated found these enforced lay-offs no great hardship at all.

The real problem arose when a ship entered port looking for a new crew. The lotus-eaters of Sorento proved strangely reluctant to sign on – so reluctant that when the moment came to take them down to the docks they were nowhere to be found.

We attempted to solve the problem by obtaining advance news of incoming shipping and – a few days prior – placing the seamen under what virtually amounted to house arrest. They were then loaded on to lorries for transmission to the docks. The drivers of these lorries were under strict instructions not to stop en route in any circumstances.

If the seamen themselves are to be believed, the lorry drivers nonetheless fell victim to a form of collective madness which compelled them to do so. The matelots who arrived back at the hostel footsore and dusty all told the same story.

At some point the lorry had stopped – quite without their knowledge or consent. They had got down to stretch their legs. The lorry had driven off, leaving them stranded. They had been forced to walk all the way back.

The drivers had of course been bribed. We eventually stamped the practice out by fining culprits so heavily that the punishment outweighed the value of the bribe.

*   *   *

What couldn't be obtained through bribery tended to be pilfered. A particular target was the balloon-type tyres fitted to service vehicles. Thousands disappeared every day. Half the taxi force of Naples was to be seen driving around on them. To bring the situation under control we set up a police cordon around the city centre. Taxis were stopped, directed into a side street and relieved of their surplus equipment. Stranded in this manner, the drivers were not best pleased and their language had to be heard to be believed. The operation was nonetheless a great success because by ten o'clock the following morning there was not a taxi to be had anywhere in the city.

If there were shortages and restrictions, these applied rather less to the occupying forces than to the indigenous Italian population. The Allies had access to a weekly bottle of whisky at 7/6d and cartons of two hundred cigarettes at an even more ridiculous price. As it was possible to smoke and drink only so much, a great deal of the surplus found its way on to the black-market.

Cigarettes, especially, represented real currency. Bargains abounded. I bought three velour bolts of cloth – ideal for making ladies' hats – for ten cigarettes. Finding myself short of cash on one occasion, I took my gold watch into a jewellers to find out what it might fetch. The overjoyed proprietor said:

'Help yourself to lire from the till. As much as you can stuff into your pockets!'

To my eternal shame – but financial gain – I did. For all this I believe the transaction was very much to our mutual benefit. The lira was almost valueless.

*   *   *

These were difficult times. People existed from hand to mouth and from day to day. Survival required constant and sometimes cunning adjustment – not only on the part of the defeated. The so-called victors could also find themselves in difficulties.

In Naples I happened by an extraordinary coincidence to encounter one of my pre-war accountancy clients, a man named George Taylor, who had run a building business in Chertsey. At the outbreak of hostilities he and his thirty-strong work-

81

force had formed a volunteer artisan unit within the regular army. Their brief was to follow in the wake of the advancing Allied forces and repair electricity and telephone supplies as well as general amenities.

One weekend, discovering Taylor was based at Salerno, I requisitioned a Ministry car and driver and went to see him. Having recently been in England, I was able to reassure him that his wife and family were well. He returned the compliment by inviting me to the opera, where the great Italian tenor, Gigli, was performing.

Unfortunately, when we arrived at the concert hall, it transpired that the box reserved for Taylor's unit seated six. With me we were seven. We circumvented this by having George and his ticket-waving colleagues exit and re-enter the box at such bewildering frequency that the Italian theatre attendants ultimately gave up the unequal struggle to distinguish the genuine patrons from the bogus ones.

Gigli gave an incredible performance that night. The memory of it has remained with me all my life. A short, dumpy individual with no stage presence whatsoever, he possessed a voice of divine beauty. Because he had espoused the Nazi cause with rather more Latin fervour than sense, his defeated compatriots (many of whom had acted in a similar manner) were unsure whether to applaud or to hang him. To our own – and everyone else's – delight they decided to let him sing.

*   *   *

My Italian trips proved invaluable in terms of experience. As a result of them I became very much more aware of the *types* of fraud fostered by war. To put this experience to good effect I decided to go next to Cairo – a city even more synonymous with sharp-dealing.

Compared to the luxury of modern-day air travel, the journey was long and arduous. I flew firstly from England to Marseilles by flying boat, then across the Mediterranean to Castelle Benito. From here I progressed along the coast to El Adem and finally by flying-boat to my destination.

A room had been reserved for me in Cairo at Shepheard's Hotel, the fame of which had preceded it. Like so many cities which possess only one hotel of renown – the King Alfred in Jerusalem, the Grand Brittagne at Athens, Raffles at Singapore and Gaulle Face in Colombo – it appeared to me to be resting on its laurels. It was full to overflowing with wealthy travellers but the service was appalling.

I moved to the company's sister hotel, the Continental Savoy in Opera Square. Being less well-known, this proved much more accommodating. It remained my base throughout my time in the area. In between tours I stored my enormous metal trunk containing my mosquito net, tropical kit and various 'disguises' in the basement.

The last-named were not really disguises, merely the equipment needed to clothe the alter-egos I was sometimes required to adopt. For instance, the entire north coast of Africa was American controlled. As a civilian I should have made no progress whatsoever. However, the Americans dearly love – and tend to be impressed by – a uniform. So when in North Africa I wore the uniform of a Lieutenant–Colonel. (They would not have been aware that it was the uniform of a Lieutenant–Colonel in the Home Guard.) Similarly, when in Turkey I passed as a civilian. To have posed as a soldier would have been to risk internment.

* * *

Then as now, Cairo was the largest city in Africa, with a population of several millions. The very epicentre of Saracen culture, it stands on the banks of the Nile, a river containing more general effluence than I had ever seen in my life. It has been said – probably with some authority – that anyone unfortunate enough to fall into it would certainly contract typhoid and die within a matter of days.

In the course of this and subsequent tours I came to know one or two sites which were not then on the tourist route. One of these was the Mena House Hotel, which pandered to the needs of guests who were engaged but not married. Under Mohammedan law any connection prior to marriage was not only frowned upon but strictly forbidden.

In order to circumvent this, the Mena House thoughtfully provided adjacent suites with inter-connecting doors. This satisfied the needs of Western guests whilst enabling the hotel to charge for two rooms where only one was used. Although I never personally availed myself of these facilities, I recognised that they represented the perfect pragmatic compromise – reconciling Western needs to the deeply ingrained Eastern desire for profit.

I discovered an equally fascinating establishment opposite my hotel in Opera Square. Run by a Madame Badier, it was officially designated a 'playhouse'. It was a great favourite with the troops, not least for the saucy shows it produced. Officialdom turned a blind eye because the place was considered a wonderful morale-booster.

Many of the patrons of Madame Badier's establishment were cavalry officers billeted at the Casr–El–Nile Barracks in the centre of Cairo. When not in use, these gentlemen's fairly elderly chargers were unofficially loaned to a riding club. As this was situated within five minutes of my hotel in Opera Square, I became a fairly regular customer. I found a twenty-minute gallop and canter to be the perfect tonic.

On one such visit I was pointed in the direction not of my usual rather hacked-out mount but of a magnificent Arab stallion. Positioned at its head was an equally magnificent Nubian soldier, lofty in the extreme and upright of bearing. I approached him only to be informed – in the haughtiest of tones – that this was: 'The mount of King Farouk'. Sure enough, a few moments later the King's sister, the Princess Farida, glided out for her morning ride.

I slunk away, my tail between my legs, in search of my own poor nag.

*　　*　　*

Cultivating the kind of contact recommended by Desmond Tighe, I came to know the dragoman at the door of my hotel. Tall, bearded and very aristocratic-looking, he had considerable presence and charm. In addition to the professional help he was able to afford me (always of course for a 'consideration'), we became friends and on one occasion he took me out to a village where we witnessed a lengthy mounted procession wending its way through the streets.

The dragoman told me that this was an Arab wedding. He somehow acquired mounts for us and we joined the procession. I was greatly enjoying the experience, but was not able to sustain it for long. Although I considered myself a reasonably competent horseman, the mount which had been found for me – so mysteriously and at such short notice – was impossible to ride. It jogged about in a very eccentric manner and I simply couldn't get comfortable or even very stable. The animal's attendant found this very amusing. When I finally handed the creature back to him he explained that this was a *dancing* horse – and that it was simply doing what it had been trained to do, prance about to the rhythm of the band.

*　　*　　*

My work in Egypt was not of course limited to Cairo. I had also frequently to travel to other locations, notably Alexandria, surely the most famous of all the cities scattered over the East by Alexander the Great. At the height of its splendour it had rivalled 'the glory that was Greece and the grandeur that was Rome'. Since ancient times it had been one of the great commercial centres of the Mediterranean. In the early Christian era Roman galleys had docked here; as had the great tall-sided sailing barques, preparing to take on grain for Rome. The dockside would have been laden with a motley of goods – piles of native wheat, bars of tin from the British Isles, bolts of silk from China, cotton fabrics from India. The whole scene would have been dominated by the gigantic Pharos – the first of lighthouses and one of the seven wonders of the world.

If modern Alexandria bore few traces of this ancient city, it was – like Cairo, to which it is connected by the Nile – the most cosmopolitan of centres. I found its quays and bazaars thronged with people of every description and race.

*　　*　　*

Through one of my contacts I came to learn that someone was perpetrating a 'dunnage' fraud. Dunnage is a form of timber-racking used to stow cargo in transit so that it remains free from movement or damage. Once the cargo has been off-loaded the dunnage becomes redundant.

The Egyptians stacked it away in the customs sheds at Alexandria and forgot about it until it was time to add to it. At one time there was dunnage worth almost half a million pounds awaiting disposal in the Customs sheds of Alexandria.

I made enquiries and discovered that this stock had been drastically reduced. I also learned that two enterprising RNVR lieutenants had decided to save the Ministry a job and dispose of the material themselves. As Egypt has almost no trees, they used the dunnage to manufacture furniture. There were practically no overheads attached to this little venture, and in the course of two years the two men made a killing. The material had cost them nothing. The furniture itself was manufactured by Egyptian carpenters and joiners employed in the dockyards for low wages paid by the British government. The end product was delivered to the purchasers in government vehicles.

Once the fraud was uncovered, its perpetrators disappeared, together with their ill-gotten gains. To the best of my knowledge neither they nor the money have been seen since.

*　　*　　*

Much of my work involved attempting to thwart pilfering of this nature. Much of it occurred from ship-repair yards. It was costing the Ministry millions of pounds a year. One such yard, situated on what was known as No. 1 Bis Island, close to Port Said, had done sterling work during the earlier part of the war, but the conflict had moved on and it was now practically redundant. I decided to close it down.

During my tour of inspection I noticed a ship's boiler, the size of two large houses, lying on its side close to the water's edge. Two days later I was informed that this leviathan had disappeared – literally overnight. It seemed an impossible feat, but then we were dealing with formidable opponents – the descendants of the men who had built the pyramids.

It transpired that hundreds of Egyptians had descended upon it and somehow manoeuvred it into the Mediterranean. They had then towed it out to sea and sunk it at a safe spot from which it could be recovered later and sold for scrap.

Pilfering of this nature was rife in the Middle East because in the absence of a stable economy, barter had become the common currency. At another ship-yard, in Haifa, I found no work in progress other than the unauthorised manufacture of cheap cigarette lighters, which were also used as currency.

*   *   *

On one of my earlier tours I had occasion to visit the British Consul at Eskenderun in Turkey. A number of routes were suggested to me. They looked excellent on paper. However, I had learned from past experience to be deeply suspicious of such time-tables. They seldom took the human factor into account and allowed impossibly short times for transfer, sleep or recreation.

The first option was to fly by air from Cyprus to Ankara. From Ankara I was to proceed to Eskenderun by train – a journey of some six hundred miles. This I flatly refused to do.

The second option was to travel by air to Aleppo. This was also rejected because it was impossible to establish whether such a route existed and – in the event that it did – which airline might be flying it. A similar problem plagued the third route: a journey via Lydda and Beirut.

On paper, the fourth option looked a great deal more promising: a direct flight from Cairo to Adama in Turkey and thence to my destination. The various air and train journeys appeared to dovetail perfectly – a little too perfectly. I decided to investigate. The train times were inaccurate and the air flight had been abandoned long since.

By now, GHQ was beginning to feel a little guilty. It had formulated no less than four plans all of which had proved to be either nonsensical or downright inadequate.

The fifth option was rather better. It proposed that I should fly from Cairo to Haifa. Here the Ninth Army would lay on a motor-car to carry me to Eskenderun. The Ninth Army returned a signal that no motor transport was available. GHQ at last lost patience and wired back:

'You will – *repeat* will – *provide motor transport.*'

*   *   *

When I approached the bookings-desk at Cairo airport to arrange the first leg of my flight I encountered a further difficulty. The duty officer, a female corporal, informed me that as I was travelling as army personnel I was subject to army regulations. These stipulated that I must report to the airport not later than noon on the day prior to the flight, complete with baggage. I explained that this was quite impossible, not least because a goodly part of my luggage was still at the laundry.

The girl was sympathetic. She appealed to the duty officer, the original 'Jobsworth'. He informed me that regulations were regulations. They could not be altered – not for me, not for anyone.

I pointed out that this particular rule was an absurd one. I was not strictly speaking a member of His Majesty's forces. Nor was I physically capable of complying with the order. None of this made the slightest difference.

'I quite understand,' said 'Jobsworth'. 'But rules are rules.'

I was by now ready to throttle him.

At my insistence, higher authority appeared on the scene in the form of a squadron–leader, a cool-looking individual who said: 'What's the problem?' I explained.

He gave me a look of appraisal and said: 'Yes, all right. Just this once. But if you're found to be carrying anything in excess of what's allowed – well, frankly, old chap, you've had it.'

With this he walked away.

*   *   *

I finally left Cairo at a quarter to five in the morning. The flight was uneventful. When I arrived in Haifa it was clear that the Ninth Army had taken GHQ's ultimatum seriously. A Chevrolet was waiting on the tarmac to take me on the three-day drive to Eskenderun. On the front passenger seat the driver had thought-fully stock-piled some provisions: three large loaves, a pot of jam and a supply of tea. They proved invaluable.

We headed for Tripoli where we had lunch at the N.A.A.F.I., washed down with quantities of Guinness. We next stopped at Latakya where the adjutant of a unit of Foresters gave us tea and replenished our supply of petrol.

On leaving Latakya we began a three-thousand-foot climb along the coastal road to the border which separates Syria from Turkey. Here we were detained some time, albeit not for any sinister reason. The Syrian guards were clearly bored and did everything they could to detain us in conversation. We were only allowed to proceed after promising to return in two days and take tea with them.

Departing the Syrian border-post we traversed the two hundred yards of no-man's-land to the Turkish frontier. Here we encountered a very different order. I was marched into the hut of the chief customs officer by two soldiers with fixed bayonets. These they appeared more than anxious to use. The customs officer spoke no English. I spoke no Turkish. After what seemed an interminable length of time, a scruffy-looking interpreter was produced. Like his master, he spoke no English. He did confess to a limited grasp of French.

Haltingly, I explained my mission. After an hour or so we were allowed to proceed. I climbed back into the car under no illusions. Our presence had been noted. From this point on it would be minutely tracked.

This opinion was reinforced when, thirty miles later, we stopped to ask directions of a local policeman. He indicated the road we should take. As we drove off I glanced into the car's rear-view mirror – and saw him running like a hare, no doubt in the direction of the nearest telephone.

We arrived at the British Consulate at Eskenderun shortly after midnight. I tumbled gratefully into bed. I speedily concluded my business and the following day set off on the return journey. Once again, the customs official at the Turkish border proved obstructive. We were delayed for more than an hour whilst he telephoned the Consulate at Eskenderun to confirm the nature and validity of the visit.

As I had suspected they might, the Syrian border-patrol had anticipated my return. They greeted me with tea, biscuits, a basket of apples and a great deal of laughter. They pressed me to stay the entire day, insisting that in one of their hill villages there was an old man who had never seen an Englishman.

En route to base, the car developed a problem with the air filter. We were further delayed by a puncture. When we arrived in Beirut, at eight o'clock in the evening, more bad news awaited me. The naval officer who had been detailed to reserve my accommodation was nowhere to be found. He habitually made a nightly tour of the city's bars and seldom returned much before midnight. When he did he was invariably the worse for wear.

A diversion was afforded by a group of naval officers who took me to their wardroom, showed some interest in my exploits of the previous few days, and bought me drinks. Learning that I had nowhere to sleep, they logged me into the sick-bay of the British Hospital as a casualty. I never did learn the ailment.

It might have been better if I had. Without knowing it, I was very far from well. I had been forcing my body to adapt to an unnatural routine for far too long. It was about to exact its revenge.

Returning to Port Said and faced with a heavy workload, I suddenly felt distinctly unwell. I made a dash for the toilet. I awoke to find myself on the cloakroom floor, nursing a large bump on the back of my head. I was taken to the British Hospital and examined by a doctor who seemed very Scottish. He diagnosed appendicitis, changed his mind and plumped for malaria. Neither verdict was correct. I was eventually found to be suffering from exhaustion. I was ordered to rest for ten days. On the evening of the second, my Scottish physician popped his head round the door and said:

'Now . . . if you were to fancy a wee dram, you might consider popping down to my consulting room about eight o'clock this evening.'

This was hint enough. If I was sick, by the end of the evening we had rendered his bottle of scotch even more so.

The following morning I discharged myself.

CHAPTER THIRTEEN

THE CASE OF THE DANCING OLIVES

Running around as I was, I naturally spent great deal of time aloft. Indeed, there was a period when I seemed never to be out of an aircraft. Not all of these trips were without incident. On one occasion, flying from Cairo to Haifa, I found myself the only passenger aboard a very small and flimsy aircraft. There was a crew of two: a pilot of about eighteen and his engineer, whom I estimated to be about fourteen.

The plane took off without incident. However, when we reached the point along the coast at which we turned out to sea, the pilot handed the controls over to his junior, retired to the rear of the plane and promptly settled down to sleep. When Haifa came into view, the boy-wonder awoke his superior who returned to the controls and brought the aircraft safely to earth.

This was by no means my most terrifying experience. On another occasion I found myself trapped at Algiers by adverse weather conditions. I heard that an Anson of the R.A.F. had somehow received permission to fly to Malta. By dint of a good deal of fast talking, and by making a great deal of my Priority Two Clearance pass, I persuaded the squadron–leader in charge to add me to the passenger list.

The Anson is a two-engined monoplane. It seats six. It is not called a 'crate' for nothing. This one was more crate-like than most. The route chart showed that we were likely to encounter very heavy cloud conditions, with winds gusting up to sixty miles an hour. There would be rain up to thirteen thousand feet – which, as the Anson was incapable of climbing above thirteen thousand feet meant in our case *continuous* rain.

Just before we took off on the first leg of the journey to Tunis, the orderly officer came across the tarmac waving a piece of paper. He said: 'Listen, old man, are you really sure you want to make this journey?'. I said that I did. He looked at the piece of paper. 'In that case the message I have here was received after your departure. But I can tell you one thing. You're in for a very rough ride.'

He was wrong. I was in for a nightmare. Because of the continuous thick cloud we were flying completely 'blind'. Turbulence produced an almost continuous series of bumps and lurches. That was bad enough. What followed was unquestionably the most frightening incident of my entire flying career. Cruising at two or three thousand feet, the plane suddenly encountered an air pocket and began to drop like a stone. We lost height at a phenomenal rate, dropping perhaps a thousand feet. Some jars of olives stacked on the floor by my feet rose into the air and danced about before my eyes. A gap in the clouds showed the sea below. It was a great deal too close for comfort.

When we recovered our composure we noticed that one of two W.A.A.F.s on the flight – too superior to use her seat belt – had inadvertently knocked herself out by hitting her head on the aircraft roof.

Once, while waiting at Tunis to fly to Malta, the winds were gusting at more than a hundred miles an hour. I encountered a squadron of British spitfires waiting to fly to Italy. They had been grounded for three days. On the fourth, the wind having abated a little, they decided to risk it. They returned within the hour having calculated that battling such a headwind would have meant that they would have run out of fuel long before they could reach their destination.

*   *   *

My longest sea-flight was from Singapore to Colombo, a distance of approximately a thousand miles. We flew in a Sunderland which, during the early part of the trip, was cumbersome to manoeuvre due to the nine hundred gallons of fuel required. As we left Singapore we were afforded an excellent view of the fleet of picturesque Chinese junks. High-sterned and square of bow, they had lug-sails made of canvas or matting. Despite the flimsy nature of their construction they were capable of sailing enormous distances – in the dry season as far as Mombasa.

Once clear of Singapore, we saw no further land until we touched upon the northern tip of Sumatra. At Sabang, the plane circled a small and desolate airfield before dropping a bag of mail. Receipt was acknowledged by a wave from the tiny and solitary figure on the ground below.

Having risen at three in the morning in order to make this flight, I was not best pleased when, some twelve hours later, we were given only cold food for our lunch – cold tinned salmon, cold tinned carrots, tinned cheese – and, of all things, a dog biscuit. Later in the day we ran into a thunder storm, the turbulence of which shook us around a great deal.

*　　*　　*

Landing didn't always bring an end to one's troubles. Arriving by air at Gibraltar just before dawn for a meeting with the island's head of the Ministry of War Transport, I found the Dockyard gates exit guarded by Gurkhas carrying rifles with fixed bayonets. It was an important meeting and I assumed that my arrival had been anticipated. It had not. They would not allow me through. I endeavoured to explain the position but to no avail. Because of the earliness of the hour, they were not prepared to ring the man I had come so far to meet.

In the end, and in complete desperation, I flashed a piece of card under their noses which testified that I was a member of the Wimbledon Squash and Badminton Club. The effect was electric. The sentries presented arms and opened the gates.

When I later related this incident to the Ministry's head he was both highly amused . . . and more than a little concerned.

In order not to be hobbled in my work, I frequently found it necessary to bend – if not quite to break – the rules in this manner. Flying from country to country nearly always occasioned delays and to some extent these were unavoidable. It was the avoidable delays which caused me to fret. The people of the Middle East have a horror of disease. Consequently, it was necessary to wait at almost every airport and border-post while a medical orderly was found to administer an inoculation.

The orderlies were not always very expert and there were times when I felt like a close relative to a dart board. Nor was one always sure whether the needle was clean or what the syringe contained. This caused me some anxiety.

However, with time I came to appreciate the workings of the system and thereafter always carried with me an official-looking form testifying that I had been inoculated against every disease known to man. It was of course a fabrication. As I had not had a single day's real illness in two and a half years I felt justified in carrying it.

*　　*　　*

Rudyard Kipling once described Egypt as 'A country which is not a country but a longish strip of market garden'. The same could not be said of the Sinai desert. Here the dry grains of sand slide readily one upon the other, a phenomenon caused by hidden springs or gas. This produces a peculiar crackling sound. The 'singing sands' of the Sinai are said to resemble the sound of an Aeolian harp. The extent of the 'singing' depends very much on the amount of moisture present. Too dry or very wet and it produces no sound at all.

As we flew, it was possible to see the wind re-landscaping the terrain below, demolishing hills and dunes and raising up valleys. Further east – a little west of Basra – a member of the crew pointed out a vast swampland covering many thousands of square miles. This was inhabited by Marsh Arabs, a reclusive tribe which neither sought nor achieved much contact with the outside world.

Flying low, we were able to distinguish swatches of green, where mosquito-infested rushes had been cut and burned to lessen the risk of malaria. Channels of water radiated out from the tiny villages, trickling through areas cleared to allow the inhabitants to fish or to hunt for birds. Pelicans and flamingoes abounded. The noise of the aircraft caused a herd of wild buffalo to stampede, ploughing into a swamp up to their necks.

This was almost as astounding a sight as the one I had witnessed during the course of a journey from Cairo. Owing to bad weather, the aircraft was forced to alter course. In consequence we passed over the battlefield of El Alamein, where in October and November 1943 Montgomery had taken on and defeated the might of Rommel's Afrika Corps. Looking down, I could see dozens of metal skeletons – all that remained of the wreckage of aircraft and burned-out tanks. The sand was marked by hundred of tracks, crossing and re-crossing the desert, For all I know they may still be there, the ageing blue-print of that long-ago battle.

I enjoyed my time in Egypt enormously. Sadly, by the time of my last tour, in the Spring of 1946, there had been a marked deterioration in diplomatic relations between Great Britain and the host country. Everywhere I went, anti-British feeling was rife. English shop-signs were being replaced by Arab ones. Those which remained were liable to desecration or destruction at the hands of the roving mob – a mob which did not always understand the complexity of the British nature. When a ship bearing troops home to England passed through the Suez Canal near Port Said, a hostile crowd of Egyptians assembled to heckle. They shouted: 'British Out! British Out!'. The troops came to the rails to witness this demonstration. They thought it something of a free entertainment. As such, they decided on a little audience participation and set up even louder chants of: 'British Out!' At this the Egyptians – non-plussed and dumbfounded – grew silent. After a few minutes they began to disperse. From the receding ship came the faint sound of three resounding cheers.

Violence and unrest were an everyday feature of Egyptian life. The night before I left Cairo a large and noisy crowd gathered outside my hotel in Opera Square. Half a dozen mounted police, equipped with long staves, were vainly endeavour-ing to keep order. A force of about thirty more suddenly appeared in a lorry.

Leaping over the tailgate, they began attacking the crowd with truncheons. It was reminiscent of a riot in Alexandria a few weeks earlier where one of the policemen, aiming a mighty wallop in the direction of a rioter, missed his aim and caught his own sergeant a cracking blow on the back. The sergeant was rendered immobile with pain and amazement. When he unfroze he whacked his colleague back. They then both turned round and got on with the business in hand.

Considering that Egyptian policemen only received the equivalent of about £1 a week, the force was lucky in attracting men of the right calibre. They were all very respectable-looking, albeit rather subservient. They supplemented their earnings in a number of ways. Having attended a function in Alexandria, I emerged to find that my car had a puncture. I was dressed in evening clothes. I was not keen to soil them. However, I knew that to leave the car overnight in such an area was to invite disaster. I found a policeman and explained the situation to him. He said he'd be happy to look after the vehicle on my behalf but only until six o'clock in the morning, when he was due to report back to the station. Fifty piasters persuaded him to remain at his post until eight and risk the wrath of his sergeant. He was as good as his word. When Ministry of War Transport officials came on duty at 6 a.m. they saw him asleep, sitting on the front bumper, cradling his rifle in his arms.

*　　*　　*

If parts of Egypt resembled a market garden, India, in contrast, was akin to a vast estate divided into three widely differing sections: the inhospitable mountainous terrain of the Himalayas, the deserts of Sind and Rajputana, and the fertile ranges of the Deccan plateau.

Occupied by almost one sixth of the human race, I found it a continent of fascinating and almost infinite contrast. A year or so prior to my arrival, Calcutta had been devastated by famine. Yet at the Great Eastern Hotel the quality and quantity of the food was lavish beyond description. Plates came so laden that each course was the equivalent of an entire meal. One evening I ordered snipe. I received six. Perhaps in order to increase the total amount of the tip, the head waiter arranged things in such a manner that guests were served by as many waiters as possible. On one occasion I was waited upon by ten. This had the opposite effect to the one intended because by the end of the evening I was quite unable to distinguish one from another.

I quickly found that in India the population was divided into numerous races. They spoke more than two hundred different languages, professed countless shades of religious belief, supported more than two thousand social castes and were distributed across seven hundred provinces and minor states. Despite a civilization stretching back more than five thousand years, more than ninety percent of the population was illiterate.

Their way of thinking was very different from our own. Visiting the Chief of Police in his office in a Calcutta back street one day, my attention was distracted by the noise of a group of rioters. In their progress down the street they were overturning stalls and belabouring the traders with heavy sticks.

When I asked the Chief of Police what action he proposed to take he said: 'None. You'll see, they'll go away in a minute.' Which they did. The traders then picked themselves up, dusted themselves off, righted their stalls and carried on as though nothing had happened. Violence was endemic. Incidents of this nature were an everyday occurrence.

*　　*　　*

My work frequently took me to Bombay, one of the most populated of all the continent's cities and known from its peninsular location as 'the Gateway to India'. Its harbour was almost as beautiful as that of Naples.

On one of these trips I had no sooner descended from the train than I was greeted effusively by a turbaned Indian who immediately adopted me. He followed me everywhere, becoming a kind of unofficial servant and bearer. He carried my bags up to my room in the Taj Mahal Hotel, unpacked the contents and brought me a cup of tea.

I at first thought I might be dealing with a madman, but soon discovered that this was quite normal practice. The poor man had no home and slept wherever he could find work – in this case on the floor of the corridor outside my room. I paid him, I think, three rupees a week. He supplemented this by taking a small commission from tradesmen when purchasing items on my behalf.

The Taj Mahal Hotel proved to be one of the most curious buildings on the Indian continent. It had been designed by a British architect who was invited to fly out from England to attend the opening ceremony. To his mortification he discovered that whilst it had been constructed exactly to his specifications it had been sited the wrong way round, so that the back faced towards the sea and the magnificent front elevation overlooked a clutch of hovels and a compound filled with dustbins. The architect is said to have committed suicide.

During my time in Bombay I made a seventy-five-mile excursion to Poona for a day's racing. Although I think I made a modest profit, the trip was less memorable for the sport than the journey which preceded it. The train was crowded, smelly and stuffy. It travelled very slowly and stopped at intervals for no apparent reason. As soon as it did so, hoards of monkeys descended from the trees and clambered through the windows, grabbing everything edible and one or two items which were not. They were accomplished little smash-and-grab artists and as soon as the train began to move again they scampered away, retiring to the trees to examine their prizes.

When my work in Bombay was completed, my Indian bearer insisted on packing up my things and carrying the suitcase down to the car which was waiting to take me to the airport. As I opened the door, he endeavoured to squirm in before me. With a tinge of sadness, I explained that it simply wasn't possible to take him with me to Delhi. By way of consolation I handed over two rupees.

*   *   *

If Naples had represented a little slice of America, I found Delhi to be exclusively British. The place was bristling with military, none of whom seemed to hold any rank under that of brigadier. Realising that as a soldier I should have no standing whatsoever, I decided to adopt my civilian persona.

Before I could set to work I contracted the form of dysentery known colloquially as 'Delhi belly'. This laid me up for some days. I was placed in a transit bungalow, consisting of one large room fitted with a basin, and a smaller one beyond which contained the 'thunder-box'. To this I made numerous trips.

Lying in bed one night, feeling very low and unable to sleep, I became aware of a soft sound . . . like whispering in a far-off room. I looked down to see a snake rustling sinuously across the floor towards me. It was about five feet long. I held my breath and lay rigid, peering at it at long intervals over the top of the sheet to establish what progress it had made – and in what direction. After what must have been about ten minutes – but seemed like an hour – it departed as quietly as it had come.

*   *   *

My fifth tour took me to Ceylon, sixty miles south-east of India and rightly known as 'the Pearl of the Orient'. We flew in an Imperial flying-boat via Bahrain and Dubai. The captain, a man named Colvin, was known as 'Captain Colombus Colvin' because, some time previously, he had discovered two new islands thrown up by a volcano close to Karachi. He diverted the aircraft in order that we might see them. With a tinge of sadness, he told me that the discovery did not in itself confer any proprietorial rights.

96

From the air, the scene was one of utter desolation. When not over the sea, we crossed endless miles of desert, mountainous volcanic ranges and estuary swampland. There was little or no vegetation and the monotony was broken only by views of small, squalid-looking villages and hutments.

By contrast, the scenery of Ceylon I found to be truly magnificent. Rolling plains covered most of the island, rising in the south to lofty mountains. The most elevated of these was 'Adam's Peak', visible for some way out to sea and sacred to Buddhists as the peak from which the Master ascended to heaven.

The vegetation was lush and tropical: tall ferns, blood-red rhododendrons, magnificent palms and valuable trees of ebony and satin-wood. The island also housed what is claimed to be the oldest tree in the world, the famous Bo tree of Anuradhapura, planted in 245 B.C. from a cutting of the Bo tree of India, under which Buddha is said to have received the inspiration which led to the founding of the religion which bears his name.

The population was a considerable racial mix – Tamils from southern India, Moors, Malays, and Veddahs – generally thought to have been the original inhabitants – who lived in tree-houses in the wildest and least accessible part of the island. By instinct vegetarian, they existed mainly on exotic fruit.

About two-thirds of the population was composed of Sinhalese, the descendants of immigrants who had arrived in Ceylon from northern India about 500 B.C. The Sinhalese were a curious race, many of the men being easily mistaken for women. They had delicate features, wore earrings and a wrap-around hip-cloth similar to a skirt. They held back their long hair by means of combs.

At the time of my visit, Ceylon ranked second among the tea-producing countries of the world. As Great Britain alone then imported about 6 lbs of the commodity each year for every man, woman and child, it was of vital importance to us.

I made my base in Colombo, the island's capital and largest city, where I was introduced to the country's Tea Commissioner, a gentleman named Saravanamuttu. His deputy, a man called Fernando, took me on a tour of the island's plantations, some of which covered hundreds of acres, the low-set bushes being set in endless rows about four feet apart. This made the hills appear as though they were covered with continuous grey-green foliage.

Fernando explained that tea benefited from being cultivated at high elevations because the ground is that much cooler and produces a leaf grown rather more slowly than at sea-level and with a far more delicate taste.

Life in Ceylon afforded some leisure. I visited the Tanglin Club, just outside Colombo, and made an excursion to Candy, where I witnessed a vast parade of elephants, each highly decorated. Pondering them as they passed, it seemed to me that they merited the title 'King of Beasts' far more than the lion. Ten feet tall, with enormous ears, they were at once fearsomely powerful and extraordinarily gentle. I was particularly fascinated by the manner in which evolution had fashioned their trunks to serve as a kind of hand and their teeth into spears of ivory. In the East they had supplanted the dog as man's most patient and faithful servant.

Returning from Candy, I stayed overnight at the Grand Hotel at Nuwara Eliya. Here I experienced one of the worst thunder storms of my life. My room afforded a grand sweeping vista across a low-lying plain, bounded by a range of mountains. Across the peaks of this, fragmented lightning ran and sparked, illuminating the district for many miles around. Sometimes the flashes descended in long thin and concentrated spirals, sometimes in a thick mass of strands which at a certain point disintegrated, like the skeins of an unravelling rope.

Through my contact with a Ceylanese tea-planter named Hayward, I was invited to spend a week-end shooting in the jungle. For thirty rupees I acquired a pair of sandals. My host was kind enough to loan me a pair of shorts and a bush shirt. He, his son, myself and a friend set off in a dilapidated automobile to make the seventy-mile journey to Nicawerstiya.

The heat was unbearable. After driving about ten miles, Hayward found the steering tracking heavily to one side. We investigated and found that one of the tyres had almost melted. Rubber was oozing from a great crack where the tread had pulled away from the wall. We replaced it with the spare wheel. This proved no great substitute. Every few miles it was necessary to stop and cool the wheels by dousing them in cold water. At Nikawerstiya we found a rest-house to accommodate us for the night.

As we were seeking only birds, we were the complete antithesis of the big-game hunter and carried only twelve-bores. The terrain was mostly malarial swamp. It should have been otherwise. In the days of tribal warfare a victory in battle had been celebrated by the building of a dam – and thus another reservoir with which to water the territory reclaimed. Unfortunately, no one tribe had been capable of dominating any other for any significant length of time. In consequence, as the vanquished became the victor they destroyed the dams, re-flooded the villages and returned the area to swampland.

This was the kind of terrain in which I now found myself.Most of the day was spent calf-deep in eighteen inches of mud. My sandals – even at thirty rupees – quickly proved a bad buy. I tried binding them with cord – not only to hold them to my feet but as a pathetic form of protection against the bites of insects, snakes and reptiles. It had little effect; I felt them rotting under me.

Quite apart from what was happening to my feet below, I found it necessary to be on my guard every minute. The jungle is a startling and dangerous arena. It may look tranquil. It remains static for no more than a few seconds. From the undergrowth came to greet me a lizard (which I first mistook for a crocodile) seven (or possibly eight) feet long. I contemplated running, only to discover that, like the little boy featured in the old Victorian legend who failed to clean his shoes, running was far too heavily-weighted an option. As it transpired, the lizard/crocodile was, anyway, capable of running considerably faster than me . . . fortunately it chose to do so in the opposite direction.

My rib-cage had only just begun to accommodate the normal beat of my heart once more when I heard a loud splash – a turtle dropping from a rock into the water of the pool below.

I proceded into the clearing beyond. Here I encountered a day-old buffalo calf, flanked by its very belligerent-looking parents and other burly relatives.

In panic, I turned down the only path I could find – only to meet a wild-cat. Fifty monkeys greeted my entrance (and the exit of the wild-cat) by scampering away, screeching wildly. The week-end was rapidly turning into a nightmare. It was not at all what I had envisaged.

For all this, it had its consolations. We were mainly after snipe and golden plover, which were plentiful. Our task was rendered the easier by the fact that most of the birds – including such exotics as the lesser bee-eater, distinguished by its bright-green plumage – tended in flight to be less erratic than their English counterparts. As such they represented relatively static targets.

The morning of the second day we left the rest-house before first light, heading for a series of 'tanks' (or reservoirs) up-country. Hayward drove the car. The rest of us rode 'shotgun' on the bonnet by turns, loosing off shots at the wild-fowl which crossed the pitted jungle paths over which we were bumping. We sighted several. We killed only one.

In contrast the afternoon found us in swampland in search of duck. Due to the overhanging foliage, we could hardly see. Nevertheless, I followed my intrepid host into the brackish, swampy waters. We were never less than knee-deep and often up to our armpits.

*   *   *

My next tour of duty threaded me through the needle's eye of the Malacca Strait, along the great trading route of the Far East to the island city of Singapore, twenty-seven miles long and fourteen broad, lying midway between India and China.

The harbour was one of the greatest in the world. In times past its pale-green waters had accommodated small ocean-going liners, long lines of Chinese coaling-ships and innumerable sailing craft from sampans to dows – an aggregate each year of more than twenty-five million tons. Now, the huge floating dock, constructed in England and towed more than eight thousand miles to its final destination, could house the greatest liners ever built, with thirty feet draught to spare.

I arrived in this haven six months after the withdrawal of the Japanese, who had captured this seemingly impregnable fortress in February 1942. What Churchill described as 'this heavy and far-reaching defeat' was encompassed with the minimum of violence. In anticipation of a massive naval invasion, all the guns and fortifications had been positioned seawards. The Japanese simply traversed the Malay Peninsula on bicycles and came in via the North, the back door. The island's fall had deprived the Allies of their only dry dock between Durban and Pearl Harbour.

Now the residents were stealthily feeling their way back to freedom and safety. It was a slow and painful process. Old memories refused to fade. One of the tea planters, a prisoner of the Japanese, told me that he, his colleagues and their wives had been reduced by their captors to the role of beasts. Forced to act as surrogate donkeys, they had dragged carts out into the countryside in search of wood. They were routed back to camp past their former homes. Here they witnessed the wives of their usurpers reclining in deck chairs on manicured lawns, refreshing themselves with long, cooling drinks.

*　　*　　*

All in all, my seven tours aggregated more than a hundred and seventy thousand miles – the equivalent of more than six times round the world. The last of these – fittingly perhaps – was to Egypt once more, the very centre of knavery and deceit. One of the native shipping yards at Port Tewfik had returned a highly inflated bill for the repair of one of our vessels. If the time-sheets were to be believed, the work-force had toiled round the clock for four months, resting no more than one hour in every twenty-four.

I found this difficult to believe. With a view to winning me over, the chief engineer took me to the best rug salesroom in Port Said, where he helped me select three magnificent Persian rugs. It was evident that he had been here before and was regarded as a valued customer. This had the effect of considerably reducing the price. But when I went to pay he said: 'Please – not now. Let me send you the bill. You can deal with it when you return home'.

There was something about his manner which implied that the 'bill' would never arrive, would be quietly settled by the company, leaving me under a moral obligation which I might have had difficulty in discharging. I paid out of my own pocket.

The bill for the repair of the ship was ultimately reduced by more than half. The rugs? I have them still.

*   *   *

The incident served to impress upon me the complexity of the Arab mind. I found it to be a peculiar mix of cunning and servility which occasionally bordered upon the comical.

In July 1945 the Egyptian captain of a tug-boat known as 'Sturdy No. 7' rammed a ship of the British navy in Cairo harbour. Although there was no loss of life – or indeed any serious injury beyond the sinking of the tug – I was able to attribute the accident to no definable cause. I therefore wrote to the captain of the tug-boat asking him for an explanation. I reproduce his answer in all its glory, as it was translated from Arabic:

REPORT OF SINKING OF STURDY NO. 7

20 July 1945

I, Abdul Mohamed Rali, am the humble raies (captain) of the tug Sturdy 7. My crew is all good mans but one he is Rastus Hassan may his liver rot. He is surely the first-born son of Satan, Effendi, and a very bad man.

Your Honour, Effendi, I give you this report and wait humbly for your Almighty decision, Effendi.

While steering towards No. 66 Quay I am suddenly lying down and someone is beating me with a big shovel and it is Rastus Hassan may his liver rot he is a very bad man. He is drinking sometimes from a great red bottle, and as he drinks he makes upon me a fresh attack,

I am very busy being beaten so I do not steer and there is a big noise and we are all in the water. I am looking for the tug . . . but there is no tug, only pieces. It was a big ship hit us in your Navy Effendi.

It is all the fault of Rastus Hassan may his liver rot he is a very bad man. I am a sad raies I have no tug and many children.

Trusting your Excellency is in good health this year and have no worries like,

Your obedient servant – Abdoul Mohamed Rali.

101

*   *   *

At last, my job with the Ministry of War Transport was over. In the course of it I had visited more than forty countries on financial and political missions. It was time to come home. My large cabin trunk, stored so long at the Continental Savoy Hotel in Cairo, came with me. I was careful to pack it very carefully, inter-leaving between my clothing several bottles of liqueur and cherry brandy.

On arrival in England, I had to unpack the contents for the benefit of an inquisitive customs officer. Having satisfied him, I hurriedly repacked it and went on my way. When I opened the thing in the privacy of my room at the Farmer's Club in London's Whitehall Court I discovered that several of the bottles had shattered – impregnating my dressing gown, dress shirts, dinner jackets and white shorts with green chartreuse and cherry brandy. It was a grievous loss to me.

I spent the evening of my return endlessly washing and rinsing the desecrated items in the bath. As I had spent the previous three years washing the dirty linen of others, it was perhaps a fitting end.

CHAPTER FOURTEEN

THE ATHLETIC MARATHON

 One weekend, during my sojourn at the Farmer's Club in Whitehall Court, I happened to be glancing through the *Sunday Empire News* when I came across a feature concerning the diamond sculler, Harry Fullick, who was training for the 1947 Henley Regatta. As rationing was still in force, he was finding it difficult to obtain the right kind of food in sufficient quantity. Through the columns of the *Empire News* he was issuing an open challenge to an athletic competition – the loser to pay the cost of a rump steak dinner.

This sounded like a marvellous idea and I immediately telephoned the newspaper to pick up the gauntlet. The following morning, when I arrived at my office in the Brompton Road, I found a photographer from the *News* camped on the doorstep.

The newspaper – for whom this represented marvellous free publicity – arranged for us to meet and establish the ground rules of what became known as 'the steak battle'. It was agreed that we should each nominate fifteen events. The *Sunday Empire News* would arrange the venues and supply the necessary invigilators and officials. The whole thing would be captured on film by Gaumont British News.

We experienced some difficulty in coming up with thirty different events and were ultimately forced to include such non-athletic pursuits as billiards, snooker, drafts, cribbage – and even shove-halfpenny. It was agreed that we should meet every Wednesday for six weeks, competing against one another on each occasion in five events. The venues would alternate between London – my home base – and Fullick's native Worthing.

*   *   *

It began to occur to me that I had been rather foolhardy. At 33, Fullick was six years my junior, at least two inches taller and of a superior build. If I was fit, he was fitter. I could only hope to lessen his advantage by approaching the competition with utter

103

Marathon Athletics – Harry Fullick with Frank Taylor

dedication. Consequently, each morning before breakfast I ran a complete circuit of Hyde Park, a distance of approximately three miles. At first this took me about twenty minutes. As I became more used to the exertion my time began gradually to improve. Every lunchtime I swam and high-dived. In the evenings, when I was not seeking to improve my squash, badminton and table-tennis, I practised shooting on the miniature rifle range of the Royal Automobile Club in Pall Mall.

All this required a considerable effort. The worst effort of all was to get myself into shape for the boxing. I had been reasonably proficient at this at school but had not boxed since.

Through the Amateur Boxing Association I was introduced to a professional boxer. This man lived in the area of London Bridge and had access to the gymnasium at Guy's Hospital. I booked three lessons with him at weekly intervals. At the first of these he taught me how to deliver a straight left. The second week he taught me how to dodge one. The third week he taught me how to deliver *and* dodge a blow simultaneously. This was pretty basic stuff. It did at least serve to boost my morale.

*   *   *

Several events produced surprise results, most notably the river sports. Fullick was an expert single diamond sculler. I was nothing like as proficient. Nor was I used to a sliding seat. Consequently it was decided to run the event in skiffs. Here I was far more at home and managed just to hang on to win. At punting I beat him with comparative ease. I expected a similarly comfortable victory in the three-mile cycle race. In youth I had cycled a great deal. Utilising the great leg-drive which he had developed as a sculler, Harry won in style.

Two other events also gave me unlooked-for problems. The first of these was the shooting, at which I considered myself a good deal better than average. We were each to fire at decimal targets ranged at a distance of twenty-five yards. I ultimately scraped home by the narrowest possible margin, ninety-three points to ninety-two. As a result of my intense training, I also expected to do well in the swimming pool. In all but the underwater distance event, Harry proved superior.

*   *   *

It had originally been intended to hold the boxing competition in the gymnasium of the promoter, Jack Solomons. However, when we learned that by doing so we should become professionals ourselves, the venue was switched to Kline's gymnasium in Fitzroy Square.

As I had suspected might be the case, boxing proved to be my weak suit. To all but a professional, three two-minute rounds is a very long time to hit and be hit. At the opening bell I came out full of fire and for the first round had Harry back-pedalling. The second two minutes were more even. By the start of the last round, however, I was so desperately tired that I could hardly lift my gloves to defend myself.

Perhaps the most ludicrous of our encounters was the point-to-point, held on Worthing Downs. The *Empire News* arranged for a local stable to provide us with mounts of more or less matching ability. They were allocated by the toss of a coin. At Harry's request, the race was run over the flat.

I established an early lead and slowly increased this until I could no longer hear Harry's horse at all. However, about a quarter of a mile from home I caught the distant sound of pounding hooves.

I spurred my horse on. To no avail. The sound of the hooves came closer and closer. From the corner of my eye – and about a hundred yards from the finishing line – I glimpsed the tip of its nose as it came alongside. The nose was quickly

105

Training for the Athletic Marathon, 1949

Marathon Athletics. Start of Freestyle Swim, Fullick left, F. H. T. right

followed by the rest of the animal. To my surprise and relief, Harry was no longer riding it. He had fallen off some way back.

The billiards and snooker matches were held in the hall of the billiard-ball manufacturers, Burrows & Watts, at 19 Soho Square. They were a large concern and it is said that vast numbers of elephants had to be slaughtered every year to keep them supplied with ivory.

On my arrival I was greeted by the club secretary, who said: 'Where's your cue?' I explained that I didn't possess one – and was rewarded with the most disdainful look I have ever received in my life.

To make matters worse, the hall itself was arranged in a very intimidating manner, the billiard tables being flanked on every side by row after row of tiered seating which seemed to me to rise almost to the roof. As Harry and I were deeply inexpert at both games, they took an eternity to complete and after the initial

107

amusement they occasioned must have been a bore to watch. Harry eventually won them both.

Throughout this two-man Olympiad our progress was documented weekly in the *Sunday Empire News*, each of the articles being supplemented by photographs. I ultimately won the 'steak stakes' eighteen events to twelve. The promised rump-steak dinner was held at Kettner's pretty little restaurant in Soho, the food being brought to our table by the head chef in person. While other diners looked on in amazement, we were filmed eating by a newsreel cameraman.

All in all it had proved an interesting episode. The disruption to my business life had been expensive, but I was now a great deal fitter than I had been for some years.

For all his efforts, Harry Fullick never did win the diamond sculls at Henley, nor did he qualify for the Olympic team. It may be that he simply wasn't good enough.

My own opinion is that he lacked sufficient thrust. He seemed quite content to work as a blacksmith from a small forge adjacent to his home in Worthing. He was not an ambitious man and when each week he had made sufficient gates or wrought iron lamp-standards to cover his outgoings he shut up shop and worked no more.

A year after the competition he decided to emigrate to Majorca. He and his wife loaded two small cars with household effects and quietly departed. I never saw him again.

I have often wondered what became of him.

CHAPTER FIFTEEN

CITY LIVERYMAN

S hortly after the end of the war I became interested in the work of the Livery Companies of the City of London. This came about as a direct result of my war-time work as a Finance Director with the Ministry of Food. One of the commodities for which I had responsibility during part of that period was yeast. As yeast was and remains an essential ingredient of bread-making, the regulation of its continued production was considered of vital importance.

It was then produced in just five factories. Three of these were owned by the United Yeast Company, a subsidiary of the Distillers Company.

U.Y.C. was responsible for eighty-five percent of all production. This meant that I spent a great deal of time in consultation with its senior executives. In the course of time I became friendly with the chairman, Ernest Huxtable. I did not, however, allow our friendship to incline me towards favouring the firm in my dealings with it – if anything rather the opposite.

*   *   *

It became clear that due to its size U.Y.C. was making enormous profits. I had no particular objection to this but felt that they were being made at the expense of the company's two smaller competitors. I therefore devised a scheme for increased production angled at benefiting the minnows.

The way trade was then disposed, it became clear that under my scheme the increase to the minnows would be minimal while U.Y.C.'s profits would leap. This seemed to me entirely wrong. To even the balance I suggested that U.Y.C voluntarily agree to a Government levy whereby their increased earnings under the scheme were taxed in direct ratio to the profit made. To their everlasting credit, the Distillers Company accepted my proposition and paid up.

Over the years, Huxtable and his principals at Distillers proved very helpful to me. On another occasion they willingly agreed, at no small cost to themselves, to convert their Scottish whisky distillery at Alloa so that at a push of a button it could switch from whisky-making to the production of yeast. This the Government considered a vital reserve in the event of one or other of the five main yeast-producing factories being rendered useless by enemy action.

* * *

By the end of the war, Ernest Huxtable and I had become well acquainted. I considered him a good friend and often stayed with him and his wife at their house at Amersham.

I discovered that he was a member of the Worshipful Company of Bakers, one of the great Livery Companies of the City of London. One day he tentatively suggested that as I was qualified to do so through my wartime associations with the industry, I might consider becoming a member myself. It was also pointed out that whilst, perhaps, I might be no great shakes as a baker, as an accountant I should at least know how to cook books.

Knowing nothing of the Company, I resolved to learn a little about it before coming to a firm decision. What I discovered proved fascinating.

* * *

Perhaps with one notable exception, the baking of bread might be said to be the oldest profession. Savages kneaded dough on their primitive hearths; and Genesis tells us that Pharaoh 'hanged the chief baker'. In contrast, the bakers of ancient Rome were greatly revered. They were not only the one group of tradesmen automatically granted the freedom of the city but even had their own seat in the Senate.

It had long been the practice in many countries for men in a particular trade to band together into guilds for mutual protection and interest. In London many craft guilds were established as early as the 12th century.

The origins of the Bakers' Company are lost to us. It would almost certainly have begun with a group of allied tradesmen who had similar religious affiliations. This spiritual foundation is preserved today in the appellation 'Worshipful'; and in the Company's motto: 'Praise God For All', which also forms the traditional Grace.

The Worshipful Company of Bakers is first mentioned in the Pipe Rolls of Henry II in 1155. As such it can lay a (somewhat tenuous) claim to be the second oldest recognised guild in London. At this date its members were known as the 'Bolengarii'. The Company acted in a regulatory capacity and was empowered to

110

impose fines (and sometimes to draw teeth) where its members were found guilty of selling short weight or adulterating their flour with sand or sawdust.

More serious offences entailed the convicted man being dragged through the dirtiest streets of the City on a hurdle, the offending loaf being hung as a pendant around his neck. A second transgression saw the miscreant placed in the pillory. Anyone offending a third time had his oven demolished and a decree issued against him forbidding him ever to practice the trade again.

The Court of the Company was summoned not only for the purpose of dealing with rogue members but for many other reasons besides, notably the indenturing of apprentices and the granting of Livery status to new members.

The term 'livery' derives from the distinctive apparel worn by the members to distinguish them one from another. The Freemen wore a surcoat, the Liverymen a surcoat and hood. Only the Master wore a hat.

The original Bakers' Hall was housed in the converted mansion of John Chichele, a 15th-century Chamberlain of London. It was purchased in 1498. It was destroyed by the ravages of the Great Fire in 1666 (a fire which is reputed to have started in a baker's shop in Pudding Lane, a fact which the other Livery Companies have been slow to allow us to forget).

A second Hall was destroyed by fire in 1715. The third fell victim to enemy action in 1940. The Company's present home, completed in 1963, is housed in the lower portion of a large office block in Harp Lane. It stands on a site which has accommodated the Company for five hundred years. It is currently leased to us at a 'peppercorn' rent which is not in fact a peppercorn at all but three white and three brown loaves, payable yearly at midsummer.

*　　*　　*

I was accepted as a Freeman of the Company in 1947. I was inaugurated on the same evening as Tom Arnold, the producer of the ice extravaganzas. As I had been proposed for membership a few days prior to him, it fell to me to deliver our joint speech of thanks. I was amused to learn that by ancient statute I was now entitled to keep a cow within the precincts of the City and to drive a flock of sheep across London Bridge.

*　　*　　*

Thirty-four years later, in 1982, I was appointed the Company's 497th Master. The year which followed was a busy one and required my attendance at a hundred and ten official functions. Not surprisingly perhaps for a man born in a Weymouth pub,

I greatly enjoyed the social side of these elaborate banquets. Most of them required gentlemen to wear white tie and tails. That aspect of City life is now beginning to retreat. Slowly, dinner jackets have become the order of the day. It may be that this is symptomatic of a general lowering of standards relating not only to dress but to every aspect of business life, especially to speech and to ethics. When I first crossed London Bridge as an articled clerk, more than sixty years ago, the bowler hat and the furled umbrella were essential emblems of respectability. Nowadays City-workers arrive at the office in jeans, trainers and open-necked shirts.

* * *

In addition to my own inauguration ceremony, my duties as Master of the Worshipful Company of Bakers included attending meetings of bakers' guilds in Zurich, Vienna and Scotland; receiving new members into the Livery; overseeing the Rent-Giving Ceremony; presenting prizes at numerous trade conferences, gatherings and fairs; and making an inordinate number of speeches.

I was also invited to attend banquets given by other Livery Companies. These were always great fun but did nothing for my waistline. In the October I was present in my official capacity at the Mansion House to mark the City's 'Salute to the Falkland Forces'.

A foreign banquet – at Zurich – was especially memorable, not least because it incorporated a novel version of the Company's own Loving-Cup Ceremony. I was required to introduce myself to – and to take a glass of wine with – each of the 119 guests. The proceedings took a total of nine-and-a-half hours. They required a fair degree of stamina. The event commenced at six o'clock in the evening and terminated the following morning at 3.30.

During my term of office I also sought to establish a closer tie between the Company and the World Trade Centre at St. Katherine's Dock, hard by the Tower of London. To this end, and as Master of the Bakers' Company, I unveiled an inscribed slab of Penrhyn slate as a founding-stone for the Great Hall. This was one of the first ceremonies of its kind. Since then many other City Livery Companies have followed my example.

World Trade Centres were then a relatively new concept. I had first become interested in them some years previously when I had been asked by Peter Drew, a director of the building firm of Taylor Woodrow, to become a member of the council of the London branch. There are now numerous Centres worldwide and the one in London plays an important role in City and World Trade life.

World Trade Centre. Laying the Foundation Stone

*   *   *

With the exception of the high-flyers who have aspirations to become Lord Mayor of London – and consequently need to acquire the allegiance of as many of their colleagues as possible – most City Liverymen restrict their membership to one company. I should almost certainly have done the same had I not, in 1967 and at the age of sixty, acquired my private pilot's licence.

As I was also then a member of parliament, the Press picked up on this and – no doubt having no better story to run – made something of a feature of it. In consequence I was approached by the Guild of Air Pilots with a suggestion that I might become one of their number. I agreed to do so – initially to further the interests of the Parliamentary Flying Club, which I had helped to found. I very quickly found myself out of my depth. The majority of the members were professional pilots employed by large commercial airlines. For all this I greatly enjoyed the social life of the Guild.

*   *   *

There are those who look askance upon any kind of institution with a closed membership – suspect it of having sinister and self-interested motives. No doubt there are many such institutions. As a body, the City Livery organisation is not one of them. It fosters genuine instincts of camaraderie. Its officials are democratically elected. There is no element of snobbishness. At City banquets the most humble Liveryman mixes with the Lord Mayor on equal terms. Members do much for charity, by no means all of it within the confines of their own community – although they look to this also. They raise money to provide holidays for the under-privileged, and for other groups besides. They have been responsible down the centuries for the foundation of a number of famous schools.

Enough. To quote W. H. Auden: 'Goodness is easier to recognize than to define'.

CHAPTER SIXTEEN

FARMING

I n 1948, a year after I became a member of the Worshipful Company of Bakers, I purchased Whitnorth, a nineteen-room Georgian dower-house in the Surrey village of Shalford. It came with eight acres of land – much of it so overgrown that it looked like a jungle – a coach-house, a studio, and a large garden enclosed by a lofty wall.

Before the war, the property had been owned by a Colonel Gate, a member of the family which produced various dairy products under the label Cow & Gate. Something of an eccentric, Colonel Gate had an unusual way of acknowledging the men under his command. Instead of saluting them he called out 'Hi-de-Hi!', to which they called back: 'Ho-de Ho!'. This response ultimately led to disciplinings all round – and for all I know to a modern television series.

*   *   *

During the war, Whitnorth had been requisitioned by the London County Council for use as a residential nursery-school. By the time the school vacated in 1946 the property was in an appalling state of disrepair.

Bringing order out of chaos posed a considerable challenge. I brought in workmen to restore the brickwork and then to re-plaster. The place had to be entirely re-wired. The main bedroom, distinguished by a beautiful antique doorway and bay windows with superb views over the grounds, was carefully restored to its former glory.

The grounds themselves were a problem of a different order. Over the years they had become so entirely overgrown that they were practically impassable. Taking my courage in my hands, I edged my way gently into this forgotten jungle. I half expected to encounter snakes and tigers. What I found in actuality were two wonderful weeping-willow trees situated beside a lake which I had not known existed; a large but dilapidated summer house; and a wide variety of apple trees.

Whitnorth, Shalford, Surrey, front view

* * *

With the help of local labour I managed to convert the area immediately behind the house into a vegetable and flower garden. As we cleared away the detritus of the years we also uncovered a large rose pergola and a goldfish pond. Miraculously, some of the fish were still alive.

The ten-foot wall which enclosed the garden accommodated a grape vine. I had high hopes for this. Sadly, although it annually produced a profusion of fruit, it was wrongly situated and saw almost no sun. In consequence, none of it ever ripened.

Looking for items with which to fill the house, I frequently attended country house auctions together with my second wife, Mabs. At one of these we encountered a turkey named Rufus. This creature looked so bewildered – so lonely and unloved – that in a moment of madness we purchased it. We brought it home – with some difficulty – in the car and installed it in the enormous conservatory, six hundred square feet, which linked the main house to the stables.

Somewhat naively, we proposed fattening Rufus up for Christmas, then three months away. Rufus – who had a mind of his own – had other ideas. From the moment of his arrival he came to the conclusion that this was *his* house – that he was the master and we the servants. As my wife immediately fell in love with him and doted upon his every whim, this was an impression difficult to eradicate.

Rufus developed into something of a tyrant. He came to look upon his daily feed of the finest maize and corn as a kind of tribute, delivered to him as a matter of right. He would only eat it if Mabs brought it in person.

Shortly before Christmas I plucked up courage and broached the subject of the brute's demise. Mabs said: 'Eat Rufus? Impossible!'

There are unquestionably times when discretion is the better part of valour. This was one of them. In order to feed us over Christmas I went out and bought another turkey. A dead one.

Rufus?

I gave him to my mother who, having no emotional involvement, found Rufus delicious.

*   *   *

In a curious way, Rufus – coupled with my wife's penchant for the downtrodden of this world – led us indirectly into the keeping of pigs. Some time after the demise of the tyrannical turkey, we were wandering around Guildford market on the day of the weekly pig sales. The auctioneer was putting a family of eight-week-old weaners under the hammer. They each fetched £5, which seemed to me a reasonable price.

The auctioneer then produced the runt of the litter. Like Rufus before him, he looked frightened and bewildered. Like Rufus he had about him an air of defeat and rejection.

'What am I bid?', asked the auctioneer, casting a rheumy eye over the group of disinterested farmers leaning on the boundary fencing of the pen.

Mabs said: 'Shall we give him a home?' It was the work of a moment to put up my hand and bid fifty shillings.

* * *

We installed our little purchase in a shed in the garden. Life had not treated him kindly and he allowed it to show. Being the weakest in the litter he had been half-starved and was still painfully thin. He had a perpetually suspicious look about him. Consequently we christened him P.C. Richard.

Like Rufus, P.C. Richard appealed to Mabs enormously. Under her tutelage he grew into a contented little fellow – although his eyes never quite lost the look of perpetual suspicion and uncertainty instilled during the first weeks of his life.

Inspired by his example, we bought other pigs, including a boar – christened Jasper – from whom we bred. In the course of time we became the owners of a substantial pedigree herd of large whites and also some saddle-backs. My name duly appeared in the Pig Breeders' Herd Book. I registered our young gilts under the name 'Whitnorth Winnie 1st' and so on, to identify them with the house.

* * *

By 1950 the war had been over for five years. Meat – of any description – was still in desperately short supply and rationing was strictly enforced. Food production was hedged around by a bristling and confusing armoury of restrictions.

Pig-farmers were not permitted to kill their livestock personally; and the needs of the public were so great that no matter what the size of the herd, owners were allowed only one animal a year for their private consumption.

Due to an edict issued by the Ministry of Agriculture, which decreed that the shape and size of an animal were more important than its quality, market forces prevailed. Consequently it was necessary to fatten one's stock as quickly as possible. To this end it is said that the more unscrupulous breeders inserted pellets of lead into the feed of their live-stock during the last few weeks of their life.

Although Jews and Mohammedans regard the pig as in some way unclean, it is really no more so than any other animal. In its natural state it is exceptionally hygienic. Domestication is thought to have begun in China about seven thousand years ago. The pigs found in Europe are descended from wild boars.

Of all livestock, pigs are the most economical producers of meat. Every part of the carcass can be utilized; and for every four or five pounds of dry feed consumed they produce a pound of meat. In beef the amount of dry feed required would be more than double that. When dressed, a good fat pig yields almost eighty percent of its live weight, a cow a mere sixty percent.

As my stock of pigs expanded, it became necessary to hire a man to look after them. I also took on a local chap to care for the poultry. I could usually be found in this small farm myself most mornings by seven o'clock and again in the evenings, after my return from the office.

Life was busy and fulfilling. However, the work-load was such that there were moments when it threatened to get mildly out of hand. At some point I bought a litter of pigs only to find that I had no sty in which to house them. Now, unless they are closely confined during the fattening process, pigs over-exercise, which keeps them thin and wiry. The building of the sty was therefore of paramount importance.

I set to work at once, hammering in posts and erecting wire fencing. Pigs are intensely curious creatures. They stood to one side, watching me intently. When the job was done I ushered them into their new home and retired indoors for a cup of tea.

An hour or so later I received a telephone call from a neighbour who said: 'Of course, it's none of my business, old chap. But I thought you might like to know that some of your pigs have decided to go shopping in the main street.'

I flew out of the door like a dervish. It was true. The new arrivals had not been watching me so intently merely to while away an hour. They had spotted a weak point in the construction of the sty, tunnelled beneath it with their snouts and vanished. They were not easily recaptured.

*   *   *

A rather greater problem than the pigs themselves was the man I had hired to look after them. I discovered that he was cheating me. It was my normal practice to weigh the young growing animals once a week in order to establish the weight-gain-to-cost ratio. One weekend there were twenty such animals, all about four months old. I told the pigman to sell them. I also indicated the price I required.

When I returned from the office a few days later, he greeted me very effusively: 'I've sold the pigs', he said. 'Here's the money', and he thrust a bundle of notes into my hand.

Other than being mildly surprised at the speed with which he had closed the sale, I thought nothing more of the matter until I came to look over the list he had given me of the animals' selling weights. These were significantly less than the weights I had recorded for them three days earlier. In some cases animals appeared to have lost as much as twenty pounds overnight. It was clear that the pigman had sold them at underweight prices to a henchman with whom he had split the difference.

I later discovered this was not the only ruse he employed for lining his own pockets. My pig-meal was delivered by lorry in five-ton loads from West Surrey Farmers' Organisation. In the normal way it was tipped straight into the granary. However, I began to notice that loads were no longer lasting quite as long as they once had ; and on this account I decided to monitor the next delivery rather more closely than normal.

I discovered that when the driver of the tipper truck put the mechanism into action to lower the body of the vehicle back on to the axle, there was still half a ton of feed left on it. This, no doubt, would in due course have found its way to another of my pigman's cronies. I sacked him on the spot. Some time later I read that he had been sent to prison for defrauding another farmer.

I replaced him with a *pigmaid*, a young woman who was planning to emigrate to Australia with her fiancé, where they hoped to run a farm. In order to get herself in shape for this, she wanted to spend six months doing hard manual labour mucking out pigs. I was happy to oblige and gave her a little room in the studio which we christened 'The pigmaid's parlour'.

In contrast to her predecessor, she was entirely trustworthy. I came to like her very much. At the end of the six months she duly married her fiancé and emigrated. I hope she prospered.

As anyone who has ever kept a hundred pigs will know, they generate a great deal of manure – far more than we could possibly use ourselves. At one point I had a surplus of fifty cubic yards of the stuff, which had been shovelled into a channel behind the sties. This I offered for sale, local people being invited to submit tenders for its purchase and removal. A number of individuals displayed a passing interest, but took so long over the matter that by the time I received an acceptable offer the manure had shrunk to almost half its original size.

*   *   *

At the height of my pig-keeping activities I was invited to take one of my larger beasts to a fête organised by the Old Rutlishians on the sports ground at Merton Park. The idea was to raise a little money by charging people sixpence for the privilege of guessing its weight, the nearest approximation winning the pig.

Some of the guesses were ludicrously off-target . . . in both directions. The winning one came from a highly nervous and eccentric lady who lived quite near to the sportsground. However, when we endeavoured to present her with her prize, she turned puce and stammered: 'I can't possibly take a creature like that home with me. Where on earth should I put it?' She stumbled away in a panic.

120

We tied a rope round the pig's neck and walked it to her house in Poplar Road, tying one end of the rope to the doorknocker. Consequently, every time the pig moved, the knocker rat-tat-tatted against the poor woman's door as though manipulated by the unseen hand of a bailiff. When she finally opened it she found her winnings staring at her balefully from the front path. This made her even more hysterical. She was only calmed by my offer to pay her the cash value of the pig and take it away.

*   *   *

Now that I had come to realise that there was rather more to it than simply keeping a few chickens, the poultry side of the business was also beginning to flourish. Poultry is an important element of general farming; and because both chickens and eggs tend to be taken for granted, their importance as a factor in the national wealth is sometimes overlooked.

The more highly organised the operation, the better the results. The poultry farmer is essentially in business for the eggs he gets, not the revenue generated by the sale of the birds. A good layer will produce upwards of a hundred and twenty eggs a year, an outstanding one can lay three hundred.

In addition to chickens, I experimented with the rearing of Black Game. I also had a gander named William G. and his five wives. Each afternoon at four o'clock William G. and his lady friends would walk in file up the path from the farmyard to the house and poke their heads round the kitchen door in search of tit-bits. Like Lord Byron – who could hardly fatten a goose for Christmas without it ending up travelling in his carriage in the role of companion – we tended to become fond of our livestock and to invest them with personalities. Consequently it was a great loss when, one night, William G. and his family were killed by a fox. We later lost twenty-two ducks to the same animal.

This was a state of affairs which could not be allowed to continue. My pig man laid some poison which the fox duly took. He found it staggering around the farmyard and put it out of its misery. I had the head and brush mounted on a wooden stock engraved with the legend: 'Whitnorth Hunt' and the date on which it had been killed. I hung this in the hall where it remained many years, a source of amusement to my friends and of great annoyance to the hunting fraternity.

*   *   *

From a nearby incubating establishment I began to purchase consignments of day-old Aylesbury ducklings, sometimes as many as a thousand at a time. These I fattened up for market with some success, occasionally producing birds of eight pounds in weight in as many weeks, which was looked upon as something of a record. Most of these went to local hostelries and hotels. It was a relatively lucrative trade, the only drawback being that the majority of my customers wanted the birds ready for the oven, which meant that my poultryman spent a large proportion of his time sitting in a shed surrounded by a sea of feathers.

One day I set off for Guildford market with eighteen live birds stacked in three boxes above the boot of the car, one upon the other. I had not gone any great distance when I was overtaken by another motorist, who shouted and gesticulated in my direction. I looked round – just in time to see the last bird parachute into the road from the top box, the flap of which had blown open.

I turned the car around and went in search of the six escapees. Two had already been flattened by passing cars. Three were cornered in an alleyway. The sixth proved a more difficult problem. A passer-by confessed to having seen a duck pad through the garden gate which led to the vicarage. I searched the vicarage garden high and low, but to no avail. He had simply disappeared. As my daughter, Margaret, was due to be married by the vicar in a matter of weeks, I didn't think it appropriate to press the issue. I wrote the creature off as a bad debt – or a very dead duck.

Margaret's wedding proved a very happy affair. Curiously, the bridegroom, Michael Comben, came from an old Portland family – the town in which my mother had been raised. I was delighted when, in due course, Margaret and Michael made me a grandfather twice over by producing twins, christened Jonathan and Gillian. A third child, Anthony, has himself recently married and I now have high hopes of being spared long enough to become a great-grandfather. (Achieved since writing.)

*　　*　　*

Each autumn I bought five hundred day-old Broad Breasted Bronze turkey chicks to fatten for the Christmas market. This too became a thriving trade. Unlike the ducklings, it had the additional advantage that most of the butchers to whom I sold were happy to take the birds away alive. Not so my private customers. One Christmas this resulted in a crisis which marked the beginning of my disillusionment with the whole concept of livestock farming.

In the year in question, Christmas Day was due to fall on a Monday. On the Friday preceding, my pigman failed to arrive, claiming to be ill. On the Saturday my poultryman also failed to put in an appearance. I was thus faced with the prospect of having to pluck and dress forty-seven turkeys myself.

FARMING

On the Sunday I got up well before dawn. I weighed forty-seven turkeys. I killed forty-seven turkeys. I plucked forty-seven turkeys. I dressed forty-seven turkeys. I delivered forty-seven turkeys. And I swore at forty-seven turkeys. I didn't care if I never saw a turkey again as long as I lived. I finished past two o'clock on Christmas morning, by which time my hands were raw and bleeding. Shortly after this incident I disposed of all my livestock. I never farmed again.

CHAPTER SEVENTEEN

THE FIRST MILLION

T itles of the kind which I have given to the current chapter usually preface an account – typed out by the thumbs of tense hacks – of the manner in which they rose from poverty and obscurity to conquer the world of high finance. In my case the million refers not to money but to miles. It covers a lifetime of driving and what I estimate must have been the consumption of more than fifty thousand gallons of petrol.

I obtained my driving licence at the age of twenty-two in 1929 – the year of the St. Valentine's Day Massacre in Chicago and the Wall Street crash in New York. It was also the year the Graf Zeppelin girdled the earth in twenty-one days – and the first four places in the Le Mans 24-hour endurance sports car race went to the large six-cylinder Bentleys. Lillie Langtry died, as did the legendary Wyatt Earp, peacefully in his sleep in Dodge City, aged eighty, his famous Colt '45 Buntline Special hanging from the brass bedpost.

I was then an impoverished articled clerk. By comparison, my brother, three years my senior, was a relatively affluent estate agent – having decided early in life to dispense with what he considered to be the nonsense of education and throw himself into the melée of the market place. He had done so to considerable effect. His first foray into mechanised transport was a Matchless motor-cycle. He progressed from this to a Jowett motor-car.

In order that I might share the responsibility of taking our parents on weekend excursions, he decided that I too should learn to drive. Motorists were not then required to take any kind of test and once they felt they had reached a reasonable standard of proficiency simply applied for a licence.

By any standards, my initial instruction was basic. George simply took me out to a relatively quiet road and said: 'This is the accelerator. This is the brake. This is the lever you manipulate to get from one gear to another. Have a go'. Which I did. I thought it very great fun indeed. I cannot be sure that in those early weeks other road users shared my enthusiasm.

I had nonetheless made an important discovery. A motor car was not only a very useful mode of transport – it represented freedom. Having mastered the intricacies of double-de-clutching, I filled in the appropriate form, sent it off, together with a postal order for five shillings, and received my driving licence by return of post. (In those days, return of post *meant* return of post.)

*   *   *

Two years later I acquired my first car, a 1929 Morris Cowley. A little two-seater tourer, it cost me £40. I purchased it to celebrate passing the finals of my chartered accountancy examinations. I paid a deposit of £20, discharging the balance by hire purchase over the course of the next twelve months.

Petrol then cost a little over a shilling a gallon. Although tyres tended to have an average life of twelve thousand miles, the state of the roads was not good and punctures were a commonplace. The concept of tread was non-existent and tyres were not considered to be expendable until the canvas showed through the rubber.

*   *   *

It has been well said that one's first love remains with one longest. This was certainly true ui my first car. I used it to transport fellow Old Rutlishians to rugby matches, one in the passenger seat, two in the dickey. There was much competition for the latter when the weather was good, none at all when it was not.

As soon as I had paid off the balance of the hire purchase agreement I traded the Morris Cowley for a second tourer, a Hillman Minx. On a Friday afternoon I would often jump into this and hare off up the Great North Road to visit with a solicitor friend who was then acting as receiver for a mining concern in Cumberland. The object of the exercise? To reach a little pub near Keswick before the calling of last orders.

I made the return journey on Sunday evening. By modern standards the roads were ludicrously under-populated and it was possible to make reasonable time.

Nonetheless, the pioneer motorist had problems to contend with which his modern counterpart does not. On one occasion I bought a brand new tyre before leaving London to make the journey to Cumberland. Although I was not aware of it, the car's front wheels were out of track. In consequence, by the time I reached my destination the tyre was completely bald and had to be replaced.

*   *   *

I didn't so much buy my third car as have it sold to me, a very different matter. A smart-looking forecourt salesman 'sweet-talked' me into part-exchanging the Hillman for a second-hand Talbot. It cost me £45. It wasn't the bargain he had represented – but as the Hillman wasn't either, it transpired that we had both been sold pups. I replaced it with an old Austin 7 which cost me £7.50.

In contrast, my fifth car was the very latest product from Vauxhall Motors – a 14.40, the younger brother of the 30.98. Like all my previous purchases, it was a tourer. The body was fashioned from aluminium and it had a top speed of ninety miles an hour. I was attracted to it by its reputation for durability, reliability and – shallow creature that I was – the fluted bonnet and the distinctive red stripe. It served me well until, one day in wet conditions, it skidded out of control along Millbank, careening into a lamp-post. The insurance company deemed it a total write-off and paid me its full value of £75.00.

I loved that car. At a cost of £5 I retrieved the wreck from the insurers, used the balance of their cheque to have the thing rebuilt, and was back on the road within a month.

*   *   *

The Vauxhall proved to be my last open car. Like most young bucks, as the prospect of marriage approached – and with it the impending mantle of respectability – I felt the overpowering urge to acquire a saloon.

In that respect, while standards in motor-car production have improved beyond all recognition in the course of my sixty years in the bucket-seat, human nature has remained remarkably static. Then as now, sports cars are the playthings of the young. They are of course occasionally driven by middle-aged men – although never by the elderly, whom they frighten. Beyond the age of thirty-five, the owner of a sports car is universally viewed as an object of ridicule, desperate to conserve his lost youth.

A middle-aged gent driving a sports car is as absurd as a man in a wig.

*   *   *

I next purchased a Baby Daimler 15, by far the most prestigious vehicle I had owned to date. For two years it served me very well.

With the approach of war, I decided it had to go. Realising that the old order was about to change out of all recognition – and that consequently every form of motoring was likely to be restricted – I acquired four separate cars at knock-down prices: two Austin 7's and two Hillman Minx. The reasoning behind this was that

126

if a period of shortage and austerity did ensue, I should at least be able to cannibalise two of the cars to furnish spares for their counterparts. As a result, I now found myself with four cars but only one garage. The dispossessed sat in the road beyond. In order to keep each of them in working order, I drove them on alternate days. When war did eventually come one of the Austin 7's became an early casualty. In one of the first daylight raids on London it received a jagged scar on the rear wing from a piece of shrapnel from one of our anti-aircraft shells.

*　　*　　*

At this date cars were relatively cheap. A new Hillman Minx cost £135 and an Austin 7 £100. In comparison the £190 I paid for my next car, a Triumph Dolomite CVB, was a great deal of money – but then I had fallen in love with it at first sight. It was exceptionally quick and along the Kingston by-pass I achieved ninety miles an hour for the first time in my life.

I used this car constantly during my time as a battalion commander in Wales; and when towards the end of 1944 I was posted abroad with the Ministry of War Transport, it came out to Egypt with me. It had to be shipped to Alexandria in a giant crate. If it had not been secured in this manner it would almost certainly have arrived minus every detachable part, including its glittering silver grille.

Due to the corruption of local officials, clearing it through Customs proved a fraught and expensive business. I had firstly to pay fifty piastres to purchase an official application form. Having filled this in, and after a lengthy wait, the car was produced to me. The officer in charge then handed me another lengthy form to complete. Among other things, this required me to state the weight of the car. I hadn't the faintest idea but appreciating that any vacillating on my part could lead to weeks – and possibly months – of delay, I estimated it at three quarters of a ton. As soon as I had done so, two other customs officials materialised and drove the vehicle round the corner to a weighbridge. The check revealed that my guess had been wildly inaccurate. It weighed the best part of a ton and a half. I was told that I had made a false declaration and as such was liable to prosecution – a threat only removed by the presentation of a fairly hefty 'tip'.

On returning to the car I found that the ignition key had been removed. As I was obstructing other traffic, I persuaded a group of loitering Arabs to help me push it clear. As soon as they had done so they crowded round for yet another 'tip'. I picked out the one who looked most like their leader and gave him fifty piastres, telling him to share it round. At the sight of the money, one of the others miraculously 'found' my key.

127

Egyptian roads were not good and one constantly ran the risk of broken suspension. On one occasion I was driving a Ministry official from Suez to Cairo. He chattered away for a while unceasingly. Then the flow of words suddenly dried up. Turning round to discover the reason for this, I saw him lying supine across the rear seat. I at first thought he had fallen asleep . . . but there was something in the way he was lying which suggested otherwise. After a moment he stirred and groaned. It transpired that going over the last bump in the road he had been hurled upwards, hitting his head a hard knock on the roof of the car, rendering him unconscious.

Fortunately, not all Egyptian roads were quite so lethal and there was one magnificent stretch running parallel to the Suez Canal on which, for the first time in my life, I was able to drive sixty miles in as many minutes, a feat almost impossible on British roads.

One day, in Cairo, the Dolomite's beautiful silver grille was destroyed by a reversing military truck. The English company responsible for insuring the car claimed that its liability was restricted to £22, the cost of replacement. I pointed out that as a replacement was currently unobtainable, the money was of little use to me. What I wanted was another grille. Failing that I should be compensated for the car's decreased value brought about by its loss.

The argument raged for many months. During this time I drove the car minus the grille. The insurers ultimately agreed to commission the manufacturers to produce a 'one off' replacement. This cost a great deal more than the sum of money I would have been prepared to accept in compensation for the loss of the original.

The absence of the grille for so many months was an unsightly blemish. As such, it upset me. It was nothing to the feelings I experienced, some time later, when I came close to losing the entire car.

On the day in question I was standing outside the Continental Hotel, talking to the dragoman and a local shoe-shine boy. The Triumph Dolomite stood at the edge of the pavement. As we conversed, a large limousine glided to a halt nose to nose with my own car. Out of it stepped the majestic figure of Ibn Saud, Emperor of Saudi Arabia, who was also staying at the hotel for the duration of his official visit to King Farouk.

Before passing into the hotel, Ibn Saud stopped for a moment to admire the Triumph. It had clearly taken his fancy. As he passed, he gave me a speculative look. I began to turn over in my mind what sort of price I should ask if he expressed an interest in buying it. The dragoman quickly disabused me. This was not the way in which emperors did business. If Ibn Saud liked the car there would be no question of him buying it. He would expect it as a gift. Fortunately, I never heard any more about the matter although I frequently saw the Emperor around the hotel during his stay. He had been assigned two entire floors for the use of his family and retinue. This included forty of his sons, each of whom looked like a miniature edition of his father. For his personal use, Farouk had put one of his own royal palaces at Ibn Saud's disposal. Perhaps as a calculated snub, this he preferred to leave unoccupied. He lived instead in a series of opulent marquees which he erected in the grounds.

His sons preferred the comforts of the Continental, the floors of which, for the duration of the visit, were strewn with red carpet. The food too seemed to take a turn for the better. The royal party struck me as impressively resplendent in their exotic robes. As the only non-Arab resident, there were times when I felt distinctly uncomfortable and out of place.

The whole of the city was beflagged and the authorities had erected at intervals a series of temporary but very ornate and decorative-looking arches. To all intents and purposes they looked as though they had stood for a thousand years. They were surmounted by enormous crowns and floodlit at night. Policemen seemed to be stationed every few hundred yards. Hangers-on were everywhere. I couldn't help wondering what exactly it might be that Egypt wanted from Saudi Arabia.

*   *   *

In 1947 I acquired my first Rolls Royce. It was eight years old, cost £1850 and had formerly belonged to the company's founder, Sir Henry Royce, who only disposed of it with great reluctance on his retirement to Eastbourne. As it had been used by him to evaluate each new refinement and invention as it rolled off the production line, it came with a number of features which were very far from standard. In 1950 I traded it for a second Rolls Royce, a Silver Ghost, which came complete with electrically operated windows, chauffeur's glass partition and cocktail cabinet.

This car seemed never to need any oil. For many months I checked the dip-stick at regular intervals but the level simply did not decrease. In time I became rather blasé about this and stopped checking entirely. One day, driving home from the office, the car began to make a series of ominous grunting noises. I managed just to limp to a garage where it transpired that lacking any lubrication the cylinders had become red hot and melted the white metal of the engine. It proved a costly repair.

*   *   *

129

In 1967 I decided to enter the R.A.C's Round Britain Rally. I chose as my map reader a friend named Jack Faucitt, the licensee of the Royal Oak at Chorley. My mechanic was an Italian, a works manager for one of Vauxhall's distribution agencies. I elected to drive a Ford Consul. As this had more than twenty thousand miles on the clock, it was rather past its prime and not quite up to the job.

The first night of the rally produced an exceptionally heavy frost. This turned the roads to glass. On the leg which was to carry us from Blackpool to southern Wales – half-way down a steep incline – the car spun out of control and came to rest broadside on to the road.

Before we could manoeuvre out of this dangerous position a Riley came hurtling towards us. It smashed into the Consul's nearside, more or less amidships, burying its nose deep in the bodywork. The cars took a great deal of separating and it was necessary to dig one of the Consul's wings out of the icy bank, into which the impact of the collision had forced it. To our intense astonishment, both vehicles were still driveable. The glass of the nearside windows had been completely shattered by the collision and until we were able to block the holes with cardboard the following morning, Jack and I were rendered almost blue with cold.

Perhaps because the old Consul now resembled a tall salmon tin which someone had attempted to squash, it became something of a favourite, both with spectators and the television camera crews which lined the route. It became the car that was nearly dead but refused to lie down. There were times when I wished it would – notably during the three-lap speed trials at Silverstone. Here I did manage to edge the thing up to eighty miles an hour, but the dent in the bodywork had so affected the aero-dynamics that it tended to swerve violently and unpredictably.

*   *   *

In January 1968, and having developed a taste for the sport, I entered the Monte Carlo Rally. Having learned from my experiences of the previous year, I chose to do so in a new Vauxhall Victor. Whilst this lacked the necessary power of acceleration to win any kind of class prize, it did have excellent road-holding capacity, which I knew would stand us in good stead during that section of the rally which was to carry us through the Alps.

We were sensible of the fact that we were amateurs. As such, we should find ourselves vastly outnumbered by the professionals. In order to simulate the conditions we were likely to encounter, we drove up to Westmoreland a month before the rally looking for snow and ice. We distributed the luggage we would need evenly around the vehicle and practised skidding and drifting. The experience ultimately proved invaluable.

I found the rally itself exhilarating. Of the three hundred competitors, only about six were non-professional. Many of the entrants were works teams with massive back-up facilities, including mechanics and lorries loaded with spare parts.

The rally was not without incident. We collected a time penalty – which we later made up – for failing to stop at a checkpoint in France; and at two o'clock in the morning on the second day out we all but vanished over the edge of a five hundred foot precipice in the Alps. The car stopped literally on the brink and had to be manhandled back on to the road with very great care. We later learned that this was considered a particularly dangerous bend to negotiate and that the Press

Monte Carlo Rally, 1959. Near to disaster in the Alps

cameramen tended to congregate here in the hope of witnessing just such an accident as ours.

The Victor was a small car and the only one of its manufacture entered for the Rally. It nonetheless completed the full two-thousand miles necessary to win us our finisher's plaque. We arrived in Monte Carlo amid scenes of great festivity. As we crossed the finishing line I was greeted by two close friends, Norman Smith and Andy Polson, the chairman of the R.A.C., who had travelled out specifically to congratulate us. By way of greeting, they planted a very welcome bottle of champagne on the bonnet.

The prizes were presented by Princess Grace. The winners received these in a marquee which had been erected for the occasion in front of the palace gates. It was guarded by the six soldiers who went to make up the national army.

The Victor later made a triumphal tour of Surrey garages where it was displayed on forecourts beneath a placard which read: 'One Victor Entered. One Victor Got There. This Is It'.

*　　*　　*

The car in which I logged my millionth mile was not the Victor but a Sunbeam Alpine, which I purchased towards the end of 1969. I had originally intended to acquire a two-litre Rover. This had been on order for some months but had not arrived. One day, talking to a garage manager about this problem, I asked him what he had for sale on his own forecourt. He showed me. I pointed to the Alpine and said: 'I'll take that one'.

Of my many cars, it was the first I had ever bought without first having sat inside it.

*　　*　　*

At the age of eighty-two I am currently motoring towards my second million. I have enjoyed my life behind the wheel beyond measure. Although driving is an essentially repetitive occupation it has never bored me. I have spent many years passing the same scenery. It has never palled. Why this should be I cannot say. The whole business of cars is an emotive issue. As was once said:

'In the beginning the car was a status-symbol, like a boar's tusk in a Papuan's nose.'

W. D. H. McCullough, writing in *Aces Made Easy*, had this to say:

'Since the early days of motoring there have been many changes in the apparatus designed to keep drivers posted as to any sensational developments under

132

the bonnet. In the first cars there was little or none of this form of affectation . . . Steam coming out of the radiator, or elsewhere, indicated that the water was boiling, and a radiator that slowly became incandescent showed that it had finished doing so. This was all there was to go on . . . In those days motorists *were* motorists.'

Sinclair Lewis's character, George F. Babbitt, considered his motor-car to be 'poetry and tragedy, love and heroism. The office was his pirate ship, but the car his perilous excursion ashore'.

There is some truth in this. One risks death every time one slips behind the wheel and Colin MacInnes may have been voicing no more than an unpalatable truth when he exhorted:

'Car owners of the world unite: you have nothing to lose but your manners – and someone else's life.'

Consider though, it is not always the poor pedestrian who perishes. The driver, too, has his fatal distractions. Remember Ogden Nash:

Beneath this slab John Brown is stowed.

He watched the ads and not the road.

CHAPTER EIGHTEEN

DOMESTIC LIFE

My parents were very hard-working and principled. They lived in the age before easy credit and believed in what they and most of their contemporaries termed 'paying as you go'. They seldom had much money. My own pocket-money ran to a penny a week. In the years before the First World War, when it was possible to buy a yard of liquorice for a farthing, this went further than might now be expected in more ways than one.

We lived in a world of make-do-and-mend. In accordance with this principle, I was kept in short trousers until the age of fifteen. (Scraped knees heal, long trousers need patching.)

The acquisition of clothes for three young and boisterous boys was a constant problem for my parents. When I began life in the City at eighteen, they had also to find the wherewithal for an umbrella and a bowler hat, no small piece of expenditure. The importance of money was constantly impressed upon us, usually by its obvious lack. We were taught to be strongly independent: to appreciate that no one was likely to further our ambitions but ourselves.

Because of my fierce determination to succeed, I made a conscious decision to eschew girls until such time as I had qualified. This was not as difficult as it might sound. There were no girls in my immediate family and I consequently had little experience either of them or of their ways. At the age of eighteen they seemed to me remote and slightly exalted creatures. I could not really imagine what it would be like to be in their company for any length of time. Being a romantic and an idealist, I also felt it unlikely that I should ever kiss a girl unless I intended to marry her.

*   *   *

Once the hurdle of qualification had been surmounted, I began to allow myself a glimmer of a social life. Most Saturdays, the Old Rutlishian Association held what were known as 'flannel' dances. These were convivial if rather innocent gatherings.

In those early days I could never pluck up my courage to ask a girl on to the floor. This was partly because I was cripplingly shy and partly because I had never learned how to dance.

In 1932, Alan Puxley, the Association's rugby club fixtures secretary and an active member of Toc H, told me of a dance which Toc H was running at Putney. I attended this with a friend, Ray Finch. During the course of the evening we made contact with two Scottish girls, Queenie Robertson–Dick and Dora Mackay. At the end of the evening I offered to run them home. I thought Dora a lively and attractive girl. Consequently I made her sit beside me – the luckless Ray and Queenie having to travel in the dickey.

Protocol was different then. When we drew up at the house in Bayswater where they lived, there was no question of either of us being invited in. We received no kiss, merely a warm little handshake.

I was not so naive that I failed to make a note of Dora's address.

Life has a peculiar way of disposing matters. Ray never saw Queenie again. A week or so later I telephoned Dora to ask her out. It was the beginning of my first serious courtship. As such, it was conducted along very proper lines. Sometimes we went to a little cinema in Notting Hill. Sometimes we passed the time in her bed-sit, talking and nipping at intervals from the five-shilling bottle of sherry I usually brought along. I learned that she had come to London to take a secretarial course. On its completion she had found a job with the assurance company, Canada Life.

In April 1934 I asked Dora to marry me. Because I was still relatively poor, I was forced to ask her to wait for two years. Despite this proviso, she accepted.

*   *   *

When two people decide that they wish to spend the rest of their lives together, they seldom have any real conception of the magnitude of the decision they take. Quite apart from their own characters and personalities, they inadvertently plug themselves into a complicated network of their partner's relatives.

Dora's father was a minister of a little church situated at Croy, near Inverness. A small man, he owned an enormous Norton motor-cycle, complete with side-car, in which he took his wife and occasionally his daughter, on outings. He was a pleasant individual whom I came to like very much. He seldom had much money, largely because he tended to give it away to people whom he considered had a greater need of it.

In the closed atmosphere of the manse, the news of Dora's engagement came as a bolt from the blue, especially to her mother, Mary, the more dominant of

Dora's parents and a strict teetotaller. It was bad enough that her only child had got herself engaged to an Englishman. There could be no question of them continuing to live in the same city until they were safely married.

Dora was ordered to hand in her notice and return home. Being essentially a dutiful girl, she did as she was told. Her mother then packed her off to Edinburgh on a two-year domestic science course. She also took the precaution of transferring some shares out of Dora's name into her own. In this way, she reasoned, no man – and especially not an Englishman – would be able to get his clutches on her little girl's nest-egg.

*   *   *

For the next two years, Dora and I saw one another intermittently, perhaps four or five times a year. At the weekend I would occasionally travel up to Scotland by the overnight sleeper. The atmosphere at the manse could be a little forbidding. However, after a year or so, Mary did allow me the great concession of having a bottle of pale ale with my lunch. I sometimes saw her husband looking rather longingly at this. He never dared to ask whether he might also have one.

I worked hard and I saved my money. I accumulated £500. At Easter 1936 Dora and I were married from the manse, the joint officiating ministers being her father and her uncle, Billy Barclay. The reception for about fifty people was held at the Station Hotel in Inverness. Being a teetotal affair, it should have been rather dull. The high-spirited nature of the Scottish Highlanders ensured things went with a swing.

I discovered that Billy Barclay was the minister of St. Magnus, an eight-hundred-year-old cathedral at Kirkwall on the Isle of Orkney. He found life there rather dull, remote and unrewarding. He said there was nobody there for him to convert. He ultimately gave up the living and transferred to the more heavily populated parish of Shawlands, near Glasgow, where for the rest of his life he busied himself to great effect among the poor. He was unquestionably one of the most Christian men I have ever met.

*   *   *

Dora and I were relatively poor ourselves. We nonetheless managed to afford a two-week honeymoon in Nice. We stayed at the Hotel des Princes at Bellevue, situated on the Promenade des Anglais.

Life seemed very *foreign* suddenly, especially to Dora. We obtained tickets for the famous round-the-houses motor race. During the course of this, Dora found

136

she needed to go to the toilet. These, of course, were not segregated. Dora dutifully waited her turn in the queue. When she reached its head, an over-gallant Frenchman insisted not only on ushering her to a cubicle personally, but dusting off the seat with his handkerchief and reverently closing the door behind her. She returned to me red with embarrassment.

We counted our pennies and found that we had just sufficient for a visit to the Casino. We headed directly for the roulette room. Most amateur gamblers at roulette tend to select a number on the basis of its significance to them. In our case, as I had rented a house for us to live in at 21 Coombe Gardens in Wimbledon, we chose the number 21. Extraordinarily, we won twelve pounds. This was then a large sum of money and meant we were able to afford to extend our honeymoon by two days.

Like all good lovers, we spent them in Paris.

*　　*　　*

Although my practice continued to grow, money – or rather the lack of it – remained a problem through the early years of our marriage. Fees were often not received until many weeks after the work they related to had been completed. This meant I was required to work very long hours.

I was amply rewarded when, in 1938, Dora presented me with a baby daughter, christened Margaret Mackay Taylor. At the end of the year we moved to 46 Woodside, Wimbledon, largely in order that Dora might be nearer to the shops and other necessary facilities. We purchased the house on long-lease for a consideration of £1,050. Having overcome her fear of at least one Englishman, Dora's mother lent us the bulk of the money at 3% interest.

We continued to occupy the property until the first bombs began to fall on London in August 1940. Dora then took Margaret to the comparative safety of the manse in Scotland. She remained there until my posting to the Ministry of Food in 1942, when she joined me at Colwyn Bay. A small child requires stability, not least in the matter of education. In consequence, Margaret remained with her grandparents at Aberdeen, where she attended a school run by a Miss Oliver.

One day, Dora discovered a small lump in her breast. She mentioned this to her doctor who told her that it probably had no sinister significance and might well in time go away – a piece of advice so ludicrous that in these vastly more health-conscious times it would probably result in debarment or at the very least a suit for malpractice.

The lump proved malignant. As the cancer became more widespread, Dora's health declined. In 1944 she entered Manchester Royal Infirmary. From there she

137

Wedding of Frank and Dora, April 1936

returned to me in North Wales where she lingered six months more. She lies buried in a little churchyard in Colwyn Bay.

* * *

Dora's loss devastated me. Death in any form is a disaster. The death of the young, especially as the culmination of a long and debilitating illness, is particularly grievous. We had been married for eight years. The first three of these had been entirely happy. The last five – ravaged as they were by war and cancer – brought neither of us any real enjoyment at all.

Until 1951, Margaret remained in Scotland with her grandparents. Missing her always, I then arranged for her to come south once more. I sent her as a boarder to Wycombe Abbey School at High Wycombe. We resumed our fractured relationship during the school holidays.

I took great solace from the company of my daughter, but I still missed my wife. I felt isolated and alone. As an antidote I immersed myself in work.

* * *

Things might have continued in this way indefinitely had it not been for a chance acquaintance I had met abroad. In 1946, during the course of one of my assignments to India with the Ministry of War Transport, I found myself staying in Delhi. Having a weekend to myself, I decided to travel to Agra and view the Taj Mahal. As tended to be the case with Indian trains, when I arrived at Delhi station I found the vehicle packed to capacity. There simply wasn't a seat available.

Noticing my dilemma, a young woman sitting in a compartment reserved for the use of female military personnel invited me to join her. She introduced herself as Mabel Hills. Her uniform identified her as an officer in Queen Alexandra's Royal Nursing Corps. She was travelling down to the Corps' headquarters at Agra.

During the journey she told me a little about herself. She was shortly due to be demobbed and was worried that she would not be allowed to take her pet – an alsatian dog, of which she had grown very fond – home with her to England. I found her a pleasant companion and we agreed to look over the Taj Mahal together on the following day.

Set in stately Persian gardens, it is one of the loveliest structures in existence. It had been built by the Mogul emperor, Akbar the First, and later extended by his grandson, Shah Jehar as a tomb for his favourite wife. There is a legend that the plans for it were drawn from a dream which the empress experienced and later described to her husband. He searched all India for an architect who could turn

139

this into a reality. One day an old man sought an audience and exclaimed: 'I can help you obtain what you seek'. To one of the architects he then offered a mysterious drug, commanding him: 'Drink!' Having done so, the architect saw a vision of the completed building. Under the effects of the drug he worked feverishly until the plans were finished – when he fell back exhausted.

Under the great echoing dome we viewed the cenotaphs – or empty tombs – of Shah Jehan and his empress. The sunlight filtered into this chamber through marble screens intricately wrought and as delicate as lace, lighting up the jewelled cenotaphs. (The real tombs of the royal pair are sited in the vault, side by side and devoid of ornament.)

The walls of the interior were covered with the floral designs loved by the Persians, picked out in onyx, jasper, cornelian and other semi-precious stones let into the white marble walls. Inscriptions from the Koran, the sacred book of the Mohammedans, were ornately carved in Arabic characters.

The main building has a minaret at each corner from which it was possible to view the River Jumna. Large turtles rose to the surface for half a minute at a time before disappearing into the muddy depths below. I was contemplating just how many gallons of turtle soup they represented when our guide informed us that they were fed on the carcasses of dead children, thrown into the River Jumna to save the bother of cremation.

Nearby was the ghost city of Fatehpur Sikri, abandoned centuries ago due to the failure of the water supply. Shortly after my return from Agra, I viewed the Red Fort at Delhi, built in the shape of a semi-circle and more than half a mile in length.

Ironically, during the train journey back to Delhi our carriage caught fire, probably as a result of a carelessly discarded cigarette. We spent an hour or so dousing it with mugs of water drawn from the pan of the rudimentary toilet.

*   *   *

I had made a note of Mabs's telephone number in England – but without any clearly-formed intention of carrying the matter further. The parting seemed final.

About six months later, I telephoned the number she had given me and invited her out to dinner. We spent the evening discussing our respective experiences of the war. Mabs had an interesting story to tell. In her capacity as a theatre sister she had been sent into Burma by glider as part of a team of two doctors and six nurses needed to patch up the allied wounded. Working conditions proved appalling. The jungle was infested with Japanese soldiers who formed a constant threat and distraction. The climate too was extremely unhealthy. As a result, Mabs had contracted tuberculosis. She was now about to spend six months recuperating in a Surrey sanatorium.

During her period of convalescence I visited her on several occasions. We continued to meet after her discharge. Friendship slowly ripened and in November 1948 we were married. Our first child, Martin, was born in 1950. Nicholas followed two years later. By 1970, when I was the proprietor of two successful accountancy practices, I was nurturing the hope that the boys would follow me into the business. Unlike my own father, I should have been in a position to present them each with a flourishing concern of their own. It was not to be. Neither had a taste for a lifetime of pen-pushing and ultimately pursued different careers.

*   *   *

In 1954, Mabs's tuberculosis recurred. She again spent some months in a sanatorium. This meant the boys had to be placed for the duration in nursery schools, a disruption which may have had some lasting effect on their upbringing. The guilt which Mabs felt at this in turn produced further tension within her. This did nothing to aid her recovery. She became highly nervous and prone to sudden breakdowns. Her periods of hospitalisation became more frequent. Each time she appeared to make some form of recovery . . . only to relapse.

In 1947, and in order to provide her with a safe haven, I purchased three ramshackle fishermen's cottages at Sennen Cove in Cornwall. These I gutted and had internally rebuilt as one dwelling, twenty yards from the sea and almost opposite the lifeboat house. I named the house 'Tinker Taylor'.

Life at Sennen Cove passed largely without incident. However, in January 1960 passions became inflamed by what quickly became known as 'the Mullet War'.

For centuries the fishermen of Sennen had used a communal seine net during the first three months of the year to catch the elusive mullet which periodically visited the bay during the winter months. The operation began with a handful of lookout men climbing the cliffs and watching the bay to pinpoint the position of the mullet. The vigil was often lengthy. As soon as the fish were sighted the cry of 'Hevva!' went up. Guided by signals from the men atop the cliffs, boatloads of the fishermen then took the net out to sea, casting it around the shoal which was then dragged up on to the sand. The operation usually lasted all night. Most of the men depended on the proceeds for their winter keep.

Trouble began one Sunday when six fishermen from Par, a village some fifty miles distant, came to Sennen and attempted to land a shoal of the fish with a

141

250-yard net. Resenting the presence – and audacity – of what they termed 'them furriners', the locals overturned their boat and trailer and drew knives, as though to slash their nets. Out-numbered, the interlopers beat a hasty retreat. Two days later a second small party arrived from Par but fled when they saw an approaching crowd of Sennen fishermen.

A few days after that, seeking to establish the principle that 'the sea and its contents are free to all comers', four groups from Par banded together to form a raiding-party of twenty-one men. Before leaving the village their leader, a sixty-one-year-old man named Russell Endean, told the Cornish police of the proposed venture and asked for their protection.

The convoy of cars and lorries set off for Sennen shortly before dawn. A trailer carried their boat, aptly named 'The Peace and Plenty'. The party arrived at Sennen at 8.30 a.m. and came to a halt in a car park situated on a cliff-top some two hundred feet above the village. Endean and his followers scanned the almost calm sea, searching for the tell-tail 'grain' marking which would indicate the exact position of the mullet shoal. It was estimated to be worth £2,000.

While they were brewing mugs of tea, a squad of approximately twenty police officers in cars and on motor-cycles arrived to line the cliff top. A few local men who had been on the lookout for mullet since dawn quickly retired to the village. Ten minutes later about thirty Sennen fishermen arrived to confront their rivals. It was an ugly moment. Pointing through the police cordon to the group of Par fishermen beyond, the leader of the Sennen group, James Nicholas, asked: 'Is this the circus?'

Chief Inspector Walke told him: 'Tell your men we are here to prevent trouble. We take no sides. If anyone commits an assault they'll be arrested'. Nicholas, who was dressed in a fisherman's blue jersey and wearing a peaked cap, replied: 'That's all right. We'll manage them somehow, Captain'. This provoked a little laughter. More followed when, after casting an appraising eye over the Par boat, he added: 'That's jolly good gear they've got there'.

For the next two hours as Endean and his fishermen searched the sea, the men of Sennen were forced to stand silently by on the clifftop. Their eyes never left the Par boat. The police waited nearby. From the home of the village constable progress reports were relayed by telephone to county headquarters at Bodmin.

There was no sign of any mullet. About 11.30 a.m. the sea became a little rough and the Par fishermen decided to make for home. Before doing so, Endean told reporters: 'It's been well worth the effort and we will return. We've established an important principle – that the mullet shoals are not the exclusive property of the men of Sennen, who are so lazy that they refuse to cast their nets until the fish have practically reached their front door'.

Nicholas countered by pointing out that: 'Mullet scare very easily. If the Par men drop their nets and catch only a small number, the rest will scatter never to return. That's why we're waiting. We want to scoop the lot. Our forefathers have been catching the mullet here for generations. We will not give best to the Par raiders.'

As often happens with such disputes, the Mullet War died a natural death. There has since been no recurrence.

*   *   *

We made a number of good friends at Sennen. Probably the first of these were Len Shannon and his wife, May. Len was a builder. I commissioned him to renovate the three cottages as one habitation. We later added to this an outlying bungalow. Some ten years ago, finding the main house had become too large for our needs, we sold it to John and Sylvia Cheeseman, who have subsequently also become good friends.

Mabs loved Sennen Cove. Gradually, she came to spend more and more time there. The boys joined her during school holidays. Sadly, the limitations placed on me by an ever-expanding practice meant that I was able to do so less often.

Her health continued to deteriorate and in April 1974, after more than a quarter of a century of married life, she died. She had formed a close rapport with the crew of the lifeboat. As a mark of respect they launched their craft and carried her ashes out to a point off Penmaen Head – a landmark she had loved to gaze upon from her bedroom window – and scattered them over the water. It was a very moving ceremony.

*   *   *

If I was now a widower for a second time, I at least had my family and my home. As a consequence of Mabs's desire for a healthier climate than the one provided by the low-lying property at Shalford in Surrey. I had purchased a compact little manor house high in the Chilterns called Little Colyers, situated near Bovingdon. Curiously the county boundary separating Hertfordshire from Buckinghamshire ran through the middle of the property. Sadly, this did not exempt me from having to pay rates on it.

Built in the reign of Henry VII, it once held the status of a manor house and all the privileges attaching to this, including the rights of grazing on Boxmoor Common. The interior was distinguished by a series of low-beamed rooms and the existence of a priest's hole which, during the reign of Elizabeth I – when

Roman Catholic priests were escaping to the West – is rumoured to have accommodated the Jesuit, Father Edmund Campion. The audacity of his manifesto – known as Campion's 'Brag and Challenge' – greatly irritated the authorities. In July 1581 he arrested near Wantage and sent up to London, tied on horseback, with a paper stuck on his hat inscribed: 'Campion, the seditious Jesuit'. Thrice stretched on the rack, he was tried on a trumped up charge of conspiracy. He was hanged on 1 December 1581 and beatified by Pope Leo XIII in 1886.

*   *   *

In January 1978 I again re-married. I had known my third wife for thirty years – although we had spent the majority of this time apart. We had first encountered one another after Dora's death – during my period of service with the Ministry of Food in Colwyn Bay.

I was feeling rather lonely and depressed. My secretary, a young woman named Renee, mentioned a friend who was also feeling lonely, a Welsh school-friend, Glenys Edwards, a teacher, living and working in Guildford. Glenys's work kept her fully occupied and in consequence she had made few real friends. Through Renee, I offered my services as a part-time escort.

Glenys and I duly met. We liked one another and our meetings became weekly events. We went to the theatre and I showed her something of London. When I ultimately announced my engagement to Mabs, I wrote to her – and several other girlfriends besides – terminating the relationship. Many years were to pass before I saw or even heard of her again.

*   *   *

Fate took a hand in the unlikely form of an old Rutlishian named Bill Taborn. One night I found myself sitting next to him at a Masonic banquet. I recalled that he had known Glenys. I asked him whether he had maintained the contact. He said that he had. He told me that she had never married, preferring to devote her life to teaching. She was currently in Hong Kong. He promised that on her return he would contact her on my behalf and sound out the possibility of us renewing old acquaintance. Glenys duly telephoned and we arranged to meet.

I learned that following our separation, she had moved from Guildford to Colliers Wood, Merton, where, by a strange coincidence, she had initially taken a job at my own old infants' school. From there she had opened a new infants' school, Holly Mount in West Wimbledon. She became its first headmistress. During the period of her administration the school increased ten-fold from the

Frank and Glenys at the Mansion House

original forty students to four hundred and acquired a high reputation for academic success.

Characteristically, when her mother became seriously ill, Glenys – reasoning that a parent is a great deal more important than a job – returned to North Wales to nurse her. She found herself a job as a headmistress of a primary school.

Her reputation had preceded her and she was quickly appointed a Senior Adviser to the county of Flintshire. On the retirement of her counterpart in Denbighshire, she assumed this post also. By the time the two counties merged as Clwyd, she was in charge of a combined force of about eight hundred teachers. These she had to supervise and guide. They each had their own unique problems. It was a job which took all of her very considerable energy and resource.

By the time we renewed our acquaintance, she was living in Chester. I then occupied Little Colyers, the manor house in the Chiltern Hills. This made meeting difficult. Nonetheless it has been well said that love finds a way – and on New Year's Eve 1977 we officially announced our engagement at a dinner-dance at the Royal Automobile Country Club at Epsom. We were married at Hawarden church – where Gladstone regularly worshipped – exactly four weeks later.

Because Glenys wished to be given away by her brother, William John, and because William John was a shy, retiring sort of chap who would only agree to this provided the wedding was a quiet one, it was decided that it should be attended only by the immediate members of our respective families. Frankly, I had hoped for something rather more grand, not least because I still possessed the beautiful morning-suit, made for me more than forty years previously, in which I had married both of my previous wives. Of this, Glenys would not hear – perhaps I must now concede, rightly. I wore a lounge suit instead.

*   *   *

Our hopes for a quiet wedding were shattered when, on the day in question, a vast number of the teachers for whom Glenys was responsible descended on the church, uninvited, to see her married. Although we were somewhat surprised at the time I now think it was an impressive token of the regard in which they held her. (Being naturally inquisitive, they may also have wished to establish the nature of the man she had picked out for a husband.)

William John overcame his intrinsic shyness and rose to the occasion magnificently. Sixteen years Glenys's senior, he had a very special affection for her, and she for him. Her father had died when she was just eight years old. From that date, her brother had brought her up almost single-handed, becoming father as well as brother. He was the most quietly generous of men and is still remembered as such in his home town of Bethesda. I like to think that the knowledge that Glenys was now secure was a source of happiness to him.

The reception was held at the Grosvenor Hotel in Chester. Unbeknown to either of us, Keith Williams – the son of an old golfing friend, Ronnie Williams – had trained with the manager of the hotel and arranged for him to furnish us with a number of unexpected extras. When we arrived at the entrance in our white Rolls Royce, we found a red carpet had been unfurled. A large body of staff had been lined up to welcome us. Glenys was presented with a huge bouquet of red roses. It was the happiest of days.

* * *

Shortly after our marriage, we sold our respective houses and moved into our present London home, a flat at Barrie House, Lancaster Gate, in Bayswater. Neither of us was any longer young and we set out to make up for lost time.

My various associations – among them the City Livery Companies, Parliament, the R.A.C., the Royal Society of St. George and the Society of Lancastrians in London – ensured that our engagement book was constantly full. Glenys quickly demonstrated a remarkable talent as a hostess. She likes people and it shows. She has a talent for getting along, irrespective of people's station in life, which she considers of no consequence. She has the happy knack of easy informality, so that whether it be at the Guildhall, the Mansion House, at any of the magnificent City Livery Halls or elsewhere, we find ourselves part of a group of happy friends – especially as Glenys has now attained the Freedom of the City of London and is herself a member of the Guild of Freemen.

CHAPTER NINETEEN

PARLIAMENTARY CANDIDATE

P olitics is many things to many people. Those who practise the art tend to see themselves as philanthropists – caretakers of the public good. The public tends to see politicians as unabashed self-servers and place-seekers – the dubious and smug recipients of a cushy number. This wrong-headed view has been reinforced by a formidable body of distinguished opinion, much of it uttered by men who should have known better. Theodore Roosevelt defined a successful politician as 'he who says what everybody is thinking most often and in the loudest voice'.

From my experience, this overlooks one important factor. The nature of politics is such that a general consensus simply never exists – except perhaps an uneasy one in times of war or grave constitutional crisis such as those which occurred at the time of Edward VIII's abdication in 1936 or during the Falklands campaign. Politics is by nature divisive. It is the stuff of endless argument and limited and unsatisfactory compromise.

No matter how the dominant parties of government and opposition may be constituted, Liberal, Labour, Conservative, the two major protagonists sit entrenched on opposite sides of the House, hurling their partisan arguments at one another. Each is certain that theirs is right. It is no coincidence that, since time immemorial, warring factions within the two chambers of the Palace of Westminster have been parted by two thin red lines, the length of slightly more than two extended swords.

That consummate politician, Adlai Stevenson (in American presidential elections always the bridesmaid and never the bride), perhaps summed it up best when he compared politicians to that most regal and pompous of pachyderms:

'The elephant – which has a thick skin, a head full of ivory, and – as everyone who has seen a circus parade knows – proceeds best by grasping the tail of its predecessor.'

The same individual once described Richard Nixon, very presciently, as:

'the kind of man who would cut down a redwood – then mount the stump to deliver a stern lecture on the need for conserving our forests'.

If all this goes to show anything, it is that down the years politicians have received a bad Press. Some of this has been deserved – but by no means all of it.

*　　*　　*

I was introduced to politics through my friendship with the man who rented me my first office, Tim Donovan. In his turn, Donovan had cultivated the acquaintance of the Conservative parliamentary member for South East Bristol, Sir Gurney Braithwaite.

Braithwaite was a man of great natural ability. Following a highly successful career as a City stockbroker, he had come to prominence by unseating a Socialist politician who appeared to hold an impregnable parliamentary majority in excess of ten thousand. He became my political mentor and I followed his campaigns with great interest. I studied his methods of approach. He was a superb performer on the hustings. He employed me – although 'employed' is hardly the right word – to stand at the foot of the steps which he mounted at street corners for these orations, to ensure that no one attempted to push him over.

Initially, I found the whole issue of politics vaguely amusing. With business interests to push on, I felt no strong desire to become involved. However, Gurney was the possessor of a powerful personality. He took a liking to me, interested me in a number of his political projects and invited me to visit him at the Palace of Westminster. Almost by osmosis, I began to glean an insight into the manner in which politics worked. I began to be drawn.

Tim Donovan was then a member of the 'mock' parliament of Hampstead. This was an entirely intellectual and theoretical form of local government which had no serious standing. However, as a result of Tim's urgings, I became a member.

He and I drove up to 'parliamentary' meetings from the City, usually stopping at a local hostelry en route. Here, over a pint of bitter, I received further lessons in the niceties of parliamentary procedure. As a result, I came to understand that although the inhabitants of the Commons were sometimes rather rowdy, the manner in which they addressed one another bristled with etiquette.

A member referred to a colleague of his own party as 'My Honourable Friend'. If he was a member – or a former member – of the Cabinet he became 'My Right Honourable Friend'. A member of a party of opposition was referred to as 'The Honourable Gentleman'. If he was titled he was known as 'The Honourable and Noble Gentleman'. If he had even the most tenuous association with the Law, he was termed 'The Honourable and Learned Gentleman'. Although the member in question might never have been closer to the sharp end of a bullet than a dormitory bunk at Aldershot – or a comfortable War Office desk overlooking Horse Guards' Parade – anyone in opposition with a claim to a military career was addressed as 'The Honourable and *Gallant* Gentleman'.

The members of the Hampstead 'parliament' were an unusual bunch. There was Tim himself, who never learned to drive and never owned a dinner jacket; and Geoffrey Finsburgh, through whom I made the acquaintance of David Mitchell, the proprietor of El Vino's, the famous wine bar in Fleet Street, a traditional haunt of lawyers and journalists.

In those days El Vino's was an entirely male preserve. However, in November 1982 the Court of Appeal ruled that the wine bar was breaking the law by continuing to refuse women the right to stand at the bar and be served with the men. El Vino's had no alternative but to comply with this ruling. Nothing much changed in practice except that when approached by a woman the barman grew instantly short-sighted or distracted.

*　　*　　*

It is sometimes supposed that politicians are a breed of men who have always known what they would become. As a generalisation, this may be true. It was not so in my case. One evening in 1954 I was lying in bed pondering a number of matters. I must have been looking slightly fretful, because Mabs turned to me and said: 'What's on your mind?' I said: 'I'm going to become a member of parliament'. She said: 'You're mad' – and turned over and went to sleep.

In the morning I came to realise that she had clearly mulled the matter over during the night and come to the conclusion that it was no bad idea. 'Right, my boy', she said over the tea cups, 'let's get on with it then.'

Gurney and Tim sponsored me as a potential parliamentary candidate and my name was added to the list of hopefuls kept at the Conservative party's central office in Smith Square. In due course I was summoned to be vetted. I passed the test – although I remained a little worried that in the event of finding a constituency foolish enough to adopt me, my election campaign would require me to undertake a great deal of public speaking, of which I had only the smallest experience.

To remedy this I enrolled for three or four lessons with a body set up by the House of Commons which arranged lectures in the art. Having absorbed its rudiments, I had next to see that my name was added to what was known as the Conservative Speakers' Panel, a selection of party faithful who were willing to speak on political issues.

This accomplished, I could then do no more than sit back – impatiently – and wait for some organisation or other to invite me to talk to them. The first to do so was the Women's Guild of Crawley New Town. As I drove down, I kept repeating my speech to myself over and over again, under my breath. When I arrived at the venue – the church hall – I found it locked. The caretaker was on holiday.

Despite this anti-climactic beginning, about eight elderly ladies did put in an appearance. We somehow found a substitute venue and I delivered my first political speech. It was not especially interesting and my audience was not, I think, especially interested in listening to it. (I have a strong suspicion that I was preaching to the converted.) But at least they hadn't heckled – or worse, howled me from the stage.

*   *   *

My political career remained essentially moribund until, in the autumn of 1954, I attended the Conservative Party Conference. I found myself sitting next to a man named Adams, the chairman of the pottery company of the same name based at Newcastle–under–Lyme. We began by talking about politics in general terms. I then explained that I was a potential parliamentary candidate seeking adoption.

'Come to Newcastle', he said. 'We're looking for someone to take on the sitting Labour member, Stephen Swingler.'

I accepted with alacrity. I now had one foot poised on the bottom rung of the political ladder. It proved to be a loose one. When the General Election was called early in 1955 it did not take me long to discover that Swingler was sitting on a majority of almost nine thousand. My chances of robbing him of this were minimal. I nevertheless determined to conduct my campaign vigorously and without too closely considering the prospect of defeat.

I travelled up to Newcastle–under–Lyme three weekends a month. I put up at a pub in the centre of the town and began to canvass in order to get my name better known.

I was not, initially, very good at this, possibly because the constituency was comprised of two basic workforces: potters and miners. Both were dedicated Socialists. I could see that I had an up-hill task ahead of me. By dint of hard work I managed to become acquainted with a number of people whom I thought might vote for me, but the odds were always against me winning. Swingler was a good M.P. and as such much respected in the area. An unlikely Socialist, he had been educated firstly at Stowe, one of the country's foremost public schools, and then at Oxford, one of the county's most prestigious universities, where he graduated in philosophy, politics and economics. He had taught journalism and economics.

I quickly discovered that being a prospective parliamentary candidate is an expensive business. There is no central party fund to pay expenses. The cost of

Election publicity, 1955, Newcastle-under-Lyme

152

travel, hotel bills and a considerable amount of entertaining had to be met out of my own pocket.

I was at least fortunate to have as my agent the able Colonel Bettell, a seasoned campaigner. He had a great many contacts. As such he was able to conjure up speakers to stand beside me on the hustings and endorse my campaign.

One such was Sir George Wade, the chairman of Wade Potteries and one of the most important men in the area. On one occasion, when I was due to speak at the little village of Silverdale, he pulled up in his large limousine and through the loud-hailer system affixed to it spent fifteen minutes exhorting the populace to vote for me. The entire village was solidly Labour.

As this was an afternoon meeting, all the men were at work and the audience was made up entirely of women. Sir George told them what a wonderful fellow I was and how well advised they would be to vote for me. They listened in stony silence. At the end of his oration he politely asked whether anyone would care to ask questions. This was greeted by another stony silence. Sir George thanked them for their kindness and drove away. To the right of the village green he encountered a number of cows grazing quietly in a field. Pulling alongside, he muttered: 'And no doubt you'll be voting Labour, too – like the other silly cows I've just been addressing'.

As he had forgotten to switch off the loud-hailer, this remark was heard the length and breadth of the village. Yet I honestly believe it lost me not a single vote. In Silverdale I didn't have a single vote to lose, not one.

There were, however, votes to be lost – and won – elsewhere, and campaigning now became extremely competitive. It did not deteriorate into a slanging match. Both Swingler and I restricted ourselves to criticising one another's policies rather than personalities. He was, I believe, a man of genuine probity. It could also be said that as he was defending an all but impregnable majority, he felt no need to descend to the politics of the gutter.

*   *   *

Through Colonel Bettell, I found myself addressing an audience of approximately two hundred and fifty women in a large hall no great distance from the town. I called the talk: 'Why Bother With Politics?'

I said that I felt it was a great pity that any of us *did* have to bother with politics. If each member of parliament was allowed to vote on matters according to his own conscience – rather than adhere to a party line laid down by the Whips – we should probably get a great deal more done. Unfortunately, a completely independent parliament would also be an extremely unstable one. When electing a member to Westminster, I felt that many voters were immovable one way or the other – voted the way they did because their parents and grandparents had done so before them. They never really considered the issues under review.

We needed to persuade people to think – principally about the Labour Party and the strong Communist element which utilised it as a stalking horse. I quoted from the opening paragraph of a Socialist manifesto entitled: 'Challenge to Britain', a truly terrifying document.

'The plan for Britain which we outline will involve sacrifices, not only of material benefits, but of many cherished habits and traditions. We must be prepared to send development goods abroad without any prospect of immediate payment.'

This was the Ground Nut Scheme resurrected. Worse was to follow. Manufactured goods would be 'standardized'. In simple terms this meant that the drab and poorly-made utility item would return to the shops.

Labour also announced its intention of adopting the Collective Farm System – so beloved of Stalin and so hopelessly inefficient – whereby time-and-motion techniques were applied to agriculture. Those farmers failing to reach their quarterly target per acre ran the risk of losing their property at the stroke of a pen belonging to some faceless Whitehall mandarin.

All this was simply another example of the doctrinist's love of 'standardization' and 'equality'. It took no account of the fact that production can often vary from one corner of a field to another, let alone from farm to farm. Nor, in its blind stupidity, did it seem to appreciate that people are equal in many ways – but never in their souls.

All barley and wheat would be sold to the government (presumably at prices fixed by the government). In order to ensure its quality, the Commission appointed to regulate the industry would also prescribe the quality and quantity of farmers' feed stuffs – a measure totally unprecedented in time of peace.

Packing stations would be the only buyers of eggs. Nobody would be permitted more than one egg for breakfast (a dictat which might, in practice, have proved difficult to enforce).

Workers would be required to save by having a weekly sum deducted from their wages. 'Privileged' fee-paying schools would be abolished. They would be replaced by the Comprehensive – the educational equivalent of the sausage machine. Children, too, must be rendered 'equal'.

Innumerable quangos, staffed by government nominees, would be established to regulate the production of wool, milk, potatoes, meat and anything else which seemed appropriate. Foodstuffs would be bought in bulk, although the situation

154

would be 'rationalised', which, it was claimed, meant rationing would not be re-introduced (a contradiction in terms).

There were many similar statements, all in the same vein. Nowhere was there any mention of encouraging people to work hard or to be happy. The talk was only of restricting liberty, forcing people to do what they were told . . . inexorably grinding them down. It was 'Jobs for the Boys'. Implementation would have generated the largest and most corrupt black market economy this or any other country had ever seen.

My comments seemed to find favour and the text of the speech was later reproduced as an article in the local Conservative party's magazine, *Forward*.

* * *

One aspect of this particular campaign involved a church service. Unusually, this was held on the Sunday prior to polling day rather than the Sunday after. Swingler and I met on guarded but convivial terms. We each delivered a short address after which we shook hands.

None of this, of course, made the slightest difference to the outcome of the election. Although I did manage to reduce his mandate by almost two thousand – which I considered a major achievement – Swingler was swept back to office with a majority of 6745.

I had at least gained considerable experience from my involvement in the campaign and learned to avoid some of the the pitfalls which await the unwary on every side. One of these is to remember that anyone in quest of the popular vote should never ever agree to be a judge at a dog, cat or baby show. The winner loves you. The losers will all detest you and certainly won't vote for you. I never accepted any of the offers I received to stand in this capacity – although I was always willing to present the prizes.

I had enjoyed the fight at Newcastle–under–Lyme – and was extremely amused to receive from Lord Woolton, the Conservative party chairman, the following day a telegram which read: 'Warmest congratulations on your well deserved victory'.

I should not have wished to have stood in a truly safe Tory seat – with the kind of majority where one *weighs* the votes rather than counts them – because I was aware that in such instances members of parliament often find themselves severely hamstrung by a powerful constituency committee. In a marginal, the member is much more in control of his own fate.

Telegram from Lord Woolton (but wrong result)

* * *

In order to keep myself politically in touch, I undertook a number of tours. I visited Belfast, Glasgow, Edinburgh, Inverness and Aberdeen to address political meetings and rallies.

I had been short-listed at Aberdeenshire West as a potential parliamentary candidate. Since my only connection with the country was the fact that Dora had been Scottish, I was lucky to have progressed as far as this. I progressed no further and the selection went to Lady Tweedsmuir. She proved to be an excellent MP. We later became parliamentary colleagues.

Another tour took me to Wales and the Rhondda Valley, where I spoke at four meetings. These were mostly held in pubs and working-men's clubs. The audience, predominantly pit-men and their families, was heavily left-wing. (I sometimes think they only turned up out of inquisitiveness: to see what a Conservative *looked* like.) As with most political meetings, there was a degree of good-natured heckling and perhaps some chaffing, but it had no unpleasantness attached to it, despite being laced with a good deal of beer.

I found I enjoyed the cut and thrust of debate. I was also developing the reputation of a politician who would not evade the issue by answering an entirely different question to the one posed. Moving around so much cost me a great deal of money. However, I was learning all the time and absorbing important aspects of political lore.

I applied to a large number of constituencies seeking candidates. In some cases a choice had already previously been made and the meeting of the Selection Committee was merely an empty formality required to maintain the fiction of democracy.

Strange things happened at Selection Committee meetings, some of them extremely humiliating. When I heard that the Lancashire town of Bolton was seeking a candidate, I applied and was short-listed. I was summoned to appear with two others before the committee. Shortly before the date of the meeting I was quietly taken to one side by the party agent and informed that it was 'expected' that I should be nominated. I was overjoyed.

The night before the Committee was due to sit, a group of its members suddenly insisted – quite wrongly and unconstitutionally – that the name of another candidate, Tommy Taylor, should be added to the short-list.

My namesake was a local councillor and a very popular man. Although his inclusion broke all the rules, there was little any of us could do about it. His name was added to the short-list and amid a flurry of support he was officially adopted over our heads.

Together with the other two unsuccessful candidates, I sat in an ante-room listening to the jubilant voices congratulating Taylor on the other side of a thin partition. No one came to inform us of his selection officially, nor were we offered any refreshment. Tired, annoyed and disillusioned we crept away to our homes.

Tommy Taylor had not been the instigator of this piece of sharp practice and I never held the outcome of it against him. In fact, when the time came for him to fight the seat I happily went up to Bolton and canvassed on his behalf for three days. I'm pleased to say he won. I should like to think that many of the faction on the committee which had pressed for his selection felt ashamed when they came to review their behaviour in retrospect.

If so, they never showed it. Only one of their number had the courage to apologize to me.

CHAPTER TWENTY

THE BATTLE FOR CHORLEY AND LEYLAND

I n 1956 I learned that the constituency of Chorley and Leyland was seeking a parliamentary candidate. The Conservative party agent, who knew something of my past political record, helped to see that I was duly adopted. This was excellent news but no cause for immediate jubilation. An election looked some years away.

The sitting member of eleven years was Clifford Kenyon, a nice-looking man of some erudition. In 1951, when the new House of Commons was opened, the prime minister had invited him to move the Address to George VI 'to set a standard of speech worthy of the occasion'.

Kenyon was a man of humble beginnings but wide practical experience. Educated in elementary and technical schools, he had progressed by his own merits to Manchester University. Reared on a farm, he had served both in the Royal and the Merchant Navy before returning to his roots to take up farming in East Lancashire. He had a history of community service. For twenty years he had been a member of Rawtenstall Borough Council and had served as Mayor of the borough between 1938 and 1942. His private life was impeccable. For ten years he had been minister of a church in Oldham.

He was generally considered to be well dug in – but his majority was less than two thousand. As the holder of a semi-marginal seat, this would ultimately render him vulnerable.

*   *   *

For more than three years, between May 1956 and August 1959, I put a great deal of effort into the constituency, motoring up on Friday evenings and back again on Monday morning, three weekends a month. I stayed at the Royal Oak, a cheerfully unpretentious pub in the centre of town. My hosts were Jack and Mary Faucitt. In the course of time we became friends and Jack frequently acted as my map-reader during my rallying years.

On my adoption, the *Chorley Guardian* thought it worth asking what kind of man I might be. It proceeded to answer its own question:

'He is not one of those Southerners who are surprised to find that Lancastrians do not paint themselves in woad or live in mud huts. He has travelled too widely for that.

'In fact, in a room full of people, it would be difficult to identify him with any county. He is very much a Britisher – quietly spoken, slightly reserved, but highly capable. He is a chartered accountant and he knows his stuff! In this case the geography of birth definitely does not enter into the question.

'There are those who wanted a younger candidate. Mr Taylor is *fifty*. But he is a sportsman – a former county rugby player and sculling and punting champion. He now plays competitive golf to a handicap of ten.

He is more physically active than many men ten years his junior. In fact, he has reached an age of responsibility and has a background of experience. These are qualities which the Tories have been seeking. Perhaps that is why they have taken so long.'

*   *   *

I devoted the majority of Saturday mornings to a constituency surgery, offering what help I could to the local people on a wide variety of problems. Much of the rest of the weekend was taken up in formulating plans to remedy these complaints and implementing action, usually in the form of letters to those who held the power to get something done.

I invested what little time was left in tramping the streets, knocking on doors in order to get to know potential voters. I found that in the course of a nine-hour day I could actually manage to have a few words with as many as three hundred.

The constituency was widespread and sprawling. It was largely agricultural. Industry was represented by Leyland Motors, the car manufacturers. I came to know the company's chairman, a man named Spurrier, and when the election ultimately materialised, he was kind enough to allow me to hold meetings at the factory gates.

The workforce at Leyland was highly political and the men actually took the trouble to give up a portion of their lunch hour to listen to me speak. My opponent, Clifford Kenyon, adopted a similar practice – although at different gates and on different days.

159

*   *   *

Slowly I came to know a number of influential local people who could be of use in forwarding my political aspirations. One of the most important was the Conservative party's constituency chairman, Sir Stanley Bell. The brains behind the Astley Industrial Trust, he lived in a large mansion with an enormous surrounding estate. Here he maintained a herd of pedigree cattle. In order to improve and increase the strain he acquired a bull for £3000 and implemented a breeding programme. The local Press came to hear of this and sent a reporter and a photographer down to produce a small feature.

The words 'small feature' are inappropriate – because when the editor saw the photograph he became aware that this bull had one extremely large feature, the depiction of which, in a family newspaper, might offend some of his readers. He therefore reduced its size with the aid of an air-brush.

This no doubt preserved the sensibilities of one or two maiden ladies. Sir Stanley was absolutely livid – made it quite clear that he considered it a gross libel on the manhood of a magnificent creature. He threatened to sue. Happily, the matter was settled without recourse to the law.

*   *   *

I became aware that I needed to attract more publicity to myself. In order to imprint my personality on people's memories, I decided to canvass some of the outlying farming communities on horseback. This experiment lasted two days . . . during which it rained ceaselessly.

Realising that my stint as a prospective candidate was destined to be a long one, I drew up an enormous chart, three feet long and two feet wide, showing each of the polling areas and the number of voters they contained. I used a further column to show the estimated voting strength I could rely on in each area. With the aid of this I decided that before the election materialised I would do my utmost to canvass every house in the constituency. This in fact proved an impossible task – although I'm gratified that I did over the three years manage to get round to four houses out of every five.

Clifford Kenyon confessed to the *Chorley Times* in February 1959: 'I've done a bit of this. But frankly I don't know how he does it'.

*   *   *

160

People often denigrate the young, but the Young Conservatives of Chorley and Leyland were among my greatest allies. They were full of enthusiasm on my behalf. They organised fund-raising events and sought the permission of local farmers to affix posters to their trees and gates.

I also discovered that in what they considered to be a good cause they were capable of being extremely devious. One evening I was diverted away from party headquarters on the pretext that my presence was required at a bowling alley.

In my absence, the Young Conservatives prepared the headquarters for a little entertainment of their own, a highly professional version of 'This Is Your Life' – with me as the subject. They had gone to an immense amount of trouble to obtain cassette recordings from a goodly number of my friends, associates and office staff. The evening was a great success.

I have only one regret. I was promised a recording of the event. Sadly, this never materialised. It remains now only in my memory.

*   *   *

On 8 September 1959 the Conservative prime minister, Harold Macmillan – known to the Press as 'Supermac' – made a flying visit to the Queen at Balmoral to inform her of his intention to call a General Election. At Chorley and Leyland it proved to be a two-cornered fight, the Liberals not participating.

The big guns were called into play. Lord Hailsham, the chairman of the Conservative Party, came to speak on my behalf at the Tudor ballroom. Kenyon brought along a celebrity of his own, Hugh Gaitskell, the leader of the Opposition. The hall was crowded. Many were forced to stand.

Ineptly, Gaitskell – a man destined never to hold high office – was not only late but sought to turn this to his political advantage. He told the assembled congregation of six hundred:

'I am not making any accusation of sabotage against anyone. But if the Tory government had not so frequently interfered with the investment programme of British Railways perhaps we should not have had an engine failure.'

The remark was typical of the man. It did his cause little good. The following day his comments were reproduced in the *Lancashire Evening Post* under the headline:

'Gaitskell blames Tories for engine fault.'

Hailsham was more pertinent. He pointed out that the national figure for unemployment was under two percent. For the past eight years the government – sometimes painfully – had been endeavouring to build up Conservative Britain – to set the people free from Socialist bureaucracy. Socialism, he said, had produced

161

shortages, rationing, higher prices, devaluation, crises, and the kind of black market economy beloved of spivs and drones.

He added that when the Conservatives first came to power there was little belief in the idea of a property-owning democracy.

'But we showed that we had a warmer understanding of ordinary people's needs than Labour. The Socialists thought that the good things of life – the motor-car, television sets, nice furniture and labour-saving devices – were the playthings of the rich. They thought they were to be sneered at. But we knew that they were part of the Conservative way of life – for the ordinary man and woman . . .'

*　　*　　*

Kenyon and I next crossed swords in the studios of Granada television. We appeared as part of an Election Marathon, in the course of which each candidate was given a one-minute opportunity to state his case.

I spoke first. I pointed out that life under the Conservatives had produced a better standard of living than at any time since the end of the Second World War. In his turn, Kenyon claimed that Conservative members of parliament were controlled by the Whips' Office and the party machine. When I questioned him regarding his own so-called and much vaunted 'independence', he was forced to admit that since being first returned to parliament he had never once voted against any motion formulated by his own party.

Ominously, perhaps – at least for me – he told the *Chorley Guardian* that his meetings had been serious and free from heckling. He had found much the same feeling in the constituency as he had done at the last election. He felt confident of another victory.

The *Daily Telegraph* recorded that Kenyon and I were:

'keyed up for a touch-and-go finish. At one village school meeting a few nights ago, Mr Taylor stood beside a blackboard. On this was the question: 'Describe how the Romans used to bury their dead.'

I had no idea of how the Romans buried their dead. I got round the problem by describing how I proposed to bury the Labour Party.

The newspaper went on to describe my canvassing campaign as 'The Chorley Grand Tour':

'a phrase coined by mid-Lancashire householders to describe the most intensive single-handed political doorstep activity ever waged in these parts. In two and a half years Mr Taylor has covered on foot seven hundred miles of winding roads, through sunlit farmland, smoky engineering, textile and mining areas. He has knocked at the doors of more than 30,000 electors.'

*   *   *

As the fateful day grew closer, the campaign became more fiercely contested. The *Lancashire Evening Post* accused both Kenyon and myself of 'slinging election mud pies':

'It all started on Thursday with the issue of a challenge by [Kenyon] for a public debate on certain statements Mr Frank Taylor made regarding [Labour's] proposed nationalisation of six hundred firms, including Leyland Motors. The following day, Mr Taylor declined the challenge, saying that although he would welcome it, he was already fully booked up with meetings, adding that it was "simply an election trick".'

Kenyon was adept at this kind of manoeuvre, purposely delaying issues until the eleventh hour – when there was insufficient time either to resolve or to debate them – and using this as an excuse to accuse his opponent of avoidance. He also instigated a whispering campaign aimed at assassinating generally my character.

*   *   *

Polling day duly arrived. Before most people had risen from their beds, the Young Conservatives had slipped through the letter-box of ten thousand constituents a card, surmounted by a crowing rooster, bearing the legend:

'Good morning! This is polling day. Vote early for Frank Taylor, your Conservative Party candidate'.

This dawn-patrol required a great deal of organising and the sheer physical effort entailed upon it was immense. Myself and fifteen young helpers managed to dispose of these cards before eight o'clock. We then repaired to a local restaurant which had organised for us a hard-earned breakfast.

There was no more we could do. It was now simply a question of waiting. It seemed to us that there had been a tremendously high turn-out. When the polls closed we adjourned to the town hall to watch the count. Clifford Kenyon looked deeply apprehensive. He was aware of the work I had put in – not only in the weeks leading up to the election but consistently, over a period of three years.

When the returning officer announced the result, it transpired that Kenyon had retained his seat by a mere six hundred votes.

*   *   *

Shortly afterwards I wrote a long letter to the editor of the *Chorley Guardian,* seeking to put the campaign in perspective. I explained that although I had personally not been successful, I felt the national result had been a wonderful vindication of Conservative policy. It represented an impressive vote of confidence in Macmillan and an emphatic rejection of the Labour Party's policies of national-isation. For all this, victory had brought added responsibilities. The Conservatives – and not for the first time – had a sound majority. It would not do for them to sit back and stagnate.

I was anxious that certain aspects of the campaign should not be allowed to slip from the voters' memories. To paraphrase:

'Mr Kenyon referred to the strenuousness of his three-day trip to Australia. I was surprised to hear him mention the Election in the same context. Perhaps he has forgotten – although I have not – his slighting references to my war-time career . . . carefully timed to be released three days before polling-day.'

'Let me draw a small comparison between Mr Kenyon's journey and that portion of my own war career which he sought to belittle. Practically every staging-post he refers to I have encountered many times. My penultimate trip took forty-one days, twenty-six or some part of which were spent in the air. It took me to thirteen countries. If Mr Kenyon had experienced even a fraction of this he might have something to complain about. I lived this life – to which he refers so slightingly – for more than two years.

'I hope editors will keep information of this nature in their no doubt long memories – and recall it when the time comes for the seat to be contested once more.'

*   *   *

If the defeat at Chorley came as a disappointment, I was once again able to take comfort from the fact that I had severely reduced an opponent's majority. None-theless a part of me was beginning to wonder whether I should ever achieve my ambition.

It was not as distant as I thought.

CHAPTER TWENTY–ONE

THE BATTLE FOR MOSS SIDE

I n 1960 the sitting member for Moss Side, Manchester, a man named Jacky Watts, died. He had held the seat for only eighteen months, having inherited it from the late great Florence Horsbrugh. A nephew of Agatha Christie, Jacky had made a great impact on the constituency in a very short time and his passing was deeply mourned.

The party area agent who had helped me obtain the nomination at Chorley telephoned to suggest that I apply to fight the by-election which would be a natural consequence of Jacky's death. Although I never discovered as much for certain, I suspect he also contacted the chairman of the Moss Side constituency party to promote my chances by indicating the degree of hard work and effort I had devoted to Chorley.

Following the usual procedures and interviews, I was duly selected. I was more elated than I had been for many years. For the first time I should be fighting a Conservative-held seat. At the election which had returned Jacky Watts to parliament, his majority had been in excess of four thousand. I reasoned that it would require a massive turn-around to overthrow that. I was nonetheless not prepared to take the risk of it happening by neglecting my campaign.

Having fought two elections, I was no longer a novice. I appreciated that at the time of a general election the Press is limited in the coverage it can give to the fight for any one seat. This was a by-election. It would attract the newspaper world's undivided attention.

*　　*　　*

The battle for Moss Side was joined. I had experienced nothing like it before. I was cheered, vilified, slapped on the back, cursed, applauded and sneered at – often all within the space of an hour. As there had been almost no lapse between my adoption and the commencement of the campaign, I found myself not fully prepared and slightly disorientated.

Forceful advertising by Moss Side Young Conservatives

Moss Side was almost completely residential. It incorporated such widely disparate communities as Chorlton-cum-Hardy which housed middle-class voters who nearly always voted Conservative by inclination and tradition, and the horribly depressed slum area of Greenheyes, made up of row after row of small and mean terraced cottages. Another part of the constituency was Withington Road. The four-floor dwellings here had once accommodated families of some affluence. By 1960 the majority had been converted into bed-sits, many of which contained ladies of easy virtue. They too of course were voters and most expressed an intention to vote Conservative. When asked why, one of them told me: 'Well, I shouldn't want to be *nationalised*, now should I dearie?' Sadly, I was never able to accept an invitation to step inside one of these flats and take a cup of tea in case I might be photographed and compromised.

*   *   *

166

The nature of the constituency was perhaps best summed up – albeit in rather florid prose – by an article in the *Manchester Evening News*. This described Moss Side as:

'that crumbling, oppressive slice of old Manchester, the city's 'little Harlem'. The planners have decreed that the tight-packed terraces of Moss Lane and its precincts must share their MP with the privet-hedged avenues of neighbouring Chorlton-cum-Hardy.

'They have mixed an introverted eager-to-let-the-world-go-by immigrant community with a wide-awake middle-class group in a schizophrenic forty-five-thousand-strong electoral unit . . .'

*   *   *

A fighting fund had been established to help pay the costs of my campaign. The total allowed for this was approximately £2,000. When one considers the enormous amount of literature which had to be printed, the hire of halls in which to hold rallies, and many, many ancillary expenses, this was no great sum.

One of the outstanding features of the campaign was an enormous head and shoulders photograph of myself, eight feet by six, which was placed twenty feet high on the side of a derelict cinema in Claremont Road. It probably had some influence on the electorate although there was something of the Big Brother element about it which made me uneasy.

*   *   *

With sixty thousand voters within the constituency boundaries (rather than the forty-five thousand mentioned by the *Manchester Evening News*) I once again found myself busy with the distribution of leaflets to the wards. This aspect of the campaign was not carried out as efficiently as it might have been. Some months after, I discovered a bundle of many thousands in a cupboard at a ward office – this despite a firm assurance that every last one had been delivered. This was less the fault of the party workers than that of the voluntary part-time distributors taken on to help us complete the operation.

The high spot of the campaign involved Alderman Bailey's farm. Then as now, it was common practice for all parties to send out spies in order to ascertain how the opposition was faring. We had despatched one such to a meeting of the Labour Party. He had reported back that the candidate had been asked to outline his policy on agriculture. Perhaps unwisely, he had chosen to brush the question aside, saying:

167

The Biggest Face in Moss Side, 1961

The cows vote for Frank Taylor, Moss Side, 1961

'Agriculture doesn't concern me. There's no agriculture in Moss Side at all. It's residential.'

This was not quite the case. There *was* a farm – just one – and it belonged to Alderman Bailey, who kept twenty or so cows on a small strip of land at Chorlton-cum-Hardy. Much to the Socialists' chagrin and discomfort – and my own huge delight – by the following morning all these creatures had somehow found their way to the Wilbraham Road end of their field. The rear end of each was decorated with a poster bearing the legend:

'Vote for Frank Taylor'

This novel effect had been stage-managed by Alderman Bailey's son. He had drawn the beasts in the right direction by placing their hay at strategic points along the route.

The resultant publicity did me no harm whatsoever. The Press picked up the story. So did several television stations. One newspaper headline ran: 'Even the

169

cows are voting for Frank Taylor'. The incident offered a great boost to party morale.

The Socialists were not of course our only opponents. Other parties fielded candidates and there was, I think, a total of seven. One of these, from the hard-left, had employed the son of Sir Oswald Mosley, the notorious fascist, as his agent. This caused a great deal of disruption and not a little ill-feeling. Although nothing was ever proven, I long suspected this party – and one or two others besides – of resorting to such underhand tactics as tearing down the posters of the opposition late at night. It did them little good and they received no significant number of votes – possibly because they appeared to have no definable policies.

Polling day came and went. The following morning, at eleven o'clock, all the candidates gathered at Manchester Town Hall. When the votes had been counted, I found that I had been returned with a majority of four thousand. It was one of the greatest moments of my life.

I immediately returned to London to make preparations to take my seat in the House.

* * *

Parliament is hedged around with tradition and ceremony. This is just as it should be. Taking into account the energy I had expended over the course of seven years, I would have felt deeply deflated if membership had involved nothing more than strolling into the place and saying 'Hello'.

New members awaiting induction have first to be introduced to the House by one of their colleagues, who together with the Chief Whip brings them to the Bar, a rod of Jamaica bronze which slides from its case to establish a physical barrier between members and those who stand beyond it. To be on the far side of the Bar is to be in a symbolic sense outside the House.

I was happy to have as my supporter Sir Robert Cary, the member for Withington, who had aided me in my campaign. After the House had taken prayers at 2.30 p.m., we entered the chamber in the company of the Chief Whip and awaited our summons. This seemed an interminable time in coming. I was acutely aware of the sense of history attaching to the place and as I pondered on the many great men who had occupied it, Winston Churchill wandered in to take his seat. By common consensus – and as a mark of respect – the one at the top of the front bench, immediately below the gangway, was always left vacant for his use.

The call came. The three of us advanced abreast and bowed. Processing forward, we again stopped and bowed before reaching the table on which was situated the mace – the symbol of parliamentary authority. I signed my name in a book, the contents of which were a mystery to me. I was then conducted to the Speaker, who shook my hand and congratulated me. This done, I retired behind the Speaker's chair and the House resumed its normal business.

Moss Side was not the most glamorous of constituencies, nor was it nationally known. There were those within the House who were astounded to learn that the Conservatives held it. (There were others who were even more astounded that for thirteen years I managed to retain it.)

* * *

After seven years of great endeavour I had arrived where I wanted to be. I felt horribly lost. Fortunately, most of the members were kind and made me feel welcome. Slowly I began to learn something of the history of this 'Mother of Parliaments'.

I discovered that I was now to spend my working day on the site of a former royal dwelling – hence the term *'Palace* of Westminster' – built by Edward the Confessor. Edward III added several buildings to this, including a prison known as 'The House called Hell' and another designated 'Purgatory'. There was also a third building known as 'Paradise', but its function is not clear. All three later became taverns.

This old palace was several times damaged by fire but each time patched up. In 1512 a serious conflagration left parts of it uninhabitable. It ceased to be a royal residence about 1529 when, at the downfall of Cardinal Wolsey, Henry VIII requisitioned that proud prelate's former home, York Place, and renamed it the Palace of Whitehall.

Twenty years later the old Palace of Westminster became the seat of parliament. It remained so until 1834 when it was almost totally destroyed by fire. The blaze was started by a clerk who was burning some Exchequer tally-sticks – thin wooden batons on which notches were cut to serve as accounting records – in a faulty stove. It was several hours before the flames took hold and during this time the members' feet were roasting in their boots and the chamber of the House of Lords was so full of smoke that it was impossible to see the throne. Yet nobody thought this worth investigating.

The people of London treated the blaze as a free entertainment. Constable came and Turner – inevitably – brought his sketch pad. As flames and sparks belched from the chimneys, opponents of the Climbing Boys Act (aimed at curbing the practice of sending small children up flues to clean them) set up a derisive chorus of 'Sweep! Sweep!'

Not surprisingly, Sir Charles Barry's new Palace, chosen from some ninety-seven designs, made little use of wood. Particular attention was paid to the devising of an efficient method of ventilation and every effort was made to avoid the twisting and idiosyncratic construction which had characterised the previous building.

Barry's success may be judged by the fact that if all the doors were suddenly thrown open simultaneously, anyone standing before the Sovereign's Robing Room in the House of Lords, at the south end of the building, would have an unobstructed view through to the Speaker's chair in the House of Commons.

Today, the Palace is cooled in summer by a modern ventilation system. It is operated by a team of technicians located in a central control room. To enable them to keep track of the events in the two chambers, the room is fitted with closed-circuit television as well as a periscope, sixty-five feet in length. In an emergency, the air in the Palace can be completely changed in five minutes.

The acoustics in both chambers are excellent, thousands of tiny holes having been bored in the walls and ceiling to allow excess vibrations to escape. (The Commons produces a great deal of hot air.)

To the problem of overcrowding, which is especially acute, there seems to be no solution short of a major reconstruction. Although some additional space was provided when the chamber was rebuilt after destruction in an air raid in 1941, it has again become woefully inadequate. People are invariably astounded to learn as much, but there is nothing like a seat for every member. As I found to my cost, on busy occasions many are forced to stand or to squat on the floor, sometimes for hours at a stretch. Office space is also at a premium. Most M.P.s either have no desk within the Palace or, as in my case, share one under very cramped conditions with colleagues.

The 'Lower House', as the Commons is sometimes called, normally sits on weekdays only. It assembles at 2.30 p.m., except on Fridays when the hour is 11 a.m. In the absence of exceptional business, the sitting is suspended at 10 p.m., when a thirty-minute adjournment debate takes place. Important debates may cause the House to sit through the night and well into the next day.

The onset of Commons' business is heralded each week-day by the arrival of the Speaker, the Chamber's presiding dignitary, who is conducted to the Speaker's Chair by various officials and preceded by the Sergeant-at-Arms, who carries the mace, without which the House cannot sit. Prayers are then said, during which members kneel on the benches, a legacy from the days when the wearing of swords precluded kneeling on the floor.

Although members do of course occasionally do so, there is a tradition which states that no one ever actually dies at Westminster. Because it remains a royal palace, such an event would involve the Queen. To make the appropriate arrangements for the removal of the body she would be put to the very considerable bother of signing an Order in Council, something which is normally only invoked at times of great national crisis. In consequence, whatever the unfortunate individual's true condition, on being taken from the House he is always registered as 'dead on arrival' at Westminster Hospital.

Another tradition attests that with the singular exception of George VI, who opened the rebuilt chamber in 1950, no sovereign has been granted entry to the House of Commons since the day in 1642 when Charles I attempted to arrest in person five of its members at sword-point. The ceremony in which the monarch opens parliament from the House of Lords is a consequence of this – and a mark of the House's long memory.

Since 1605, when the Catholic Guy Fawkes endeavoured to blow up the Protestant James I at the official Opening of Parliament, it has also been the practice to search the vaults prior to that ceremony. The task remains the prerogative of the sovereign's foot-soldiers, the Yeomen of the Guard. Despite the fact that the cellars are now electrically lit and will already have been minutely examined by modern scanning devices, they utilise oil-lamps to probe each nook and cranny with the same conscientiousness as they have done for centuries.

During my time as a member of parliament I frequently had to entertain visiting dignitaries. Nearly all of them enquired about 'Big Ben' – the name of a bell within the Albert Tower rather than the tower itself – and the manner in which it came by its name. Opinion is divided. One source claims that it was named after Sir Benjamin Hall, Commissioner of Works at the time the bell was installed.

A romantic and equally plausible version attributes it to the Victorian prize-fighter, Ben Caunt, who at the age of forty-two became something of a national hero after fighting a bare-knuckle contest lasting sixty rounds. Prior to its installation, the bell had to be dragged to Westminster from its foundry by a team of sixteen white horses, one for every ton of its weight.

The clock itself keeps excellent time, losing less than a tenth of a second a day. At one time, adjustments were made by adding to or subtracting from a small stock of coins lodged in a tray affixed to the pendulum. Until recent years, it had only stopped once – when a member who was explaining the function of the mechanism to a party of visitors inadvertently allowed his umbrella to become entangled in it. The mechanism is smaller than might be expected. It was made by Dents of Pall Mall, who for many years used to send an employee to the Palace twice a week to wind it up. The driving mechanism took a long time to wind.

Everything about 'Big Ben' is larger than life. The four dials of the clock-face stand two hundred feet above ground level. A double-decker bus could be driven with ease through any one of them. The minute spaces are a foot apart, the numerals two feet high and the minute hands – each of which weighs two hundred pounds – fourteen feet long. The huge central rose which fastens the hour and minute hands is the size of a small dining-table.

*   *   *

The old clock which stood here before 'Big Ben' was known as 'Great Tom'. It also has a fascinating history – one aspect of which will serve to round off this chapter rather fittingly.

In the reign of William III a sentry on duty at Windsor Castle was charged with being asleep at his post. He refuted the allegation by claiming that at the time in question – midnight – he had heard the bell at Westminster strike thirteen. The Court Martial rejected his story as preposterous. Fortunately, the man's friends took the trouble to check – and the authorities confirmed that it was true. The man, whose name was Hatfield, was granted the King's Pardon and survived to a hundred and two.

I have a strong suspicion that if the death penalty applied to politicians falling asleep at their posts today, the numbers of all parties would drastically decrease overnight.

This might be no bad thing. At least those remaining would be assured a seat.

CHAPTER TWENTY–TWO

PARLIAMENT

Within an hour of being officially inducted into the House of Commons I received an astounding piece of news. It came as a terrible shock. I was called to the office of the Chief Whip and informed that Barbara Castle, one of the most prominent members of the Opposition front bench, had long been incensed by my views on immigration and proposed that very day to deliver a speech attacking me.

I found this deeply distressing. I had no idea what she might say, and therefore no way of preparing a defence in advance. Added to this, I knew it was established wisdom that to be in too great a haste to deliver one's maiden speech was dangerous. Before putting one's neck into the noose, it was wise to learn something of the lore and traditions attaching to the House. To be manoeuvred into doing so within hours of one's arrival – intimidated by one's new surroundings and deprived of anything but the barest opportunity to prepare notes – was the stuff of which nightmares are made.

Fortunately, even to contemplate launching an attack on a member of such short duration was quite without precedent or parallel. Wiser and more civilized counsels prevailed and Mrs Castle was persuaded by her Whips to withdraw the threat. In my subsequent – and thankfully limited – dealings with her I found her to be an unpleasant and vitriolic woman whom age has mellowed only fractionally.

My new role required me now to juggle my business commitments with my parliamentary responsibilities. I had also to endeavour to spend three weekends out of every four in my Manchester constituency where, among other things, I held surgeries aimed at helping local people with their problems. As Moss Side was deeply cosmopolitan these were many and varied. To begin with, there was a large body of Sikhs, many of whom spoke no English whatsoever. They nevertheless formed a religious brotherhood the history of which dates back to the sixteenth century.

I found their faith to be a curious amalgam of Mohammedanism and Hinduism. The influence of the latter means that they are grouped into countless castes, half social, half religious. Originally there were just four – priests, warriors, farmers and labourers. They have subsequently been sub-divided again and again until it is now impossible to tell the number. Estimates vary between two and three thousand distinct groups. Members of professions such as potters or jewellers tend to form separate castes which amount to trade guilds or unions. Generally speaking, a person may not marry outside his caste nor may he touch or associate with a member of a lower one. Until quite recently, certain very high-caste Hindus felt that they were profaned if even the shadow of a European fell upon them or their food. Where this happened, they were forced to undergo elaborate rites of purification.

My own constituents were nothing like so 'racist'. I met them frequently and they made me welcome at their temple. Here we sat on the floor, men and women segregated and some distance apart. In order to comply with the rule that no one may enter a Sikh temple with their head uncovered, I fished my handkerchief from my pocket. I have no doubt I looked a comical sight – more suited to Brighton beach than a place of worship.

A substance was handed round for us to sample. It resembled brown maize which had been left to soak in water for a fortnight. I could not of course follow the service but found the experience utterly fascinating. A cynical colleague remarked:

'What do you do while they're praying to Allah? Pray for votes I shouldn't wonder.'

* * *

Moss Side also boasted a strong Polish Conservative community. I went among them frequently. I felt an especial affinity towards them. Like many others, I remained profoundly grateful for the contribution made by their airmen in exile during the Second World War.

As a result of this connection, I was made vice-president of the Anglo-Polish Association, a position I still hold. It has headquarters in London's Exhibition Road. On one occasion I attended a function there to hear an address delivered by the Association's president, Lord Carrington.

Five minutes before this was due to start, I was approached by the chairman, who appeared agitated. He explained that Carrington had been delayed in the House by vital parliamentary business. As a result, he would not be able to attend. Would I give the address in his place? As had been the case with the Barbara

Seeking votes. Sikh Temple, Moss Side

Castle incident, my blood ran cold. I had nothing prepared and no time available in which to make any notes. In consequence I was forced to speak extemporaneously. Although the audience appeared to enjoy what they heard, it was, quite frankly, a deeply unpleasant and nerve-wracking experience. I profoundly hope never to be subjected to its like again.

*   *   *

A particularly knotty constituency problem concerned a family of Hong Kong Chinese called Chan Ying Fong, who ran a laundry in Moss Side's Great Western Street. They had five children. In consequence the wife had little time to devote to the business, which was consequently short-staffed. The husband's mother was still in Hong Kong. She had applied for entry into the United Kingdom on several occasions but without success. Could I help? Her residence here was vital. She would be more than happy to look after the children, thus releasing the wife to help her husband in the laundry.

It took many months of letter-writing and persuasion but I was ultimately successful in obtaining an entry visa. This transformed the family's life out of all recognition. As their prices were low, the laundry prospered. It was a source of considerable gratification to me. It must also have been so to the family because they continue to send me a card every Christmas and on my birthday.

With this and similar problems to unravel, I was now kept busier than I had ever thought possible. Consequently, some of my former interests were forced to give ground. My golf handicap of ten became one of the earliest casualties. Willie Whitelaw – a former captain of the Royal and Ancient, who had a handicap of five – was kind enough to commiserate.

I was one of eight members representing Mancunian constituencies. Among the Socialists was the Labour politician, Gerald Kauffman, for whom I never cared. In contrast, I found the brothers Lesley and Harold Lever extremely likeable. Although both held relatively safe Labour seats, neither was in my opinion a Socialist at heart.

Lesley Lever was an eccentric. He was blessed with a facility for attracting publicity which amounted almost to genius. Every member of parliament feels very proprietorial towards his constituency. It is an unwritten rule that one meddles in no other. Yet on those occasions on which I held garden parties or similar functions in Moss Side, Lesley invariably sent a telegram apologising for his inability to attend. He had not of course been invited, but he knew that it was common practice to read such telegrams to the assembled throng. This had the double benefit of keeping his name in the forefront of their minds and establishing him as a man of great politeness and consideration.

For all this, there was no real harm in him. He was a man impossible to dislike. I was deeply saddened when in later life he contracted a debilitating illness and was confined to a wheelchair.

His brother Harold was perhaps the most intelligent of all Labour members. Unlike Lesley, he shunned the limelight. Now Lord Lever, he ultimately found himself a beautiful Lebanese lady who – like her husband – was a millionaire, which Harold, in his dry way, always gave as his chief reason for marrying her.

*   *   *

Initially, like many new members of parliament, I was over-diligent. I sat in the chamber day after day, listening to every debate. This was because – in common with the incredible Mr Toad – I wished 'to know all there was to be know'd'.

```
Charges to pay                                                          No.
   Tariff  £              POST      OFFICE              OFFICE STAMP
   V.A.T. £                TELEGRAM
   Total  £      Prefix.  Time handed in.   Office of origin and Service Instructions.   Words.

RECEIVED
From                                                                   At              m
By            44 12.10 HOUSE OF COMMONS 19             To
                                                       By

        TAYLOR MP  C/P CONSERVATIVE OFFICES 617A WILBRAHAM

        ROAD CHORLTONCUMHARDYMANCHESTER 21 =


        YOUR ATTENDANCE ESSENTIAL 7PM AND 10PM TUESDAY 26TH

        JUNE = PYM +


   ++:COL  617A 21 7PM 10PM TUESDAY 26TH JUNE PYM +

   For free rep     TS 675      phone "TELEGRAMS ENQUIRY" or call, with this form
   at office of                 I be accompanied by this form, and, if possible, the envelope    B or C
```

Three-line whip

I quickly came to realise that this was both a foolish ambition and a great waste of time. I therefore decided to attend only those debates covering subjects of interest either to me or to my constituents – debates to which I might make some useful contribution.

The remainder of my time was spent in a room, shared with six colleagues, at the top of the House, overlooking the river, where I toiled to dispose of the mountainous pile of correspondence which forms part of the everyday life of all members of parliament.

I had also to spend time in my constituency, planting rose trees and opening fetes. From time to time I was also called upon to open schools. On one such occasion – at Wilbraham High School and for the benefit of a number of Labour councillors present, who then had control of Moss Side at local level – I mentioned how sad I found the widespread deterioration of standards within the educational system. I mourned the loss of the grammar school and the growth at its expense of that monstrous hybrid, the comprehensive.

I added that in our quest for 'equality' we were in danger of neglecting the talented at the expense of those less fortunate. Something had to be done for them too. But by inflicting rigid dogma of this nature on the education system we inevitably produced a low morale which permeated every corner, affecting even the teachers. It perpetuated a vicious spiral. Demoralised children produced demoralised teachers – and thereby even more hopelessly demoralised children.

Twenty years later, standards have deteriorated even further. Tests have shown that one in six children beneath the age of seven can barely read. Within this age group more than a hundred thousand are incapable of spelling bat, cat or mat.

Martin Turner, an educational psychologist commissioned in 1990 by the government, reported that:

'such a striking down-turn in reading scores has not been encountered before in peacetime in public education in Britain. It represents a conspiracy of silence among education experts and bureaucrats.'

I believe the problem rests, initially, with those who have control of educational policy at grass roots level. When Annis Garfield, a Cambridge graduate employed by the Examinations Board to mark papers at A–level recently applied for a job as a teacher, she was rejected by no fewer than five colleges as 'too old-fashioned'. It was suggested that she might better look for a job as a dinner-lady. A sixth college asked her 'what ethnic minority literature' she had read and seemed 'unreceptive' when she said she preferred Jane Austen and Shakespeare.

Mrs Garfield has a Classics degree and twelve years' experience as an examiner in English literature. Her father was president of Wolfson College, Oxford. Her mother wrote a number of books on reading. Her brother is the headmaster of a preparatory school.

Mrs Garfield is a courageous woman. She believes in practising what she preaches. When she found her daughter, Emmie, was falling behind at school due to the methods employed, she tore up the text books and resolved to teach her herself. As a result, by the age of six, Emmie had a reading age of eleven.

*　　*　　*

My first real sense of parliamentary occasion was provided by Budget Day. The House filled up very early. Those unable to find seats squatted on the steps. Many Conservative members wore morning dress. The flamboyant Labour politician, Leo Abse, came in a stove-pipe hat, which some aspect of the dress code – introduced no doubt in the Victorian era, and never repealed – continued to permit.

The day was a memorable one, not least because it produced my first parliamentary gaffe. Being anxious not to miss a minute of the proceedings, and having

Opening New Wilbraham High School

learned that it was possible to reserve a seat for a single day, I attended the House very early and collected a ticket from a box just inside the Chamber. Not wishing to appear presumptious, this I placed on the top seat of the third row below the gangway.

The moment the House opened I rushed to my place, my exhilaration only slightly tempered by the fact that a number of elderly members who came in shortly afterwards appeared to look at me rather oddly.

I discovered the reason when an extremely distinguished old gentleman approached, fixed me with a stare and said: 'I have occupied that seat for twenty-five years'. He was Sir Thomas More – a descendant of the saint of the same name. He had not inherited all of his ancestors' traits of forbearance. In terms more commonly reserved for dealing with children and simpletons, he informed me that the entire row in which I was sitting was, by hallowed precedent, reserved for members of the Privy Council. I fled in embarrassment and confusion to the backbenches.

181

*   *   *

On Tuesday 10 April 1962 I delivered my maiden speech. By tradition this had to be politically non-contentious. Consequently I chose to deal with the subject of direct taxation, a matter then very much in the news. I spoke for twelve minutes. I said that motivating people to earn money whilst at the same time balancing the need to prosper the community has always posed a knotty problem. The highest tax bracket then stood at almost ninety percent. Consequently there was little inducement for people to work harder. An umarried businessman earning £10,000 a year lost forty percent of this to tax. Yet a similar man, with a wife and three children, could earn £700 a year without attracting any tax whatsoever. This seemed to me quite wrong.

A climate had developed in which tax evasion had come to be viewed as no more than a minor misdemeanour and even, perhaps, rather clever. I felt that we needed a fiscal system which promoted a full week's work whilst at the same time lightening the impact on the Friday pay-packet. This could only be done by cutting tax rates.

If this meant an immediate loss to the Treasury, so be it. It would ultimately be compensated for by increased productivity. It was called the law of increasing returns. As such, and some years later, it was adopted by Margaret Thatcher as part of her policy of de-regulating the economy in favour of market forces. It anticipated the very real need for politicians to take the people into their confidence.

*   *   *

In accordance with my resolve to participate only in debates in which either I or my constituents had a special interest, I next spoke to the House on 3 March 1964. The subject under review was the Air Defence Estimates – the R.A.F.'s budgetary requirements for the coming year. The debate was marked by verbal assaults and accusations from all sides of the House. By the time I rose to speak a little before eight o'clock in the evening, it had been raging for the best part of four hours. The principal bone of contention had been the massive cost of aircraft and ancillary equipment – some of it running into many millions of pounds. My own point, while not of the same magnitude was, I believe, of equal importance – if only because it concerned men rather than machines.

For some years, servicemen posted abroad had been made extravagant promises regarding the quarters they would occupy. This was especially so in the case

182

of married personnel. Yet married quarters were everywhere at a premium. In bases such as Malta, Gibraltar and Aden, where servicemen and civilians formed a mixed community, it was felt that the latter tended to receive preferential treatment. This caused considerable resentment and lowered morale. Where married quarters were available they were often sub-standard. Due to archaic administrative procedures which entailed much form-filling, it could be as long as eight or ten weeks before a wife was able to join her husband.

A part of the reason for this dearth was financial. Married quarters cost three times as much to maintain as quarters occupied by a single man. This was a curious anomaly when even the Inland Revenue's tax allowances conceded that two can live more cheaply than one.

During a visit to Aden as part of a parliamentary delegation, I had witnessed the problem for myself. Many of the quarters were wholly dependent on air-conditioning. Consequently, the windows had not been made to open. When the air conditioning broke down, the fug became unbearable – far worse than if air conditioning had never been installed. Other quarters had air conditioning in one room only. This tended to lead families to live and sleep together in one very small area of a dwelling.

I appreciated that hiring accommodation could be expensive. Buying and maintaining property was even more so. There was a general consensus among the servicemen themselves that the situation might best be resolved by making tours of duty considerably shorter – limited perhaps to twelve months – and that families should not accompany.

*   *   *

I was on my feet on 29 April 1965, to query aspects of the Manchester Corporation Bill. This was designed to give the local authority powers to redevelop the city. It was a thoroughly good Bill in principle but went far beyond what was necessary. It contained a number of provisions far removed from the needs of simple town-planners.

Hidden among the clauses and the legal jargon were a number of rather murky aspects of Socialism at its most sinister. For instance, under Clause 48 the authority was to be empowered to reserve to itself a guaranteed supply of solid fuel. In order to do so it proposed to subsidise the manufacturers – thereby encouraging them 'to increase output'. This could only be done by a sharp (but undefined) increase to the rates. The rate-payers had not, of course, been consulted. Neither had they been asked whether they wished to have solid fuel forced upon them. I was able to tell the House that many of my own constituents found that solid fuel burned poorly and emitted obnoxious fumes. The price too was unpopular, not least with pensioners.

Could Clause 48 be a clandestine attempt to introduce nationalisation via the back door? Nor could I see why the local authority needed to underwrite private enterprise in the first place. Provided the market is available, industry – in whatever shape or form – increases its productivity automatically.

Clause 9 I found equally sinister. It allowed for the local authority to enter into agreements with developers on ridiculously advantageous terms. It was in contravention of the 1962 Town and Country Planning Act and was both impudent and wholly unprecedented. No such clause had ever been introduced into a Bill before.

*   *   *

My next speech, in June 1965, was also intended to guard against the abuse of privilege. It focused on the impact which the immigrant population was having on our educational system. At this date there were some areas of London, including Paddington, where there were no more than two or three white children to a class. The situation in Birmingham and Liverpool was in some instances just as bad. In Bradford, certain schools had immigrant pupils exceeding fifty percent.

I believed then – and I believe now – that the indigenous population was in danger of swamping the educational scene. It was not simply a matter of numbers but the rate at which those numbers appeared to be increasing. In Manchester there were four times as many five-year-old immigrant children as eleven-year-olds.

Many of these had been born abroad. They spoke little or no English and as such required special help if they were fully to integrate into the community – help they were not receiving. Figures showed that far and away the most backward children were of West Indian origin. Many spoke only a kind of unintelligible patois based – ironically – on eighteenth-century English.

These views were not of course fashionable or popular and I have in the past been described as a racist. Yet the solution I proposed to this specific problem was not to restrict immigration even further but to import teachers who had a closer affinity with children of their own race. Unfortunately, although more than adequately qualified, they had inherited a similar problem to those whom they were required to teach. Many could not be understood even by the officers sent to interview them.

Due to the Labour government's misguided policies, during the years 1961–63 more than half a million immigrants flooded into Britain from every corner of the globe. Not all of them were coloured, although the majority of them were.

En masse I believe they stood in the van of an inexorable tide which is destined to change the face of an entire society beyond recall.

There were ancillary problems. Many immigrants lived at what can only be described as near slum level. They tended to congregate in cities plagued by acute housing shortages. The resultant overcrowding tended to place them high on the housing lists of local authorities. This did nothing to generate good relations with the indigenous population.

As a result of the utterly disastrous policy instigated by Harold Wilson's Labour government – and the inevitable children it generated – the maternity wards of local hospitals were soon overflowing with immigrant wives, further aggravating the problem of bed shortages. Immigrant unemployment stood at three times the national average.

This said, I was very aware that many immigrant families were extremely anxious to integrate – and I said so in the course of my speech. A significant number attended church on a regular basis – far more than their British counterparts, whom in this respect they put to shame. By and large, their children tended to be well cared for and beautifully turned out. They were generally well behaved.

Nonetheless, there were certain facts which could not be gainsaid. We were desperate to integrate those whom we had taken in. This desire was not always shared. It seemed to me that there was a proportion of immigrants who, whilst seeking – and usually finding – a better way of life, wished to retain their culture exclusively. They made no effort to learn English, adopted none of the customs or attitudes of the country of their adoption.

Although I had devoted the greater part of my speech to the specific subject of the educational needs of immigrants, I divined that after I had been speaking for about a quarter of an hour Denis Howell – who as Labour's Joint Under–Secretary of State for Education was scheduled to reply – was growing extremely restless. I said:

'I gather that the Minister feels that I should conclude. I thought it reasonable to speak for twenty minutes'.

I sat down. In characteristically arrogant manner, Howell rose and said:

'Not if the Hon. Gentleman wants a good answer'.

I retorted:

'I wrote to the Hon. Member and said I should speak for twenty minutes. I said that if this were not satisfactory we could make other arrangements. I have had no reply.'

This Howell completely ignored, preferring to launch into a personal diatribe which was both offensive and factually inaccurate. He said:

The Hon. Member for Manchester, Moss Side, came very near to abuse of the decencies of the House in that he asked for an Adjournment debate on the problems of the education of immigrants and went on to make a political speech on almost every subject under the sun dealing with immigration except education'.

This was not only appallingly bad English but deeply unfair.

He continued in the same vein:

'If the Hon. Member did a disservice, I do not want to follow him into a general political argy-bargy at this time of night' (eight minutes past midnight, no great hour for politicians).

He then proceeded to do just that. In the course of the next ten minutes he sought to develop a number of shambolic arguments which purported to show that the current problem was due not so much to the Labour goverment's 'open door' policy on immigration but to some indefinable consequence of what he continuously referred to as the preceding 'thirteen years of Tory rule'.

To everyone's relief, at twenty-two minutes past twelve o'clock, the Speaker, John Selwyn-Lloyd, adjourned the House.

*   *   *

During my time in the House I came to know many Speakers. Selwyn-Lloyd kept order in a statesman-like manner but, being a former lawyer, worked very much to precedent. As such he revered the established order of things fractionally too much. He had very little sense of humour but interested himself in such disparate good causes as the Methodist Homes for the Aged and the Liverpool School of Tropical Medicine

After holding the post for five years, he was succeeded as Speaker by Dr. Horace Maybury-King, a very different type of man. He lacked any real aptitude for the job, not least because of what can only be termed his intense sociability. By tradition, the Speaker leaves the chair in the hands of his deputy between the hours of 7 and 10 p.m., when he retires to entertain visiting dignitaries. Horace enjoyed this aspect of the job very much – perhaps a little too much – with the result that from time to time he would return to the chamber looking rather the worse for wear and with his wig slightly askew.

George Thomas, now Viscount Tonypandy, reigned as Speaker from 1976 to 1983. He was very much his own man. His voice had an attractive Welsh lilt and his charm lay in his imperturbability. He had a genius for employing an under-

186

stated sense of humour to defuse situations which might otherwise have quickly deteriorated. He is one of the kindest men who has ever lived. Glenys and I are privileged to count him among our friends.

For the past seven years the Speaker has been Bernard 'Jack' Wetherill. By a curious coincidence, his father donated a golfing cup to the City Livery Golfing Society to be competed for by veterans – a cup which I have won on four occasions. It may be that I have been assisted in doing so by one of the rules of that competition: that entrants are entitled to add half a stroke to their handicap for every year they have managed to survive beyond the age of sixty-six.

In November 1984 'Jack' Wetherill wrote to me to congratulate me on my latest win. He said:

'Because of his gammy leg, my father's golfing style was always unorthodox, and he used to select carefully the courses on which he played, so that he could ride round on a bicycle! Apart from his business, golf was his passion and it is very good to know that he is still remembered in the Cup which he presented so many years ago to his favourite Golfing Society!'

As I am sure 'Jack' Wetherill would be the first to attest, the role of the Speaker today is a thankless one. When I first entered the House a sense of decorum was everywhere displayed. Dress was subdued and there was very little rowdiness. The authority of the Speaker was absolute. Although debates were often heated, they seldom developed into a full-scale row. Eloquence, nowadays, is almost a thing of the past. The most that can be hoped for is articulateness. With the advent of television, publicity-seeking members have entered into their own. Many now actively plan stunts some way in advance in order to get themselves suspended. They do so for no better reason than that it keeps them in eye of a public which – if they knew it – detests them. I rate them on the same level as certain modern tennis players.

*   *   *

Each year the calendar of the House sets aside a number of Fridays on which members can present a Bill of their own choosing. When I was fortunate enough to be successful in the ballot, I decided to introduce a Bill which sought to increase the previously fixed pensions of public service and armed forces personnel, many of whom, due to the increased cost of living, were experiencing quite appalling hardship. It was really an attempt to introduce what are now called index-linked pensions. As such it was a significant Bill and one which I am pleased to have been able to seek to promote in its course through the House.

A member of the Royal Air Force, who retired on a fixed pension in 1961, found that seven years later his equivalent in rank was able to leave the service on a pension forty percent higher. I received a letter from a widow – who missed her pension by just four days after twenty-five years of happily-married life. A seventy-eight-year-old teacher, whose pension had been allocated many years previously, wrote – with great pathos – to explain that she was discovering that: 'malnutrition is no great respecter of persons'.

A policeman, who retired in 1955 after 25 years' service on a fixed pension of £303 found that within thirteen years the real value of this had been cut by almost half. This erosion seemed to me deeply iniquitous. It was made the worse by the mental anguish it entailed. Recipients often spent many months – and sometimes years – coming to terms with the fact that the situation was 'under review'. Any long-distance retrospective adjustment might well depend on the degree of public awareness they could muster in their defence. In most instances this was slight.

For the most part they were forced to suffer years of anguish as their pensions were inexorably – and frighteningly – eroded by inflation. My own proposals were that a commission be set up to ensure that reviews took place at regular intervals, were completed within a fixed period, and tied pensions to the cost of living.

At the time I promoted the Bill the Labour Party was in power. They cast a jaundiced eye over my proposals and rejected them, albeit only by a mere fourteen votes.

*　　*　　*

Perhaps the most heated debate in which I participated occurred on 14 July 1969. It concerned boundary changes to eight Manchester constituencies, including that of Huyton, held by the prime minister, Harold Wilson. I had no sooner risen to speak than the temporary chairman of the House, Sir Barnett Janner, was forced to call for order.

When I was able to continue, I expressed support for the findings of the Boundary Commission. As it would cause two Labour seats to become one I could hardly have done otherwise, despite the fact that it also brought about changes to my own constituency which ultimately cost me my seat. However, I was careful to point out that the Commission's findings should be accepted in toto, not piecemeal.

For purely political reasons, this the Labour government was loathe to do. At one point I briefly crossed swords with Jim Callaghan. I told him I considered the government was disenfranchising voters in a thoroughly nasty manner. I concluded:

'I hope that the electors will remember that it is this Government, and the prime minister – who is not here – who are unscrupulous. I hope that they will realise that the prime minister is absolutely outstanding. During this century there have been only two men in the same class – himself and Horatio Bottomley.'

This was not well received on the government benches and a Labour member rose to say that Opposition feelings seemed always to run high when the subject of Huyton was introduced into debate. It generated a good deal of spite. At this a member of the Conservative opposition rose to counter:

'Our spite is not for Huyton but the man who represents it'.

*   *   *

One of the last debates in which I featured occurred on 3 February 1972 and concerned the Horserace Totalisator and Betting Levy Board Bill. The government was seeking to decide whether the tote should be allowed to collapse or whether it was in the general interest to maintain it. In either event, legislation was required.

I explained that I had no special reason to love bookmakers – if only because every time I plunged on to a sure thing I had cause to regret the investment. However, it seemed to me that the Bill had been drafted in such a manner as to operate against the interests of the bookies. There was a clause whereby it was proposed to allow the tote to open betting shops using loans guaranteed by the government. This virtually amounted to the Levy Board giving the tote money.

This was worrying, not least because it appeared that the tote had run a number of similar shops in the past. I was concerned to know whether or not this had been a satisfactory venture. Had the shops now been sold – and on what terms? If the tote, as I had heard, was really planning to open something in the region of five hundred shops, this would require a massive investment of government money and – as they were plunging into competition with experts – against no very certain return. My own inclination was to permit the tote to be administered by a consortium of bookmakers; or to allow them to run tote business through their own shops. The Bill was endlessly altered and amended before ultimately passing into the Statute Book.

CHAPTER TWENTY–THREE

A HIGHLY EXCLUSIVE CLUB

In the course of time I developed an interest in some of the internal procedures of the House, including the role played by various Committees. These were open forums at which outside parties objecting to a Bill were given the opportunity to put their case to the government officials charged with prosecuting it. Where the matter under review had far-reaching ramifications, there were often large numbers of objectors. Many of them chose to be represented by counsel. Consequently, the audience tended to be littered with legal gentlemen whose white wigs stood out like snowflakes against a background of dark cloud. The proceedings were conducted somewhat along the lines of a court. Like a court, the findings of a Standing Committee were seldom overturned.

I was ultimately elevated to chairing some of those committees relating to Private Bills. These enabled me to have a genuine influence over the way in which change was structured. I found this considerably more effective and fulfilling than the mere delivery of a speech on the floor of the House – the contents of which, in all probability, would be forgotten before the raising of the mace.

Two such Committees were abruptly terminated. The first was appointed in 1965 to examine the merits of a Bill introduced by Sidney Silverman.

Sidney Silverman was a diminutive politician fervently opposed to capital punishment. To this end he introduced a Private Member's Bill in the hope of having it abolished. I was not in favour of this and said as much. I felt that for parliament to railroad a Bill through the House on such a vital issue and without consulting the public was quite wrong.

I knew from personal experience that public opinion was very much against the Bill. I myself had received some fifty letters from constituents, including prison officers, policemen, their wives – and even a convicted murderer – pleading that hanging be retained, if only for murders committed in the furtherance of theft. I had received only one document in favour – a slip of paper on which had been written: 'Thou shalt not kill'.

As a member of the Committee, I was in the middle of setting out my arguments when J. C. Jennings, the Chairman, brought his gavel down sharply on the table, signalling its recess until the following morning.

That evening – appreciating the importance of the issue – the government decided to bring the Bill out of committee stage and debate it on the floor of the House. Consequently, when we arrived to resume proceedings the following morning, we found ourselves out of a job and the Committee was disbanded.

The second Committee to meet a premature end had been set up in 1968 to investigate the viability of constructing the Channel Tunnel. It was a contentious subject to which there were expected to be many objections. I was selected to chair this Committee and made what at the time appeared to be the very prudent decision to book the room in which we were due to sit for a period of at least two weeks.

The night prior to the opening of the proceedings, the government called a general election. As the Bill had not reached the point at which it had become enshrined in law, the issue of the Tunnel was shelved. It was to be many years – and long after my departure from parliament – before it was raised again.

*   *   *

The House then had many characters. One of the greatest was unquestionably Gerald Nabarro, the member for Kidderminster, a constituency which, it could be said, he did much to put on the map. He had a flamboyant manner, a fine bushy handlebar moustache and a passion for motor cars. When I first entered the House the present underground car park had not been built and I used frequently to see one or other of Gerald's three Rolls Royces standing about the courts and alleyways of the Palace, distinguished by their 'cherished' number-plates: NAB 1, NAB 2 and NAB 3. On Budget Day he took great delight in vyeing with Leo Abse, on the other side of the House, in the matter of eccentric dress.

Nabarro would have been the first to endorse the theory that in addition to being a great chamber of debate, the Palace of Westminster is also a highly exclusive club. In my time its members socialised on a regular basis.

Thanks to the generosity of a French lady who remained inordinately grateful for the Allies' liberation of her homeland, we annually played a golf match on a course she owned at Deauville. She was also the proprietress of the Casino at Deauville and we were invited each year to send out three teams of parliamentarians to challenge their counterparts in the French assembly at tennis, golf and sailing. With the exception of our travelling expenses, we paid for nothing during the three or four days of our stay.

For several years I was privileged to be included in the golf team. I found that the conduct of the French deputies often left a good deal to be desired. Not to put too fine a point on it, they cheated at every available opportunity. On one occasion, having driven his ball into a bunker, the deputy concerned entered the bunker to play it. I observed his club flash five times in the sunlight before the ball emerged. He quickly followed, confidently announcing: 'Played two'.

For the most part we tended to ignore this kind of conduct, reasoning that the result of the match was of no lasting consequence. The goodwill it generated was.

Despite this and various other forms of sharp practice, I once managed to win the singles competition. As the result was determined by aggregating the players' net scores over the two days of the match, this was a source of some pride to me. Sadly, these enjoyable trips ceased with their sponsor's death.

Each year, on the last day of the Queen's Shoot at Bisley, a match is held between members of the House of Commons and members of the House of Lords. I was fortunate enough to be selected for the Commons every year. In spite of their grouse-moor heritage, and the regular inclusion in their team of Lord Swansea, a former Commonwealth Games gold-medallist, the Lords tended to win only about one year in three.

I recall that in 1962 one of the members of the Lords' team was Lord Lucan. His dim-witted grandfather had been responsible for misinterpreting Lord Raglan's ambiguous order which resulted in the Charge of the Light Brigade at Balaclava. He himself was later found guilty in his absence by a coroner's jury of murdering the family nanny, Sandra Rivett – whom in the darkness he is thought to have mistaken for his wife. Given such a history of family incompetence one might reasonably have expected Lord Lucan to have shot himself in the foot. In fact, he returned a score of 87, only three points behind my own.

We generally fired over three separate distances, the targets being ranged at two, five and six hundred yards. They appeared very small. However, one year I did manage with the regulation seven shots to achieve five bulls and two inners at a range of five hundred yards. The year following I came within a whisker of achieving the best score of my life. At six hundred yards I registered five bulls and two inners, giving me thirty-three points out of a possible thirty-five. But shooting over five hundred yards I mistakenly fired one shot at a target which was not mine . . . and the chance was gone, probably now for ever.

It was a Lucanesque error and for me very much out of character. As such, it continues to rankle.

*   *   *

During my years in the House I was able to extend the range of leisure activities available to members by founding the Parliamentary Flying Club. I did so not only to promote an interest in flying as a pastime but in the hope that it would promote the subject generally. It seemed to me that whenever the Minister for Air addressed the House his audience was abysmally ignorant of the content of his speech.

This was certainly true in my case. I decided to remedy the matter. I took lessons at the Aeronautical College at Cranfield.

Piloting the aircraft I found relatively easy. Having to return to school, at the age of sixty, and learn the principles of flight, aeronautics and navigation proved much more difficult. I nevertheless stuck at it. In due course I was rewarded with my private pilot's licence. Perhaps because of my age, the Press picked up the story and it received wide publicity. As a result I was invited to become a member of the Guild of Air Pilots.

Together with Commander Anthony Courtney – the only other member of the House to hold a current pilot's licence – I founded the Parliamentary Flying Club. We recruited members and acquired the use of a Beagle Airdale aircraft.

Ultimately, Anthony Courtney turned out to be a rather sad individual. In addition to his parliamentary activities, he ran a business which imported goods from the countries of the Eastern Bloc. He loved Russia and went there frequently. On one trip he noticed that British diplomats were driven around by Russians. In Britain, Russian diplomats were chauffeured by their own nationals. This seemed to him quite wrong if only because – as he later told the House – 'It means the Russians have a friend in the car, the British a spy'.

This remark deeply angered powerful factions in Moscow.

I received some intimation of what was to follow when, during a reception at the Czechoslovakian Embassy in London, I was informed that the Russian Ambassador wished to speak to me. He said: 'I understand that Commander Courtney and yourself are planning to attend the Moscow Air Show by flying there in a private aircraft'.

He stated this not as a question but as a fact. Russian intelligence had clearly been at work.

He continued: 'I also understand that you intend to fly there in a small aircraft which you will pilot yourself'. He gave me an icy smile. 'This we do not recommend. You may easily lose your way. You might wander into restricted areas where we have military installations'. He gave me a second icy smile. 'I am sure you take my point.'

I did. The inference was clear. We would be shot down.

'However, if you would care to come to Russia aboard a civil airliner, we will make you most welcome. Your friend, Commander Courtney, is persona non grata.' He waved his hand in a gesture of dismissal. 'You may tell him that'.

In fact, Anthony was allowed back into the country. At the time I wondered why. The answer wasn't long in coming. Shortly after arriving – perhaps in the circumstances too shortly – he made the acquaintance of a pretty girl. She invited him back to her flat. They made love. The entire thing was photographed and filmed by the K.G.B. They sent copies to Courtney's wife, to the prime minister, and to the chairman of the poor man's constituency committee. His wife divorced him, his constituency disowned him and he went out of business.

*   *   *

Courtney was one of many casualties of the Cold War. All members of parliament were specifically warned against accepting invitations to cocktail parties issued by any of the London embassies belonging to countries of the Eastern Bloc. Such invitations arrived on my desk at regular intervals, perhaps every three or four months. Being very much my own man, when I received one inviting me to a private lunch with the First Secretary at the Russian Embassy I informed the Whip's Office that I proposed accepting.

The event always proved something of an anti-climax. My host was urbane and civilised. Our conversation covered a wide range of topics. The food was excellent, the wine superb. We were joined by no Mata Haris nor was any foreign substance slipped into my drink. I was nonetheless acutely aware that I was playing a dangerous game and that my host was probing for any weakness in my personality which might be exploited to his country's advantage.

I do not flatter myself that I was the only member of parliament singled out for such treatment. Many similar invitations were sent out. With the example of Anthony Courtney before them, most M.P.s either refused or came accompanied by their wives. It has been well said that 'he who dines with the Devil had best bring a long spoon'.

I found this out for myself when in 1967, as part of a delegation of eight, I was appointed a delegate to the inter-parliamentary annual conference in Paris. This was held in the National Assembly and was attended by delegates from sixty-three nations.

I was preceded to the rostrum by a Russian. In the course of his speech he made a slighting reference to the British system of colonization – a system of which, he added, we should be heartily ashamed. He rather foolishly held his own country up as a role-model. 'Russia has never colonized anyone.'

When my turn came to speak, I pointed out that there were many among the assembled delegates who might consider the manner in which Russia has treated those of its neighbours now reduced to the status of satellites as even more disgraceful.

The Russian delegates listened to this in stolid and stony silence. They became even more withdrawn when I broached the subject of aid to the under-developed nations of the world, on which their record was abominable.

I thought no more of the matter. The conference ended, I returned to England. But from that day forward I received no further invitations to wine and dine at the London embassies of the Eastern Bloc.

The KGB had written me off as a bad debt.

* * *

The inter-parliamentary conference at Paris had been convened to discuss the problem of aid to developing countries. This was a subject in which I had a keen interest and on which I held strong views.

Together with many of the delegates from other countries, I was anxious to see as much as one percent of each of the so-called developed countries' gross national product devoted to aid. However, this would not be easy. With sixty-three participating nations, I had little doubt there would be sixty-three differing interpretations of 'gross national product'.

I was sure that where aid was concerned, the secret of success lay in setting reasonable targets. Provided long-term progress was made, it hardly mattered if these were occasionally not attained. 'Too little too late' had become something of a political cliché in discussions concerning aid. I felt we should not allow ourselves to be depressed by it. 'Too little' was better than nothing at all. The economies of developed countries had been built up slowly and over many centuries. It was natural that the under-developed ones were in somewhat more of a hurry, but this sometimes produced dangers of its own.

I had been disturbed to learn that the conference had tabled a resolution calling for 'a pure redistribution of wealth'. This, I felt, was naively idealistic. Redistributing existing wealth to countries unused to handling money was as fruitless as a rich man giving away his fortune to a child. Then, as now, what we needed to do was to educate the under-developed countries so that they were able to generate wealth in their own right and by means of their own skills.

I have never felt that any one country was under any legal obligation to provide aid to another. There might or might not be moral grounds. That largely depended on the financial plight – and political attitude – of the country concerned. It was clear that whilst the deprived nations were making progress, their wealthier neighbours were progressing even faster, thus causing the gap to widen rather than to close.

The entire question was a fraught and delicate one. On the one hand we wished to help. But aid had to be furnished in a co-ordinated manner. The overriding consideration had to be the needs of the recipient. There were times when this would be regarded as unwarranted interference in another country's affairs. Our job was to reconcile these anomalies.

*   *   *

The inter-parliamentary conference at Paris was one of many which I attended as a delegate over the years. The first, in my days as a parliamentary candidate, was to Strasbourg. With the exception of myself, all eight members were old Etonians. As Eton and Harrow then furnished the Conservative party with a significant number of parliamentary contenders, this was not as unusual as it at first appears.

A third delegation was to Iceland at the time of the so-called Cod War, when British trawlers were accused of violating Icelandic waters. It was always intended that we should return; but when the situation became more acute, the second excursion was abandoned.

Having always felt that if you have a problem you should talk about it, I was convinced that this was the wrong approach. Consequently, my wife and I decided to go as a delegation of two. The Icelanders appreciated the gesture. They proved friendly and very hospitable. We found they lived only along the foggy coasts, the centre of the country being three thousand feet of perpetual ice.

Only one seventh of the land was inhabitable. The remainder was a barren and weird hinterland of boiling mud springs and geysers which hurled torrents of water high in the air. The great volcanoes were capable of stupendous eruptions and produced earthquakes which wiped out great tracts of cultivated land.

The Icelanders still remembered the fearful eruption of Mount Laki in 1783. It destroyed four-fifths of the livestock, devastated much of the land and – together with the resulting famines and epidemics – killed over one-fifth of the population. Although the surrounding oceans make Iceland warmer than its latitude would suggest, we found the climate not unlike our own.

The major difference of course is that in January Iceland is never light and in July never dark. As we were privileged to be there in the latter month, we witnessed the most extraordinary setting of the sun I have ever seen. It simply dipped below the horizon for five minutes before rising to begin another day.

Parliamentary Delegation Greeted at RAF Bruggen, Germany, 1964

*   *   *

Shortly after our visit to Iceland, I was sent as part of yet another delegation to the Southern Arabian Federation. Beneath a vast marquee in the Hadhramaut Desert, we were entertained to a great banquet. There was an enormous amount of food – although none of us was particularly delighted to be offered sheep's eyes, which

197

our hosts considered a great delicacy. We ate with our fingers, there being no knives or forks.

I watched the Sheiks with some curiosity. For good or ill, Arabs are what Arabia has made them. Our hosts occupied gaunt principalities composed mainly of billowy sand-dunes within the frightful Ruba–el–Khali or 'Empty Quarter'. As the name suggests, this was a vast ocean of well-nigh lifeless sand. Until 1931 no European had ever crossed it. The first man to do so was Bertrand Thomas. He made the remarkable nine-hundred-mile journey in fifty-eight days.

A Sheik is chosen for his power to rule. His subjects obey him blindly. Life is considered of little consequence and therefore death is never far away. An Arab ruler – as we are now re-discovering – is at once civilized and a brute.

A great civilization flourished in Arabia ten centuries before Christ. There is a strong tradition of hospitality. A stranger must always be fed and sheltered. However, when he departs, his host may follow and rob him – but not until four days have elapsed, the period which is required for the last of the host's food to leave the guest's body.

Is the 'Arab mind' really that much different from our own? I believe that it is. Each of the Sheiks approached each member of the delegation by turn. Oil had been discovered in Bahrain. Our hosts claimed that their soothsayers had told them that their own territories possessed vast untapped quantities of the stuff. Naively, they requested we use our influence with the government to persuade the British to provide sufficient financial resources to tap it – the profits to be shared on an equal basis.

In the course of our visit we were taken to see the Federation's new parliament building. This was constantly referred to as 'a great symbol of democracy'. It had been constructed as a smaller version of the Palace of Westminster. There was, however, one important difference. At Westminster, there are two voting lobbies, one for the 'Ayes' and one for the 'Noes'. The Federation's parliament had only one – for the 'Ayes'. Arabs do not brook dissent.

*   *   *

Why it should be I cannot say, but many of the delegations to which I was privy had an eerie knack of arriving in a country either just prior to – or just after – the eruption of trouble. This was especially true of our visit to Czechoslovakia in 1968.

We arrived during the period which afterwards became known as 'the Prague Spring'. The preceding January the Czechoslovak Communist Party had produced a new leader in Alexander Dubcek who had a reputation as a reformer and – in Eastern European terms – a liberal.

A sharp-featured man, he was the first Slovak to lead the party. This was of some significance because then, as now, Czechoslovakia was a country divided. We found that the Czechs were largely concentrated in industry. They congregated in towns. They were as fun-loving as the regime would permit and were fond of alcohol. The Slovaks tended to be country folk. They were employed in agriculture and ancillary pursuits. They were somewhat dour and lived in primitive conditions.

Dubcek had ousted the pro-Moscow stalwart, Antonin Novotny. He was expected to ease the heavy-handed controls on the press and encourage more candour in political discussion. All this duly came to pass. To our delight, we found there was real news in the newspapers – and on television and radio as well. There was exposure of corruption in high places, criticism of housing conditions, low wages, bureaucratic ineptitude and oppression.

However, in the May following, alarmed by this liberalising tide, Moscow began moving tanks through Poland and East Germany to the Czech border. On 22 August they struck. As the tanks rolled into Prague, people could be seen climbing on to them and arguing with the men inside. Others bared their breasts in defiance before the advancing gun barrels. It was deeply moving, but it was not of the slightest use. Russian officers entered the headquarters of the Czechoslovak Communist Party and took Alexander Dubcek away. As they did so, he cried:

'How could they do this to me? My entire life has been devoted to co-operation with the Soviet Union. This is my own profound personal tragedy.'

This was true. But then Dubcek was neither the first nor the last to bate the Russian bear to his cost; and tragedy takes many forms. One of the worst must surely be dire personal poverty. I encountered this frequently during my delegational travels.

It was especially marked in Jamaica, where I found primitive corrugated-iron shacks nestling in the lee of some of the most luxurious hotels in the world. All forms of employment were extremely labour-intensive. Mechanisation was possible but not encouraged. To have introduced it on a large scale would have been to create mass unemployment.

*   *   *

True to my habit of visiting a country at a period of turbulence, I arrived on a delegational visit to Malta the winter prior to Dom Mintoff being swept to power. Despite the heroic assistance it had rendered Britain during the Second World War,

Malta's history thereafter had been dogged by trouble and dispute. Most of it had to do with money.

In April 1958 Dom Mintoff had resigned the office of prime minister in protest at Britain limiting aid to the island to five million pounds. The British governor assumed command and declared a state of emergency. In 1961 the Colonial Secretary, Iain Macleod, announced that the island would be returned to self-government. In fact, in March 1962 it was granted full independence.

Nine years later, in January 1967, the then prime minister, Borg Olivier, hinted that Britain's forces on the island were no longer welcome. In June 1971 Dom Mintoff's Socialists were returned to power. Mintoff immediately scrapped the ten-year defence treaty with Britain. Talks were instigated but collapsed after Mintoff demanded twenty million pounds as an annual rent for British bases. As a consequence NATO was forced to pull its Mediterranean headquarters out of the island.

Our delegation spent a morning with Mintoff. I personally found him to be not only anti-British but anti-Tory. He held sway over his kingdom like some medieval despot. His policies all but ruined the economy.

In contrast, the island itself was a delight. It had been a British possession since 1798. From the British navy's point of view it was of intense strategic importance.

The country people, who cultivated tiny farms terraced into the hillside, were descendants of the ancient Phoenicians who had colonized Malta more than a thousand years before Christ. They spoke a dialect of mixed Phoenician, Arabic and Latin origin. The townsfolk were an admixture of Italians, Greeks, Turks, Jews and Arabs.

I might have remained in politics beyond 1974. I would not conceal that I have always wished – to quote a phrase from a bygone age – 'to get on'. There is no point to life unless it involves progression in every sphere of life.

At Westminster, due largely to circumstances over which I had no great influence, progress was virtually impossible.

For reasons which are entirely valid, those seeking ministerial office must demonstrate their impartiality and immunity from partisan influence by eschewing any serious involvement in business. As the sole proprietor of a relatively small accountancy firm, this I was unable to do. It remains a source of great regret to me.

By the time the General Election of 1974 arrived I had fought no fewer than seven such battles, some in my capacity as a parliamentary candidate, rather more as a sitting member. In order to understand the changes I had lived through during my time in the House it is necessary to look at these in a little detail.

In 1961 Anthony Wedgwood Benn – dubbed by the newspapers 'the reluctant peer' – was refused entry to the House of Commons after doubling his majority at the Bristol South East by-election. It was argued that as Viscount Stansgate he properly belonged in the Lords. He was allowed to sit in the public gallery of the Commons and listen to members wrangling over his case.

After a long and costly battle – in the course of which he demonstrated great strength of character – he succeeded in renouncing his title and was admitted to the Commons as plain Anthony Wedgwood Benn. In his unceasing quest to become the exemplar of the common man, he announced that he should be addressed for the future as Anthony Benn. Imperceptibly, this was shortened to Tony Benn. I doubt he will be completely satisfied until he is known simply as 'Tone'.

He is a man of great intellectual ability and no sense. His causes, which are those of the extreme Left, can never succeed. He nevertheless has the facility for uttering the most ridiculous statements in a seductively avuncular manner. Only his eyes betray. They are the eyes of a fanatic.

Equally fanatical was the Reverend Ian Paisley, the burly, bigoted and deeply unpleasant Democratic Unionist member for North Antrim. He had first hit the headlines in January 1969 – soon after the resurrection of the ancient 'Troubles' – when violence flared in Londonderry at the end of a seventy-three-mile civil rights march from Belfast. Paisley's car was overturned and set on fire. He was later briefly imprisoned – a situation which he relished – but freed under a wide-ranging amnesty.

An unquiet priest who promotes neither union nor democracy – and only his own very limited brand of religion – this passionately wrong-headed 'reverend' has a long history of disruptive behaviour. As far back as January 1974 he was employing his techniques in the Northern Ireland Assembly. The fracas occurred following the resignation of Brian Faulkner as leader of the Unionist Party. As one source wrote:

'The Northern Ireland Assembly was reduced to an unworkable shambles today as hard-liners protested vigorously at Protestants sharing power with Catholics in the new Executive Council. Unionists spat at Unionists, the mace was seized and passed from hand to hand. Police forcibly removed the Reverend Ian Paisley.'

*　　*　　*

1961 – the year which saw Anthony Wedgewood Benn's initial rejection from the House of Commons – also heralded the government's introduction of tighter immigration controls, a measure for which I had been pressing for some years. In March 1962 I experienced the general dismay caused by the most sensational by-election victory of a generation when at Orpington the Liberals overturned a Conservative majority of almost fifteen thousand and converted it to an eight thousand majority of their own.

In July 1962 – and just twenty-four hours after a second huge Tory voting collapse in a by-election – I was astounded to hear that Harold Macmillan had sacked seven members of his Cabinet in what the newspapers described as 'an act of ferocious political butchery'.

The following March, the Secretary of State for War, John Profumo, came before the House to make a personal statement denying any 'impropriety what-soever' in his relationship with a twenty-one-year-old model named Christine Keeler.

The resulting scandal wrecked his career. It was a tragedy of the first order. He had been a marvellous Minister for War and was in essence a good man. He left the House and devoted the rest of his life to charitable causes. The loyalty of his wife, the actress, Valerie Hobson, was an inspiration both to him and to those who wished both of them well. His work for charity was later rewarded with the CBE. I know of no man who has paid so dearly for one foolish lapse – or who has worked so hard to make amends for it.

*   *   *

Two months after Profumo lied to the House over the Christine Keeler affair, Sir Winston Churchill, who was then eighty-eight, announced that he would retire from the House of Commons at the next election. He had been sixty years an M.P. I had witnessed the last years of the career of this parliamentary colossus with interest. I had come to admire and respect him. Towards the end, his great faculties had begun to diminish. His achievements never can.

When he died, in January 1965, I was privileged to attend his funeral, held in St. Paul's Cathedral, as the representative of my constituents. It proved to be not only one of the last great State occasions of my career but an especially moving ceremony.

Because everything had been organised down to the last detail, there were no unseemly mishaps. Churchill's end had long been anticipated by the authorities and they had laid their plans accordingly. These were contained in a document code-named 'Operation Hope Not', a copy of which was circulated to all those likely to play any part in the proceedings.

Rehearsals took place at regular intervals, the last of them in a blinding snowstorm at 5 a.m. on a January morning. This was overseen by the Duke of Norfolk, who, as Earl Marshal of England, was responsible for the organisation of all State ceremonies. After its conclusion, the Duke took breakfast with the governor of the Tower of London, Sir Thomas Butler. As he departed, he told Sir Thomas: 'I think I am probably the only Duke of Norfolk who has ever left the Tower with his head on his shoulders'.

Following the service in St. Paul's, the coffin containing Churchill's remains was brought to Tower Wharf to be loaded on to a launch which would convey it up river to Waterloo station for onward transmission to the tiny Oxfordshire village of Bladon. Here the great man had asked to be buried.

The departure of the body from Tower Wharf produced a scene of high dignity. As the launch pulled away, the cranes on the far side of the river dipped their long slender necks to the water's edge by way of salute.

It was a moving event and one which remains longest in people's minds when they recall those four unprecedented days of homage. The Queen led the nation in its mourning and there was a spontaneous upsurge of affection and respect for this many-sided genius. It was homage on the grandest of scales. Live television coverage beamed the event to 350 million people throughout the length and breadth of Europe – a continent which Churchill had done so much to liberate. They were the highest European viewing figures ever recorded.

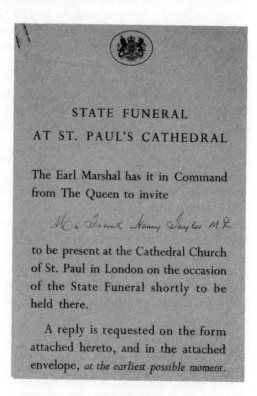

STATE FUNERAL

AT ST. PAUL'S CATHEDRAL

The Earl Marshal has it in Command from The Queen to invite

Mr. Frank Henry Taylor M.P.

to be present at the Cathedral Church of St. Paul in London on the occasion of the State Funeral shortly to be held there.

A reply is requested on the form attached hereto, and in the attached envelope, *at the earliest possible moment.*

Winston Churchill's Funeral Invitation to St Paul's Cathedral

*   *   *

203

At the General Election of 1964, Labour was returned to power by a whisker, with an overall majority of four, thus ending thirteen years of Tory rule. Stepping across the threshold of No.10 Downing Street for the first time, Harold Wilson muttered for the benefit of the gathered reporters: 'Nice place we've got here'.

For Wilson I never cared. I spent two sessions in the House during the course of his premiership. A Socialist of the old school, he clung to the hackneyed and out-moded techniques of yesteryear, first utilised by his hero, Ramsay Macdonald. He believed that all industrial disputes might be solved by bringing the trades union leaders together round a table at No.10 for beer and sandwiches.

He was in my experience the most unpleasant individual ever to hold the office of prime minister and almost certainly the most devious since Lloyd George.

His administration presided over the fruitless economic sanctions aimed at bringing to heel Ian Smith's illegal breakaway regime in Rhodesia. Re-elected to power in April 1966 with what he termed 'a clear mandate', he immediately imposed a six-month freeze on pay in an attempt to stem runaway inflation – an albatross which was to cling to him tenaciously throughout his years of office.

Battle lines were drawn up between the government and the unions. In October 1966 production was brought to a standstill at the British Motor Corporation as a result of strike action over threatened redundancies. A year later, the worst financial crisis for twenty years ended with a further devaluation of sterling. Wilson endeavoured to persuade a television audience that this had not necessarily devalued 'the pound in your pocket'.

After twenty-four hours of 'threats, sulks and high farce', in March 1968 George Brown resigned as Foreign Secretary. Possibly the most wayward politician since Charles James Fox, the previous night, during an all-night sitting of the Commons, he had quarrelled with his colleagues and generally made a fool of himself. When the announcement was made he was at home asleep. For all his faults he was an endearing man. He delighted in impassioned debate but seldom considered his words. It might have been said of him – as Churchill once said of Baldwin – 'He takes a leap in the dark, looks round and takes another'. Yet his undoubted abilities brought him within a hair's-breadth of the leadership of his party. He would not have been a good choice.

*　　*　　*

The following April, Enoch Powell, the Tory Shadow Minister of Defence, delivered a speech in which he foresaw 'rivers of blood' unless more was done to curb immigration. He described the present situation as 'like a nation busily engaged in heaping up its own funeral pyre'. The speech immediately isolated him from the party leadership.

For several years I had sat beside him in the third row above the gangway. As an individual, I had come to like him. I now felt for him keenly. He is an intensely honest, slightly enigmatic man with a brilliant academic mind. He is also sufficiently courageous to state in public what he believes in private – a trait not characteristic of politicians. His estimate of the situation was unfashionable then and even more so now. Nonetheless, much of the racial strife he predicted has come to pass. It is unlikely to decrease.

In 1970 a Bill passed through the House of Commons which, it was claimed, would afford women equal pay with men within six years. The Employment Secretary, Barbara Castle, warned that women would still expect to keep their special privileges.

*　　*　　*

1970 also brought a surprise election victory for Edward Heath. He promised the electorate 'strong and honest' government. Half a mile away, at Labour headquarters, a painful inquest began. All the opinion polls had signalled an easy Labour victory. People were asking, could it be that Harold Wilson had lost office through complacency? He had endeavoured to portray the Tories as 'Yesterday's Men'. Heath had more accurately described his opponents as: 'men of straw, trampled over by greedy, strike-prone unions responsible for rising prices'.

For all this, the first year of Edward Heath's administration was marked by more working days lost to strikes than at any time since the General Strike of 1926. There were major disputes involving dockers, national newspapers and local authorities. In January 1971 they were joined by the postmen.

Later in the year Geoffrey Rippon, the government's EEC negotiator, told a packed House that Britain's entry into the EEC was now almost certain. 'The back of the negotiations is broken.' On 28 October the decision to join was ratified by the Commons 356 votes to 244.

On the economic front, matters had not improved and in February 1972 the crisis over the miners' pay dispute deepened. Total electricity blackouts were imposed over the whole of the country. Some of these lasted as long as nine hours. In March, Heath imposed direct rule on Ulster. Anthony Barber, the Chancellor of the Exchequer, announced the government's decision to allow the pound to 'float' on the world's money markets. Clydesdale shipworkers staged a 'work-in'.

By February, Ulster was paralysed by a general strike. In December Britain reverted to a three-day working week amid rumours that unless the government could defuse the disputes now crippling industry – including the coal-mines, railways and power stations – Edward Heath would be forced to call a general election in order to seek a new mandate for his policies.

On 7 February 1974, claiming that the miners were seeking 'to change our whole democratic way of life', that election was duly called. The result was a stalemate. Labour won 301 seats, the Tories 297 and the Liberals 14. The uneasy period of the Lib–Lab pact had begun.

Heath was an able prime minister brought low by the miners' strike. A product of the grammar-school system, he seemed to me to suffer from a strong sense of inferiority when in the presence of aristocrats or those who had been educated at public school.

As a result, he tended to hold himself aloof, was given to stalking through a packed division lobby speaking to and looking at no one. Unlike his predecessor, Alec Douglas–Home, he was completely devoid of charm. His presence tended to make one feel vaguely uneasy. He has not mellowed with age. In February 1975 he was ousted from the leadership of the Conservative party by Margaret Thatcher, who became the first woman leader of a British political party at the age of forty-nine. This was an act of 'treachery' which Heath has never forgiven. He has now been sulking for fifteen years. He ungraciously refused Margaret Thatcher's offer to send him to Washington as British Ambassador; and he continues to snipe both at the government and its leader at every available opportunity. He is a sad and deeply embittered man.

In contrast, Margaret Thatcher progressed from strength to strength. She withstood the intense trials and tribulations of high office with a fortitude of character which is, of course, legendary. If she is occasionally autocratic – and it has been well said that she was 'the best man in the Cabinet' – it may be that she needed to be.

Life at the top is tough. As Edward Heath and Michael Heseltine have shown, there are always those prepared to indulge in backstairs intrigue, to move in for the kill at the slightest sign of political faltering or weakness. Margaret Thatcher I am sure will be well applauded by history.

With the exception of Winston Churchill, she is the only prime minister this century whose qualities merit interment in Westminster Abbey.

*   *   *

In the course of my thirteen years, all this I had seen and more. At the 1974 General Election I fought my corner as tenaciously as I had ever done. However, during the term of the previous government, Moss Side had suffered a significant boundary change. As a result I was voted from office. Shortly after that, and as a result of a drastic reduction in the population of Greater Manchester, Moss Side ceased to exist as a parliamentary constituency. I am proud to have been its member of parliament for so many years.

I am also proud of one of my lesser achievements – that of having made the shortest recorded speech in the history of parliament. It might almost qualify me for an entry in the Guinness Book of Records. On Wednesday 7 April 1965 the Labour politician, Mannie Shinwell, was delivering what I considered to be a long, tiresome and factually inaccurate diatribe on the subject of the National Debt. When I could stand this no longer, I stood up and retorted 'Nonsense!' This was of course no more than an interjection, not a speech.

However, due to an error on the part of the shorthand writer, it appeared next day in Hansard . . . where it remains enshrined for all to see.

CHAPTER TWENTY–FOUR

GLENYS

For her services to education, Glenys was made M.B.E. She was invested by the Queen at Buckingham Palace. There are those among our friends who feel that she should rightly have been created a Dame – if only for agreeing to marry me.

She is a woman of quite outstanding ability. She is also very adaptable. On two occasions she was sent to Hong Kong by the British Council to lecture on the new methods of education then being introduced into the English school-system. Her schedule was heavy. It included discussion with all the island's educational chiefs, members of the schools inspectorate, head teachers, principals of colleges and gatherings of students. On matters educational she was a U.K. delegation of one. In this role she had the slightly intimidating experience of having to meet the entire Hong Kong Cabinet.

Part of her programme involved spending several mornings addressing groups of five-hundred English-speaking teachers. The afternoons were taken up with similar lectures to similar-sized groups – none of whom spoke English at all. Consequently, she had to pace her address to allow for pauses in-filled by an interpreter. This continued day after day.

Within her chosen profession, Glenys is widely known and loved. She has made her mark not only in my heart and mind but within the hearts and minds of many others. In her home area of North Wales it is quite impossible for her to walk through the centre of any major town without being hailed and stopped. I find this a pleasantly humbling experience.

In her company my own achievements pale into insignificance. Being an essentially male-orientated society, there are certain formal occasions when etiquette requires that she be addressed as 'Mrs Frank Taylor'. On her home territory I become 'Mr Glenys Edwards' – receiving no more than an inquisitive glance or a casual nod . . . which is just as it should be.

In the fifteen years of our marriage she has proved to be a restraining influence. I now work only five days a week as opposed to seven. We take time to travel,

208

Glenys at the Palace displaying her MBE, 1978

Long long ago when schools were schools
And life uncomplicated,
Before the O & M and Clwyd
And Ed. Tech. were invented.

Our Glenys came from London town
A fair and lively maiden,
To organise the schools of Flints
With Moses Les & Haydn.

She brought the Infants' up to scratch
And galvanised the county,
She left her mark upon the schools
Her labour is their bounty.

Our future days with Taylor friends
Are full of trepidation,
Her days with Taylor, let's be Frank
Will shine with jubilation.

We wish her well in days to come
And thank her for her vision,

She brought the Infants' Schools of Clwyd
Up to the first division.

She is the one and only Glen,
When all the words are spoken,

And when God created her
The mould was quickly broken.

• • • • • • • • • • • • • •

Tribute by colleagues to Glenys on her retirement
to marry me, 1978

often in groups of more than a hundred organised by Bunny Morgan, the secretary of the London City Livery Club. In the course of these and other journeyings we have visited the Canadian Rockies – where we encountered a number of wild brown bears; the Far East, including Bali, Singapore and Hong Kong; Delhi and Kashmir; Rio and Brazilia. In 1990 we enjoyed a cruising holiday aboard the Cunard Princess to the Black Sea, putting in at Ephesus, Yalta and Odessa.

As part of our travels we ultimately fulfilled a long-standing ambition to make a world tour. It took us sixty-seven days. On November 1 we left our flat in Barrie House in a limousine which took us on the first leg of our journey to Heathrow. Fifteen hours later we arrived in Hong Kong, Britain's first outpost in China. In less than two hundred years it had been transformed from a desolate nest of pirates into one of the globe's most important business centres. With an area of less than thirty square miles it also represents one of the most heavily-populated.

We were taken to the home of David Lau on Hong Kong Island. We had come to know him some time previously when a friend, Ruby Lau, had written to Glenys to enlist her help in finding suitable schools in England for the family's children. After much scrambling and opening of suitcases, we were hurried away to a dinner-party to celebrate the appointment to the Executive Council of Hong Kong of Mr Liu, another fascinating character.

Liu had risen to prominence – and fortune – by recognising what entrepreneurs nowadays term a gap in the market. At one time the island's banking was almost completely monopolised by the mammoth Hong Kong & Shanghai Banking Corporation. Its branches were large grandiose structures which inhibited lowly Chinese businessmen. The astute Liu opened a tiny street-corner bank to cater for their needs. It quickly prospered. Other branches were opened and Liu became very rich.

One function succeeded another.

On the Monday we attended a cocktail party at the Hilton Hotel given by Irene Cheung, a director of the large department store 'Danmaru', to celebrate its quarter-centenary. There were eighteen hundred guests and a display of food the like of which is seldom seen. Later, Irene invited us to the Mandarin Hotel where we lunched and were treated to a preview of Sotheby's famous Jade Collection sale.

After a week packed with similar lunches and dinners we left Hong Kong for Perth, where we were scheduled to spend five days as guests of an Old Rutlishian friend, Derek Evans.

*   *   *

Remote from all other lands, the vast island continent of Australia covers a sprawling mass of three million square miles. Even New Zealand, which we think of as its close neighbour, is a four-day voyage away; and the distance to India is almost as great as from Liverpool to New York.

Though it was the last of the continents to be discovered and opened up to civilization, it is the most ancient of them all – so ancient that its mountain peaks have been worn down by the waters and winds of countless ages to mere blunt stumps.

When most of Asia and Europe was still submerged beneath the oceans, Australia was dry land. It was once connected by a land bridge with Asia – and some believe with south America also – but this disappeared beneath the surface of the ocean long before the higher forms of animal and plant life came into existence.

During our stay in Perth, Derek Evans was kind enough to take us to the Yacht Club where we viewed the America's Cup, wrested so controversially from the Americans a few months previously. He also showed me the famous cricket ground – where, by an extraordinary coincidence, I encountered four Old Rutlishians who had come out from England to enjoy a winter's cricket.

In glorious sunshine, we left Perth for Melbourne, where we were to stay with Merrell Browne and her husband Marshall. In addition to being the overseas controller of the National Bank of Australia, Marshall Browne is well known as a writer of crime stories. His Victorian home was filled with interesting Chinese antiques, a legacy of Merrell's time in Hong Kong. We were intrigued by the lace patterning of wrought-iron placed above balconies or, in smaller units, over doors.

We visited the zoo, where we gossiped with the koalas; saw our first platypus and wombat; toured an exhibition of paintings depicting Aboriginal life; and were driven to Port Campbell to view the rocks which protrude from the sea and are known as 'The Twelve Apostles'.

Some years previously, in London, Glenys had made the acquaintance of an Australian woman. She helped her load her heavy baggage on to a bus. In gratitude, she mentioned that she owned a restaurant in Melbourne. She said that if we were ever in the vicinity she would be pleased to treat us to a meal.

Glenys decided to accept the offer. She took the greatest care with her appearance, wore a fabulous dress and no small amount of jewellery. When we arrived at the restaurant we found it to be no more than a greasy-spoon cafe. To make matters worse, it was located in a red light district. The lady and her husband did put in a brief appearance; but long before our departure we had decided that this was not an acquaintance we wished to pursue.

Marshall and Merrell Browne next drove us down to Phillip Island to view the fairy penguins, dwarfish creatures no more than thirteen inches high. At dusk they suddenly appeared out of the sea by the thousand, waddling up the beach to the burrows where they passed the night. They took no notice of us at all. They did appear to be briefly alarmed by the appearance of a predatory bird.

*　　*　　*

From Melbourne Glenys and I took a relatively short flight to Sydney where we were given a palatial room in the Intercontinental Hotel with spectacular views of the Harbour Bridge and Opera House. We toured the city; visited the shopping district of Double Bay; and drove along the coast to Manley.

On 1 December we flew to New Zealand, putting up briefly at the Rose Park Hotel in Auckland.

New Zealand had been founded by a hardy Dutch seafarer named Abel Tasman in 1642. No man appears to have visited it again until the coming of Captain Cook in 1769. During the next sixty years, whaling vessels and trading schooners (seeking timber) were the only callers.

In its upper portion, we found the North Island to be a moist semi-tropical region. It was filled with amazing geological wonders. Cone-shaped volcanoes rose abruptly from its eastern plains and towards the centre there was a region of geysers, hot springs and vast crevices where boiling mud bubbled up from subterranean furnaces.

The South Island – a three-hour ferry-boat ride away – was even more magnificent. In the south-west we found the coast broken by narrow picturesque fiords, where the sea snakes its way far inland between cloud-capped peaks.

Of all the magnificent sights we encountered, one of the most glorious was the trees, graceful beyond belief. Ferns, twenty or thirty feet high, leant above the edge of ravines. The most abundant was the nikau palm, the fronds of which shoot up from the trunk at so sharp an angle that the wild parrot is forced to hang its head in order to reach the scarlet fruit.

*   *   *

In the course of a twelve-day coach tour of the country, during which we covered an average of two hundred miles a day, all this we saw and more. We visited a Maori settlement at Rotorua, enjoyed their food and watched a number of tribal dances. As a race, the Maoris are deeply hospitable. The men are distinguished by their tattooed bodies. The tattooing is carried out in patterns, the elaborateness increasing in direct proportion to the wearer's station in life. The women formerly played an important part in tribal affairs and sometimes went into battle with the men, fighting fiercely by their side.

We flew next to Honolulu. Cooled in summer and warmed in winter by the ocean winds, we found it seldom too hot and never cold. During our stay we flew over the fifteen or so enormous volcanoes which have been built up from the bottom of the ocean and now form the Hawaiian Islands. We had lunch on one, tea on another.

Looking down from the aircraft, we observed that several islands, such as Maui, consisted of volcanic 'twins', united at the base. Others were formed around a single cone. All were mountainous. In many places they rose from the sea in sheer cliffs hundreds and even thousands of feet high. The valleys were remarkable for their beautiful scenery, The swift short rivers cut deep ravines and picturesque gorges.

From Honolulu we flew across the Pacific to San Francisco, famous for its cable cars, steepling hills and the island prison of Alcatraz. We stayed at the Fisherman's Wharf, one of the prettiest of the city's enclaves and as such a great tourist attraction.

*   *   *

We had anticipated that in travelling alone we might find ourselves spending a rather solitary Christmas, thinking about family and friends back home. We had underestimated the kindness of the American people. On Christmas Day we ate lunch atop the beautiful (and expensive) Fairmont Hotel. Looking down on the city below, we found ourselves drawn into conversation with an American couple sitting at an adjacent table. After lunch they took us on a seven-hour tour of the city.

We were saddened to leave, but after five days flew on to Baltimore, a city which – we had heard – was very dull. In fact it has been much improved in recent years and I regret we were unable to see more of it,

Our penultimate flight took us to Bermuda, via New York. Through my R.A.C. golfing connections we were able to stay in a pretty pink bungalow, with a private beach, at the Mid Ocean Golf Club. It was the very essence of luxury and if, at £40 a round of golf appeared rather costly, we were at least befriended – again – by four very jolly Americans. We also looked up some friends of Glenys, Ann and Norman Brown, who gave us a guided tour of the sights by car.

Travel has a curious way of bringing one to earth with a bump at the end of a holiday. Four days after sitting in the Bermuda sunshine, I found myself racketing along on the underground's Central Line to my office in the City.

*   *   *

It has been said – although not by me – that women are incapable of keeping a secret. I have no idea whether or not this is true as a generalisation. It is certainly not so in Glenys's case. As my eightieth birthday approached, she announced that we were to celebrate it in style – with a special dinner. She would not tell me where or when.

When the momentous day arrived, we set off in the car, together with our special guests for the evening, Morgan Edwards and his wife, Alwen. I calculated from the direction in which Glenys instructed me to drive that we were heading for the World Trade Centre – of which I am a member of the Council – at St. Katherine's Dock, hard by the Tower of London.

As we travelled along Lower Thames Street, with apparent spontaneity Glenys asked me to turn left so that our passengers might view the Hall of the Bakers' Company. When we arrived at the entrance she turned to me and said:

'You can stop speculating now. We're here.'

214

*　　*　　*

Thirty years previously the Young Conservatives of Chorley and Leyland had produced a version of 'This Is Your Life' for my benefit. I had been deeply touched by their efforts. Glenys surpassed them. Single-handed, this one-woman dynamo had organised the birthday party to out-birthday them all . . . an evening to remember and to cherish.

I climbed from the car. The Hall was in darkness. However, as I was ushered through the door, the lights went up. Waiting to greet me in the foyer was my daughter. Behind her stood a group of more than a hundred old friends and associates gleaned over four score years. They included friends from the worlds of the City Livery Companies, golf, the Thames and politics. Old Rutlishians were well represented as were the associates of my business life. There was also a fair complement of Glenys's friends and relatives – many of whom had over the years become my friends as well.

Eightieth Birthday Gift from Sam Bryan, 10th October, 1987

215

The supreme feat of organisation and co-ordination required to bring such a company together – many of them extremely busy and with complex schedules – almost defies description. I am an observant man. Yet in the weeks leading up to the event Glenys had managed to receive many letters and to carry on numerous telephone conversations without my becoming in any way aware of what was afoot.

Among those present on that evening was Beryl Bryan, who became my agent shortly after my election to parliament. She it was who master-minded most of my election campaigns. As such I owe her an enormous debt. On my eightieth birthday she presented me with a painting, executed by her husband, a professional artist, which depicted me surrounded by a number of miniature alter-egos – in rugby kit, dressed as an oarsman and as an athlete. There was a propeller to mark my foundation of the Parliamentary Flying Club, a grandfather clock, emblematic of Time, the parliamentary portcullis, and a set of golf clubs, a reminder of my captaincy of the R.A.C.

* * *

My eightieth birthday is now five years behind me. Like a batsman who takes guard afresh, I am now moving – a little slower than I once did – towards my ninetieth.

I have lived an active life. At the age of sixty-four I swam sixteen lengths of Chorlton–cum–Hardy baths for charity; and a month earlier tied for first place with two other men – both in their twenties – in a twenty-mile sponsored walk.

I consider I have already had my money's worth out of life, have even shown a considerable profit. Perhaps, then, I shall make my century. I should not, along the way, wish to see a repeat of the incident of March 1970 when the *Daily Telegraph* – confusing me with my namesake, F. M. H. Taylor, a past-master of the Paternmakers' Company – inadvertently reported my death.

Despite the medical problems which have beset me in the last few years, I have no intention of ceasing to work. In 1987 I entered hospital for the removal of cataracts. The following year I had a prostate operation. The year after that I was found to be suffering from cancer of the bowel. This required a colostomy. This has brought in its wake consequences which are both tiresome and time-consuming. I endeavour to surmount them as best I can.

* * *

Nowadays, all roads lead to Glenys. The fifteen years of our marriage have been the happiest of my life. She remains a constant source of joy. We met so many years ago. We were then parted for so long. This has always been a source of great regret to me.

James Walker, the legendary Mayor of New York between the two world wars, once wrote a song which posed the question:

'Will you love me in December?

As once you did in May?'

Although I am quite unworthy, I believe Glenys does. In that respect – as in so many others – I count myself the luckiest of men.

INDEX

Aber 62
Aberdeen 137, 156
Abse, Leo 80, 191
Adama 85
Adams, Mr 151
'Adam's Peak' 97
Aden 183
Aeronautical College, Cranfield 193
Agra 139–40
Akbar the First 139
Albemarle Street 23
Alcatraz 213
Alcock, Captain John 11
Aleppo 85
Alexander the Great 84
Alexandria 77, 84–5, 94, 127
Algiers 90
Allan, Mr & Mrs 68
All Blacks rugby team 25–6
All England Tennis Club 60
Amateur Boxing Association 104
America's Cup 211
Amory, Rt. Hon. Leo 76, 77
Angle, Jack 48
Anglo-Polish Conservative Association
    176
Animal Feeding Stuffs Division 68 &
    passim
Ankara 85
Archer, Joe 26
Arnold, Tom 111
Association Sportif Française 28
Astley Industrial Trust 160

Astor, Nancy 11
Atkins Bill 44
Auckland 212
Auden, W. H. 114
Australia 211–12

'Babbitt, George F.' 133
Badier, Madame 83
Bahrain 96, 198
Bailey, Alderman 167–9
Bakers, Worshipful Company of 110 &
    passim
Baldwin, Stanley 204
Balham 54
Bali 210
Baltimore 214
Bank of England rugby team 26
Barber, Anthony 205–6
Barclay, Billy 136
Barrie House 147, 210
Barry, Sir Charles 172
Basra 93
Beatrice, Queen of Cyprus 38
Beirut 85, 88
Belfast 156
Bell, Sir Stanley 160
Benn, Anthony Wedgewood 201–2
Berlin 56, 64, 67, 79
Bermuda 214
Bethesda 147
Bettell, Colonel 153
Bettws y Coed 64

'Big Ben' 55, 173–4
Bis Island 85
Blackheath Rugby Club 27
Blackpool 75
Black Sea 210
Bladon 203
Bodmin 142
Boer War 57
Bolton 157
Bombay 95–6
Bonaparte, Joseph 79
Botha, Louis 11
Bottomley, Horatio 189
Bovingdon 143
Box, Captain 65–6
Boxmoor Common 143
Braddock, Tom 14
Braithwaite, Sir Gurney 149, 150
Breed, Peter 26
Brewer, Ernie 26
Bridport 1
Brighton 45
British Council 208
British Museum 5, 55
British Sportman's Club 25
Broderers, Worshipful Company of 12
Brompton Road 43, 103
Brompton Finance Company Ltd. 43, 46
Brown, Ann 214
Brown, Lieutenant Arthur Whitten 11
Brown, Lord George 204
'Brown, John' 133
Brown, Norman 214
Browne, Marshall 212
Browne, Merrell 212
Brownley brothers 25
Bryan, Beryl 216
Buckingham Palace 39, 54, 56, 208
Buddha 97
Burma 55, 75, 76, 140
Burnham, Roy 23, 26
Burrows & Watts Ltd. 107
Butler, Sir Thomas 203
Buttry, Frank 31

Byron, Lord George 121
Byton Chambers, Tooting 43

Caernarvon, 1st Battalion 62, 67
Cairo 77, 82–7, 90, 93, 101, 128
Calcutta 94
Callaghan, James 189–90
Campbell, Colin 32
Campion, Father Edmund 144
Canada Life Assurance Co. Ltd. 135
Candy 97–8
Capri 79
Cary, Sir Robert 170
Carrington, Lord 176
Carlisle, Colonel 59–60
Carpentier, Georges 48
Carroll family 6
Carroll, Jack 6
Carroll, Tom 6
Casr-el-Nile military barracks 83
Castelle Benito 82
Castle, Barbara 175, 176, 205
Caunt, Sir Benjamin 173
Cecil Hotel, Alexandria 77
Central Y.M.C.A. Rugby Club 28
Ceylon 72, 73, 96–7
'Challenge to Britain' pamphlet 154–5
Chamberlain, Neville 51
Charles I 173
Charles II 12
Cheeseman, John 143
Cheeseman, Sylvia 143
Chesil Beach 1
Cheung, Irene 211
Chicago 124
Chichele, John 111
Chivers & Co. Ltd. 1
Chorley 158–64
Chorlton-cum-Hardy 166–7, 216
Christie, Agatha 165
Churchill, Sir Winston 56, 71, 100, 170,
   202–3, 204, 206
City Livery Golfing Society 187

Clapham Junction railway station 89
Colombo 82, 91, 97
Colvin, 'Captain Columbus' 96
Colwyn Bay 61, 62, 68, 69, 137–8
Comben, Anthony (grandson) 122
Comben, Gillian (granddaughter) 122
Comben, Jonathan (grandson) 122
Comben, Michael (son-in-law) 122
Constable, John 171
Continental Savoy Hotel, Cairo 82, 102, 128–9
Conway 62, 63, 64, 65, 67
Conway Bridge 66
Cook, Captain James 212
Coombe Gardens 48, 137
Courtney, Anthony 193–4
Coventry 54
Cow & Gate Ltd. 115
Crawley New Town 151
Crowson, Sydney 17–18
Cuffley 7
Culloden, Battle of 50
'Cunard Princess' 210
Cyprus 38, 85
Cyrenaica 55

Daily Mail, The 35, 39
Danmaru department store 211
Delhi 96, 139, 210
Dempsey, Jack 11
Dents of Pall Mall 173
Desborough, Lord 36
'Desert Rats', The 55
Disney, A. N. 12
Distillers Co. Ltd. 109
Ditton Skiff & Punting Club 33 & passim, 39
Dodge City 124
Doig, A. J. 14
Donovan, W. Timothy 42–3, 149, 150
Dorchester 5
Double Bay, Sydney 212
Douglas-Home, Sir Alec 206

Drake, Sir Francis 49
Draper, Dr. 12
Drewe, Peter 112
Drummond, Sir Jack 70
Dubai 96
Dubcek, Alexander 198–9
'dunnage' fraud 85–6
Durban 100
Dyers, Worshipful Company of 38–9

Earp, Wyatt 124
East Africa 71, 72
Eastbourne 129
Edinburgh 136, 156
Edward the Confessor 171
Edward III 171
Edwards, Alwen 214
Edwards, Glenys (*see* Taylor, Glenys)
Edwards, Mary 9
Edwards, Morgan 214
Edwards, William John 146
Eisenhower, General Dwight D. 55
El Adem 82
El Alamein, Battle of 55, 93
Elizabeth I 38
Elizabeth II 40, 56
Elizabeth, the Queen Mother 54
El Vino's wine bar 150–1
Empire Day 6, 13
Endean, Russell 142–3
Ephesus 210
Ericson, Teddy 26
Eskenderun 85, 86, 87–8
Evans, Derek 211–2

Fairmont Hotel, San Francisco 114
Falk, Keeping & Co. Ltd. 20 & passim, 41
Farida, Princess 102
Farmers' Club, The 103
Farouk, King 84
Fatehpur, Sikri 140
Faucitt, Jack 130–1, 158

Faucitt, Mary 158
Faulkner, Brian 201
Fawkes, Guy 173
Fembey, Bill 12
Fernando, Mr. 97
Ferry Road, Thames Ditton 31
Figgures, Sir Frank 15
Finch, Ray 135
Finsburgh, Geoffrey 150
Fisherman's Wharf, San Francisco 213
Fitzroy Square 105
Florence Villas 5, 6, 11
Flower, Blossom 45
Flower, William 45–6
Follett, Sir David 15
Fong, Chan Ying 177
Fortune's Well 1
Fox, Charles James 204
Fullick, Harry 103–8

Gaitskell, Hugh 161–2
Garfield, Annis 180
Garfield, Emmie 180
Garibaldi 79
Gate, Colonel 115
Gaulle Face Hotel, Colombo 82
Gaumont British News 103
Gielgud, Sir John 22
Gielgud Mr. 22
George V 5, 17
George VI 56–7, 158, 173
German Chamber of Commerce in
    England 51
Gilbraltar 76, 91, 183
Gigli, Benajamino 82
Glasgow 50–4, 156
Goering, Hermann 54
Gordon Square 42
Gower Street 42
Grace, H.R.H. Princess (of Monaco) 132
Graf Zeppelin 124
Granada Television 162
Grand Brittagne Hotel, Athens 82

Grand Hotel, Nuwara Eilya 98
Great Eastern Hotel, Calcutta 94
Great North Road 125
'Great Tom' 174
Grosvenor Hotel, Chester 147
Groves, John & Son 2
Guildford 33, 117, 122, 144
Guild of Air Pilots 113–14
Guy's Hospital 104

Haifa 86, 87, 90
Hailsham, Lord 161–2
Hall, Sir Benjamin 173
Hammerton's Boathouse 31
Hampton Court Bridge 36
Harlequins Rugby Club 29
Harp Lane 111
Harvey, Charlie 36–7
Hastings, Major 61
Hatfield (soldier) 174
Hawaii 213
Hawarden Church 146
Hayward, Mr. 98
Heath, Edward 205–6
Henley-on-Thames 31, 103, 108
Henry II 110
Henry VIII 38, 171
Hentzner, Paul 38
Heseltine, Michael 206
Hewitt, Florrie 31
Hewitt, Sam 31
Hewitt, Theo 31, 35
High Wycombe 139
Hills, Mabel (see Taylor, Mabel)
Hilton Hotel, Hong Kong 211
Himalayas 94
Histon 1
Hitler, Adolf 49, 51, 52, 53, 54, 55, 56,
    62, 67
Hobson, Valerie 202
Hodder, Emma (see Taylor, Emma)
Hodder, Mary (grandmother) 2
Hodder, William (grandfather) 2

Holloway Bros. Ltd. 60
Holloway, Dick 60
Holly Mount School, Raynes Park 144
Holmes, Major 16
Home Guard 57–67, 96
Hong Kong 144, 177, 210
Hong Kong Island 210–11
Hong Kong & Shanghai Banking
    Corporation 211
Honolulu 213
Horsborough, Florence 165
Hotel des Princes et Bellevue, Nice 136
Howe, Brian 46–7
Howell, Denis 185–6
Huxtable, Ernest 109–10
Hyde Park 104

Ibn Saud 128–9
India 72, 75, 76, 84, 94
India Office, Whitehall 76
Inkpen, Mr. 12
Institute of Chartered Accountants 47
Institute of Chartered Secretaries 47
Intercontinental Hotel, Sydney 212
Inverness 135, 156
Ironmonger Lane 21, 41
Ischia 79

Jagger, Cannon 13
James I 173
Janner, Sir Barnett 188
'Jasper' 118
Jennings J. C. 191
Jumna, River 140

'kamakazi' cormorants 64
Karachi 96
Kashmir 210
Kauffman, Gerald 178
Keeler, Christine 202
Kenyon, Clifford 158–64

Ketas, John 132
Kettners Restaurant 108
King Alfred Hotel, Jerusalem 82
Kingston 9, 32
Kingston Road, Merton 11
Kipling, Rudyard 92
Kline's gymnasium 105
Knight, 'Tiny' 31

Lancaster Gate 147
Langtry, Lillie 124
Latakya 87
Lau, David 210
Lau, Ruby 210
Leach, Sir Ronald 69
Leeds 8
Lenglen, Suzanne 11
Leo XIII, Pope 144
Lever, Harold 178
Lever, Lesley 178
Lewis, Sinclair 133
Leyland Motors 159
Little Colyers 143–4, 146
Liu, Mr. 211
Liverpool 211
Llandudno 62
Llanfairfechan 62
Llanrwst 64
Lloyd George, Gwilym 204
Local Defence Volunteers 57
Lockwood, Major 76
London Bridge 21, 104
London City Livery Club 210
Lower Thames Street 214
Lucan, Earl of 192
Luke, Claud 36–7
Lydda 85

MacDonald, Ramsey 17, 204
MacInnes, Colin 133
Mackay, Dora (see Taylor, Dora)
Mackay, Mary 135–6

Mackay, Rev. 135–6
MacLeod, Ian 200
Macmillan, Harold 164, 202
Maidenhead 35–6
'Mainwaring, Captain' 64
Malacca Strait 99
Malden Golf Club 48
Malta 90, 91, 183, 199–200
Manchester 54
Manchester Moss Side (parliamentary
    constituency of) 50, 165–74
Manchester Royal Infirmary 137
Mandarin Hotel, Hong Kong 211
Manley 212
Mann, Steven 51
Mansion House 112, 147
Maori Settlements 213
Margaret, H.R.H. Princess 56
Marseilles 82
Maui 213
Maybury-King, Dr. Horace 186
McCullogh, W. D. H. 132
Melbourne 212
Mena House Hotel, Cairo 83
Merton Abbey 5
Messel, L. 22
Messel, Oliver 22
Metropolitan College of St. Albans 22
Middle East 75, 76
Milroy, Nevill 35, 36
Mincing Lane 72
Ministry of Agriculture 118
Ministry of Food 45, 61, 68 & passim,
    76, 109, 137
Ministry of Health 8
Ministry of War Transport 45, 67, 74,
    75–89, 91, 94, 102, 139
Minsk 55
Mintoff, Dom 199–200
Mitchell, David 150–1
Mombasa 91
Monte Carlo 130, 136
Montgomery, Field-Marshall Bernard 55,
    93

More, Sir Thomas 181
Morgan, Bunny 210
Morfa, The 65, 66
Mosley, Sir Oswald 170
'Mullett War', The 141–3
Munich 51
Mussolini, Benito 11, 67

Nabarro, Gerald 191
Naples 79, 81, 95
Napoleon Bonaparte 79
Nash, Ogden 133
National Bank of Australia 212
Neuve-Chapelle, Battle of 57
Newcastle-under-Lyme (parliamentary
    constituency of) 151–2
New York 211, 214
New Zealand 211–12
Nicawerstiya 98–9
Nice 136
Nicholas, James 142–3
Nixon, Richard 148
Norfolk, Bernard, Duke of 203
Notting Hill 135
Novotny, Antonin 199

Odessa 210
Offer brothers 32
Old Mountaineers' Rugby Club 28
Old Rutlishians Association 25–30, 41,
    120, 125, 134, 144, 211, 215
Oliver, Miss 137
Olivier, Borg 200
Orpington 56, 202
Oxford Street 23
Oxford University 152

Paisley, Rev. Ian 201
Palermo 55
Pangbourne 39
Par 141–3

Paris 27, 56, 137, 195
Parliamentary Flying Club 113, 193–4
Parliament, Houses of (*see* Westminster, Palace of)
Pastrudi, Alexandrian restaurateur 77
'P. C. Richard' 118
Pearce, Laurie 26
Pearl Harbour 100
Peat, Sir George 69
Peat, Sir Harry 69. 70, 74
Peat, Marwick Mitchell & Co. 69
Penmaen Head 143
Pen Maen Mawr slate quarry 62
Pen Y Gwryd 64
Perth 211–12
Pharos, lighthouse 85
Phillip Island 212
Phipps Bridge Road 5
Phoenix Hotel, Dorchester 5
Piazzo Loretto, Milan 67
Polson, Andy 132
Poona 95
Poplar Road, Merton 121
Port Campbell 212
Portland 1–2
Port Said 85, 89, 100
Port Tewfik 100
Posilipo, Heights of 79
Powell, Enoch 205
'Prague Spring' 198
Pritchett, Horace 43, 46
Profumo, John 202
Public School Sports 26
Pudding Lane 111
Puxley, Alan 135

Queen Alexandra's Royal Nursing Corps. 139

R.A.C. 48–50, 130, 146, 147
R.A.C. Golf Club 48–50, 216
Raffles Hotel, Singapore 82

Raglan, Lord 192
Rajputana Desert 94
Ralph & Mann Ltd. 51
Ramsgate 56
rationing (1940–56), effects of 53
Red Fort, at Delhi 140
Registry of Friendly Societies 5
Renee, F. H. Taylor's secretary 144
Renoir, Auguste 11
Reuters' News Agency 76
Rhondda Valley 156
Richard I 38
Rio de Janeiro 210
Rippon, Geoffrey 205
Rivett, Sandra 192
Rixon, Beau 36
Robertson-Dick, Queenie 135–6
Rock Hotel, Gibraltar 76
Rome 84
Rommel, Field-Marshall Erwin 93
Roosevelt, Theodore 148
Rose Park Hotel, Auckland 212
Rosslyn Park Rugby Club 29
Rotorua 213
Royal Oak public house, Chorley 130
Royal Scottish Automobile Golf Club 50
Royal Society of St. George 147
Royce, Harry 129
'Rufus' 117–18
Rutlish Grammar School 10, 11–19
Rutlish, William 12

St. Anne's, near Blackpool 75
St. Elmo Castle 79
St. John's Ambulance Brigade 2
St. Katherine's Dock 112, 214
St. Magnus' Cathedral, Orkney 136
St. Paul's Cathedral 55, 202–3
St. Valentine's Day Massacre 124
Sabang 91
Salerno 82
San Francisco 213
Saravanamuttu, Mr. 97

Savoy Hotel 25, 51
Scotland 50, 112
Selwyn-Lloyd, John 186
Sennen Cove, house at (*see* 'Tinker
    Taylor')
Shah Jehar 139–40
Shalford 33, 143 & passim
Shannon, Len 143
Shannon, May 143
Shawlands, near Glasgow 136
Shears, Mr. 69
Sheffield 54
Shennon, Colonel 62–7
Shepheard's Hotel, Cairo 82
Shinwell, Mannnie 207
Silverdale 153
Silverman, Sidney 190
Silverstone 130
Silvertown munitions factory,
    explosion at 7
Sinai Desert 92
Sind Desert 94
Singapore 82, 91, 99, 210
'singing sands', The 92–3
Singlegate Junior School, Colliers
    Wood 9
Smith, Ian 204
Smith, Norman 132
Smith Square 150
Smuts, General Jan 11
Society of Lancastrians 147
Soho Square 107
Solomons, Harry 105
Sorento 80
Sotheby & Co. 211
Southwark Bridge 39
Spurrier, Mr. 159
Stalin, Joseph 154
Stansgate, Viscount (*see* Benn, Anthony
    Wedgewood)
Station Hotel, Inverness 136
Stevenson, Adlai 148
Stowe School 151
Strachey, Mr. 71

'Sturdy No. 7' (tug-boat) 101
Suez Canal 128
Sumatra 91
Sunbury 39
Sunday Empire News, The 103 & passim
Swansea, Lord 192
Swan Upping Ceremony 38–9
Swingler, Stephen 151–3, 155
Sydney 212
Syria 87–8

Taborn, Bill 144
Taj Mahal 139
Taj Mahal Hotel 95
Tanglin Club 97
Tasman, Able 212
Taylor, Dora (first wife) 135–9. 156
Taylor, Emma Rebecca (mother) 1–2
Taylor, Frank H.—
    birth 1
    encounters George V 4
    childhood 6–10
    witnesses poverty of near
        neighbours 6
    and Great War 6–9
    acquires extra sugar rations 8
    starts school 9
    thwarted of a prize 9
    encounter the Twelve Fat Men 9–10
    awarded a scholarship to Rutlish
        Grammar School 10
    at Rutlish Grammar School 11–19
    enrols with metropolitan college 22
    embarks on a life of hard work and
        self-denial 23
    recreations at this time 23
    qualifies as a chartered secretary 23–4
    celebrates qualifying as a chartered
        accountant 23–4
    becomes member of Old Rutlishians'
        Association 25
    association with the British
        Sportsmen's Club 25

INDEX

rugby career 25–30
interest in athletics 26
rugby tours abroad 27–8
plays water polo 23
elected treasurer and then president of
O.R.A. 29–30
wins skiff doubles marathon with
Colin Campbell 32
wins punt-racing championship 35–6
camping excursion to Windsor 37
association with Thames Heritage
Trust 39
sets up own accountancy firm 42
founds Brompton Finance Company 43
encounters 'sharp end' of Blitz in
Merton High Street 52–3
career in Home Guard 57–67
war-time posting to the Ministry of
Food 68–74
war-time posting to the Ministry of
War Transport 74–89
participates in the Athletic Marathon
103–8
as City Liveryman 109–14
aeronautical interests 113 & passim
as member of the Guild of Air Pilots
113
farming interests 115–23
motoring and motor-rallying activities
124, 133
marriage to Dora Mackay 135–7
marriage to Mabel Hills 139–41, 143
marriage to Glenys Edwards 144–7
career in politics 148–207
recreational travels abroad 208–14
eightieth birthday celebrations 214–16
Taylor, George (father) 1–5
Taylor, George (brother) 13, 43
Taylor, George (client) 81–2
Taylor, Glenys (third wife) 39, 144 f.,
187, 208–17
Taylor, Jack (uncle) 1–2
Taylor, Mabel ('Mabs') (second wife)
33, 117, 139–43, 150

Taylor, Margaret Mackay (daughter) 137
Taylor, Martin (son) 141
Taylor, Nicholas (son) 141
Taylor, Tommy 157
Taylor Woodrow Ltd. 112
Teddington Reach 33
Tenison, Colonel 'Taffy' 57–61
Thames Heritage Trust 39
Thatcher, Margaret 182, 206
Thomas, Bertrand 198
Thomas, George (see Tonypandy,
Viscount)
Thurber, James 51
Tighe, Desmond. 76–7, 84
Tobruk 55
Tommy's Bar, Cairo 77
Tonypandy, Viscount (George Thomas)
186
Tooting 8, 43, 53
Tower of London 41, 112, 203
Tripoli 87
Tubbs, Sergeant 58
Tug-boat ('Sturdy No. 7') 101
Tunis 90–1
Turf Club, Cairo 77
Turkey 83, 85, 87
Turk's Head public house, Weymouth 1,
2
Turner, J. M. W. 171
Turner, Martin 180
Tweedsmuir, Lady 156
'Twelve Apostles', The 212
Twickenham 25

United Eastern Banks Rugby Club 28
United Yeast Co. Ltd. 109–10
Uphatherleigh 16
'Upstairs Downstairs' (television series) 7
Varnish, E. A. A. 13–15, 19, 42
Old Boys' opinions concerning 14
sits for his portrait 15
helps F. H. Taylor to find a job 20–1

Vesuvius, Mt. 79
Vienna 112
Vintners, Worshipful Company of 38–9
von Ribbentrop, Joachim 51–2

Wade, Sir George 153
Wade Potteries Ltd. 153
Wakefield, W. W. 25
Walke, Chief Inspector 142–3
Walker, James 217
Wall Street Crash 23, 124
Woolton, Lord ('Uncle Fred') 71, 155–6
Wandsworth, London Borough of 7
Wantage 144
'Warmington-on-Sea' 64
War Office 44, 48, 57, 58
Waterloo railway station 60, 203
Watts, Jacky 165
Waugh, Evelyn 58
Wells, Bombardier Billy 48
Westminster, Palace of 55, 148–9, 154,
    171, 191, 198
    functions & traditions 171–4
West Surrey Farmers' Organisation 120
Wetherill, Bernard ('Jack') 187
Whitehall 44, 76
Whitehall Court 102–3, 154
Whitehall, Palace of 171
Whitelaw, Viscount 178
Whitnorth 115–7
Wilbraham High School 179
Wilkinson, Miss 36
Willard, Jess 11
'William G.' 121–2

Williams, Keith 147
Williams, Ronnie 147
Wilson, Harold 188, 204
Wilson, Major 61
Wimbledon 45, 57, 62
Wimbledon Borough News 61
Wimbledon Common 60
Wimbledon Hill 60, 61
Wimbledon Park House 59
Wimbledon railway station 60
Wimbledon & South West Finance
    Company Ltd. 46–7
Wimbledon Squash & Badminton Club
    92
Wimbledon Swimming Club 23
Woburn Palace 42
Wolsey, Cardinal 171
Woodcote Park, Epsom 48
Woodside, Wimbledon 137
Woolton, Lord 53, 71, 155–6
World Trade Centre 112, 214
Worthing 103, 108
Wycombe Abbey School 139

Yalta 210
Yeoman of the Guard 173
York Place 171
Ypres, Second Battle of 57
Ysbyty 63
Ysbyty, Ifan 63

Zurich 112